ALSO BY GRACE YOUNG

The Breath of a Wok (with Alan Richardson)
The Wisdom of the Chinese Kitchen

Stir-Frying

TO THE SKY'S EDGE

THE ULTIMATE GUIDE TO MASTERY

WITH AUTHENTIC RECIPES AND STORIES

GRACE YOUNG

Photographs by STEVEN MARK NEEDHAM

SIMON & SCHUSTER

NEW YORK LONDON TORONTO SYDNEY

Simon & Schuster
1230 Avenue of the Americas
New York, NY 10020

First Simon & Schuster hardcover edition May 2010

SIMON & SCHUSTER and colophon are registered trademarks of
Simon & Schuster, Inc.

For information about special discounts for bulk purchases, please
contact Simon & Schuster Special Sales at 1-866-506-1949 or
business@simonandschuster.com.

The Simon & Schuster Speakers Bureau can bring authors to your live
event. For more information or to book an event contact the Simon
& Schuster Speakers Bureau at 1-866-248-3049 or visit our website at
www.simonspeakers.com.

Frontispiece photograph: Stir-Fried Chili Scallops with Baby Bok Choy

Designed by Diane Hobbing of Snap-Haus Graphics

Manufactured in the United States of America

10 9 8 7 6 5

Library of Congress Cataloging-in-Publication Data
Young, Grace.
  Stir-frying to the sky's edge : the ultimate guide to mastery, with
authentic recipes and stories / Grace Young with photographs
by Steven Mark Needham.
      p. cm.
1. Stir frying. 2. Wok cookery. I. Title.
  TX689.5.Y69   2010
  641.7'74—dc22
                        2009045195

ISBN 978-1-4165-8057-7
ISBN 978-1-4165-8073-7 (ebook)

In memory of my father
Delwyn Wah Yan Young
and my friend
"Sunny" Dolores Taylor
With love

Let the meats and vegetables be combined and "married," instead of meeting each other for the first time when served on the table in their respective confirmed bachelorhood and unspoiled virginity, and you will find that each has a fuller personality than you ever dreamed of.

LIN YUTANG

Acknowledgments

This book was an incredible adventure—traveling to great destinations, forging new friendships, and learning from the best. It is also a powerful reminder of how blessed I am to have extraordinary friends and family.

I have had the good fortune of Evie Righter's wise editorial counsel for all my cookbooks. For this project her initial consultation transformed the manuscript into a coherent book. My gratitude to Evie for her devotion to editorial precision, which gave this project its heart and soul.

I am eternally grateful to Laura Cerwinske, my friend and writing guru, who edited all my first drafts and helped me craft the original book proposal, thus making everything possible. I can't begin to thank Laura for her love and generosity. Scott Hunt gave me the idea of taking this project to the sky's edge by suggesting that I write about the cooking of the Chinese diaspora. With his impeccable taste and good humor I relied on him for advice on the art, design, and text.

The indescribable beauty of a stir-fry glistening from the heat of an iron wok is captured in Steven Mark Needham's stunning photography. Steve has a genius for creating gorgeous photographs effortlessly. I am grateful too for the generosity of my friends Ulrike Carpus and Stephanie Browner: Ulrike flew from Germany to assist with the food styling for the first photo sessions and Stephanie volunteered for the second half. Everyone's good humor and hard work made for some of the most enjoyable workdays.

At Simon & Schuster, my thanks to publisher David Rosenthal for his faith in this project. My heartfelt thanks go to Jackie Seow for the beautiful cover; Nancy Singer for overseeing the book's interior design; Mara Lurie for orchestrating the manuscript through production; Julia Prosser and Katie Kurtzman for their support in publicity; and Michelle Rorke for her expert management of the manuscript in its final stages. I am grateful for the impeccable proofreading of Marla Jea and Suzanne Fass. Many thanks to Ruth Fecych, for adopting this project in its eleventh hour. Most of all, thanks to my exceptional editor, Sydny Miner, who allowed me the freedom to create the text and the photography I envisioned and who skillfully shepherded this book through all its stages. It has been an honor and privilege working with you and I miss you already . . .

The moment I saw Diane Hobbing's design for the book I smiled. I never imagined the text, photographs, and artwork could be integrated so elegantly. Many thanks to my literary agent, Martha Kaplan, for her belief in this project and her enthusiasm for Chinese food, especially stir-fries.

I am grateful to Aaron Rezny for opening his prop closet to me and to Sara Abalan whose exceptional taste elevates everything. My thanks to Jennifer Baumann who gave me a mini-tutorial on how to shoot the portraits of the home cooks.

Anyone writing about Chinese cooking owes much to Florence Lin. Thank you, Florence, for sharing your culinary remembrances of China and for the wonderful stir-fry cooking session. I am indebted to all the home cooks who welcomed me into their kitchens and shared their favorite stir-fry recipes and stories. Each has taught me a different nuance of the Chinese experience through the simple act of stir-frying. Many thanks to Amy Yip, Mei Chau, Fah Liong, Peipei Chang, Lejen Chen, Maejeane Chang, Chef Danny Chan, Potsam Loo, Ken Lo, Wai Ching Wong, Justin Guo, Mei Ibach, Luis Li, Beverly Low, Kian Lam Kho, Raymond Leong, Irene Khin Wong, "Jackie" Yok Lin Chong, Rose Wong, and Joyce Jue. Special thanks to George Chew who gave me a tour de force cooking interview, and for the many memorable meals that followed. And thanks to Marilynn K. Yee, who shot the wonderful photo of George.

I also extend a special note of appreciation to all the individuals who shared their stir-fry and diaspora stories with me: Ernest Wing King, Frieda Quon, Sen Pu, Hsiao-Ching Chou, Ellen Chou, Terry Huey, Peter Lee, Terry Chung Schulze, Pang-Mei Natasha Chang, Yu-Li Pan, Curan Loh, Alejandro Lee, Maria Benavides, Renee Wan, Rita Szeto, Raquel Wong, Regina Lai, Norma Chin, John Chan, and John Kuok. Thanks to Mimi Chan, May and Joe Chan, Julio Li, Steven Picker, Vik Lulla, Anna and Richard Chu, Melissa Guerra, Jennifer Lew, Mario Chang, Angel Chan, and Darren Wan, who helped make many of the interviews possible.

My deepest gratitude to the IACP Culinary Trust for granting me the eGullet Society for Culinary Arts & Letters Culinary Journalist Independent Study Scholarship, which enabled me to travel to California, Trinidad, Canada, Germany, and Holland for research. In Trinidad, heartfelt thanks to Winnie Lee Lum for arranging countless cooking interviews and for her incomparable hospitality. I will always remember the grace and generosity of your family and friends, including your brother Frank Williams's help in Miami, Florida. Thanks to

Tony Lee Lum, Dean Lee Lum, Nicky and Michelle Fung, Gerald and Ann Sancho, and Cora and Desmond Lee Lum. Special thanks to Professor Walton Look Lai for sharing his vast knowledge of the history of the Chinese diaspora in the Caribbean. In Holland, my thanks to Leonore and Bart Neervoort-Briët for hosting my stay and for introducing me to Hengko and Wai Ming Dun. Thanks also to Cheung Shuk Ching, Cheung Shuk Kam, Cheung Shuk Tai, and Cheung Wing Yee at Azie restaurant in Vaals, Holland. And in Aachen, Germany, thanks to Fan-Zen Shiau-Blome at Dshingis Chan restaurant and the staff at Jasmin Garten restaurant. I am grateful to Winston Chang, who made it possible for me to attend the Hakka Conference and Festival in Toronto, Canada. Special thanks to my honorary Hakka sister Simone Tai for her kindness and hospitality, and most of all for introducing me to Chef Yong Soon, an exceptionally articulate and generous Chinese culinary expert.

Profound appreciation goes to my esteemed colleagues who shared their expertise and insights: E. N. Anderson, James Oseland, Robert L. Wolke, Marion Nestle, Sidney Mintz, Joyce Leung, Richard Kahn, Mark Swislocki, Shirley Shu-Liang Cheng, Fuchsia Dunlop, Cheuk Kwan, Rosalind Creasy, Kathleen Bertolani, Tom Dekle, John Kuo Wei Tchen, Laura Chen-Schultz, Barbara Kirshenblatt-Gimblett, Sue Lee, Lok Siu, Val Gleason, Chef Richard Chen, Chef Chow Chung, Jennifer 8. Lee, Linda Anusasananan, Lowell Bassett, Tom Damrauer, Gladys Tszting Lui and the instructors at the Chinese Cuisine Training Institute in Hong Kong, Susan Jung of the *South China Morning Post*, Marge Perry, David Leite, and Jacqueline M. Newman. I am also grateful for being able to do research at the Jacqueline M. Newman Chinese Cookbook Collection at Stony Brook University with the assistance of Kristen J. Nyitray.

The piece on "The Language of Stir-Frying" required the help of numerous people. First and foremost my heartfelt thanks to Julie Tay, who patiently checked the Cantonese translations and made corrections numerous times in addition to sharing her Singaporean stir-fry recipes. Many thanks to Sun-Yui Fung, Pandora Chu, Ivy Fung, Estella Tam, Szeto Keung, Katheryn Louie, Helen Fung, Walter Chu, and Herbert Fung.

A stir-fry cookbook needs a great source for woks and Tane Ong Chan, owner of The Wok Shop in San Francisco, is the ambassador for wok cooking and so much more. Tane has been an incredible friend, introducing me to many of the cooks that grace these pages. She also put me in touch with Rachel Sit Wong, who in turn demystified the world of the Chinese of the Mississippi Delta with introductions to Ellen J. Fong, Katherine Chu, Mary Ann and Ernie Wong, and Rev. Ted Shepherd.

I am indebted to Barney A. Ebsworth for graciously granting his permission to reproduce Edward Hopper's *Chop Suey*. Many thanks to his assistant Kristine Dunnigan. I owe Bill Schleining for his peerless detective work in finding the name and the exact location of the restaurant in the Hopper painting and for putting me in touch with Hopper's biographer Gail Levin. Much appreciation to my dear friend Sue Israel who coached me on how to do photo research.

Among the friends who have encouraged this book along, I thank my godmothers Anna Kwock and Ronnie Wei Gin, Andrea DiNoto, Frank Farnham, Michael Zande, David Schachter, Janice Easton-Epner, Barbara Chan, Neil Applebaum, Kim Park, Gale Steves, Alice Lowe, Pamela Thomas, Deborah Clearwaters, Eugene Moy, Aaron Paley, Judith Teitelman, Henry Talbot, Frances Largeman-Roth, Fraya Berg, Doralece Dullaghan, Terry Conlan, Andrea Nguyen, Mitchell Davis, Victoria Fahey, Kathy Gunst, Michelle Steffens, Amy Besa, Romy Dorotan, Leslie Oster, Bonnie Slotnick, Diane K. Chamberlain, Barbara Haber, Diane Harris Brown, Nancy Hebb, Carol and Mark Griffin, John Jung, Robbie Hudson, Trisha Calvo, Jane Taylor, Warren Chapman, and my godfather J. Robert Purdom, who kept me focused on making the deadline.

Sincere thanks to Roldan Lopez and Vinita Chandra who kept me healthy and fit from too many hours of sitting at the computer. And to Henley and Huggy who make me smile on good days and bad.

I am deeply indebted to my cousins Loretta and Skip Seeley who have been guardian angels to my parents and me. Their help and support, especially as my father fell ill, held me together. My heartfelt thanks to Ragnhild Sunstrom Wagenhofer, whose wise counsel and friendship steadied me, and to my Auntie Lil Jew, who came to my rescue in my moment of need. Special thanks to my brother Douglas Young, my cousins Katherine and Robert Lim, and Sylvia and Fred Chow for their support. Love and thanks to my mother, Helen Young.

Most of all, I want to thank my husband, Michael Wiertz, for never complaining even when I turned the living room into a photo studio or took over the entire apartment for my office. Without Michael's support, encouragement, and belief in me this book would not be possible.

Contents

Vegetable and Tofu Recipes   183

Stir-Frying

TO THE SKY'S EDGE

Introduction

A Stir-Fry Odyssey

Chinese cooking is a cooking of scarcity. Whatever the emperors and warlords may have had, the vast majority of Chinese spent their lives short of fuel, cooking oil, utensils, and even water.

—E. N. ANDERSON, *THE FOOD OF CHINA*

I consider stir-frying a form of culinary magic in which ingredients are transformed. Their textures are enhanced, their flavors intensified and caramelized. The alchemy of stir-frying brings a blush of color to raw shrimp and a radiance to vegetables. Meats grow plump and fragrant from browning. The stir-fry dish brings food to life.

I grew up observing my father's passion for stir-fries, developed from years of frequenting the best restaurants and knowing many of the great chefs in San Francisco's Chinatown. Later, I developed my own more consuming infatuation, because it wasn't enough for me to appreciate the pleasures of a delicious stir-fry: I needed to know how it was made.

Over time my esteem for stir-frying has only grown. I see it as a way of life, both timeless and timely. As I've observed rising food and fuel prices, I cannot think of another cooking technique that makes less seem like more, and by which small amounts of food feed many. And what could be healthier than cooking with a minimum of meat and fat and emphasizing vegetables of every kind?

This book is about a "universal longing for home" and a cooking technique that traveled the globe satisfying that desire. The story of stir-frying is one of cultural perseverance and healthy, flavorful cooking, of universality and subtle distinction, of the Chinese diaspora and local character. Each of the many cooks I interviewed lends a human face and personal technique to the vast stir-fry tradition. In the hot, tropical Malaysian village of Dungun, stir-frying enabled

Mei Chau, a young girl entrusted with feeding her family, to produce flavorful dishes while being mercifully delivered quickly from the intense heat of the kitchen. In the Caribbean, Winnie Lee Lum continues the culinary traditions her parents brought with them in the 1930s when they emigrated from China to Jamaica, as well as integrating the local ingredients and techniques she has learned from living in Trinidad for over forty years. In Redwood City, California, Fah Liong stir-fries the same simple Hakka dishes her mother taught her in Indonesia, substituting American vegetables for the Asian produce she once used. The common theme of all the stories and recipes in this book is the transformation of humble ingredients into rich, delectable, healthful meals using precious little food and cooking fuel. Regardless of whether it is a ten-year-old child who learns to stir-fry when her mother falls ill, or a ninety-year-old woman who partners with her son-in-law to stir-fry, each cook demonstrates how, if you have only tasted a stir-fry in a restaurant or cooked from a recipe taken off the Internet, you have missed the humanity of stir-frying.

I grew up in a very traditional Chinese home in San Francisco where my parents cooked the same Cantonese dishes they had eaten in their youth in China. My ideas of Chinese food were based on a strict adherence to classic food combinations that left no possibility of improvisation. For example, my mother would always stir-fry ginger with Chinese broccoli (page 190), never garlic. One of my favorite dishes she stir-fried was ginger tomato beef (page 80), a recipe she never considered making with chicken or pork. In our household, Chinese recipes were carved in stone.

Imagine my revelation at Henrica's, a Chinese Jamaican restaurant in Rosedale, Queens, which is part of New York City. When perusing the menu of unremarkable Chinese American dishes, my eyes fell upon a listing for Jamaican jerk chicken fried rice (page 262) and then one for jerk pork fried rice and for jerk chicken chow mein. Jerk chicken in a Chinese stir-fry? To my great surprise, the dish was wonderful—the spicy, robust jerk chicken was beautifully suited to the rice flavored with soy sauce and speckled with chopped onions, scallions, and finely diced carrots. I asked to meet the chef and was led into the kitchen where, side by side, a Chinese and a Jamaican chef worked at the stove. When I asked the Cantonese chef how he made the jerk chicken, he shrugged his shoulders and nodded to the Jamaican chef who, it turned out, cooked the chicken that he then turned over to the Chinese chef to stir-fry with the rice.

Not long after my visit to Henrica's, I was introduced to a Chinese Guyanese restaurant called Happy Garden in Jamaica, New York, where jerk chicken fried rice appeared alongside Guyanese dishes and typical Chinese American ones. Then I heard about a Chinese Indian restaurant in New York City called Chinese Mirch. There I sampled wildly spicy Sichuan vegetarian fried rice (page 265), made with basmati rice, and Chicken Manchurian (page 142), a scrumptious stir-fry generously spiced with fresh chilies. The Indian American owner brought me into the kitchen to meet his Cantonese chefs. He explained to me his cooks were trained to use the Chinese stir-fry technique, but with ingredients suited to the Indian palate and without the pork, beef, rice wine, or alcohol that are prohibited, in accordance with Muslim and Hindu dietary laws.

When I came across *Chinese Restaurants*, a fifteen-part documentary series produced by Cheuk Kwan, a Chinese Canadian documentary filmmaker, I was fascinated to follow Kwan's exploration of Chinese restaurants in such unlikely places as Mauritius, Turkey, Argentina, Trinidad, and Israel. In my naiveté it had never occurred to me that the Chinese had immigrated to such disparate countries. In fact, seven and a half million Chinese left southern China at the beginning of the nineteenth century because of economic poverty, with the vast majority remaining in Southeast Asia. Chinese migration continues to this day to the far corners of the globe. I began to ponder whether Chinese immigrants living abroad learned to adapt their cooking to local tastes and if they always continued the traditions of stir-frying. Were there other stir-fries like jerk chicken fried rice, invented when the tastes of two cultures merged?

My search for stir-fry recipes ultimately evolved into an almost anthropological examination of the Chinese immigrant experience worldwide as expressed through the stir-fry. I visited restaurants that served Chinese Peruvian, Chinese Mexican, Chinese Dutch, Chinese Guyanese, Chinese Indian, Chinese German, Chinese Vietnamese, Chinese Jamaican, Chinese Cuban, and, of course, Chinese American food, observing that these unique Chinese restaurants had learned to adjust their cooking to cater to the mainstream tastes of their clientele. I located Chinese whose families had immigrated to Peru, Trinidad, New Zealand, Fiji, Indonesia, Jamaica, Libya, Holland, India, South Africa, Burma, and Germany. I conducted cooking interviews and tasted stir-fries that fused various culinary traditions. These interviews often revealed the unimaginable hardships experienced by Chinese immigrants living without Chinese communities. Many of the people I met recounted how a stir-fry's aromas and tastes eased their sense of displacement, providing comfort as they adapted to foreign customs, language, and climate. Often cooks had to simplify classic dishes;

at other times they substituted, embellished, or combined local ingredients and the popular tastes of their new culture with intriguing and mixed results. Some families even learned to grow Chinese vegetables and make their own tofu.

I even became fascinated by the language of stir-frying. The distinct tossing and turning action of stir-frying captures the notion of quick change and is used in several Cantonese terms for speculation, as in "stir-frying stocks" and "stir-frying real estate," the buying and selling of stocks and real estate for quick financial gain. Surprisingly, "stir-fry" even appears in a number of colloquial expressions that have nothing to do with change or quick movement—such as "to stir-fry a person," a slang term for firing an employee. The Cantonese obsession with stir-frying inevitably leads to a discourse on *wok hay*, the Cantonese term that refers to the distinct vitality exuded when super-fresh ingredients are stir-fried so perfectly they possess wok fragrance.

I interviewed Chinese whose families were among the first to settle in towns in Nebraska, Oklahoma, Texas, New Mexico, Arkansas, and Tennessee. For many, their only means of earning a living was to open a restaurant serving Chinese American fare that included chop suey, the crude "non-Chinese" stir-fry improvisation that became a staple for Americans and provided for Chinese economic survival. Eventually I interviewed Chinese who had been raised in the Mississippi Delta in the 1930s and '40s. The story of the Chinese of the Mississippi Delta is one of the most remarkable testaments to the tenacity of Chinese immigrants anywhere. Brought to the South as laborers in the 1870s, and often living in towns in which they were the only Chinese residents, these immigrants gradually began running grocery stores throughout Mississippi that serviced impoverished sharecroppers. Without a wok and with limited

Chinese ingredients, these Chinese used local produce, such as rutabagas or turnip greens, plus a little salted pork and a frying pan to re-create their longed-for stir-fries.

Stir-frying has been a continuous comfort to the Chinese diaspora. Even when deprived of Chinese produce, condiments, and the wok, the Chinese have always managed to find a way to stir-fry.

I have tasted my share of mediocre stir-fries. It is easy to produce uninspired dishes when stir-frying is approached with the attitude that it is merely the quick cooking of bite-sized pieces of meat and vegetables in oil with no sense of its refined artistry. In this cookbook I share with you all the stir-fry principles and knowledge I have learned from home cooks, master chefs, and cooking teachers from around the world. I offer detailed recommendations on all aspects of stir-frying at home, focusing on the challenge facing most cooks: working with stoves that do not produce the ideal amount of heat for stir-frying.

In truth, stir-frying is a cooking method of great subtlety and sophistication. In Chinese cuisine a system of classifications exists to distinguish "dry" from "moist" stir-fries (depending on whether broths, sauces, or liquids of any kind are added). The term "clear stir-fries" is reserved for ingredients that have been stir-fried in a little oil and deftly seasoned, thus enhancing the pure essence and character of the main ingredient. "Velvet stir-fries" involve the coating of an ingredient, such as chicken breast, in an egg white and cornstarch mixture, which is then blanched in hot oil or water and stir-fried until the texture becomes silky and succulent.

Stir-frying is a technique of tradition and innovation. This cookbook mainly comprises classic stir-fry dishes from the traditions of Guangzhou (Canton), Hong Kong, Shanghai, Fujian, Sichuan, Hunan, and Beijing. These recipes are the essentials for any stir-fry repertoire. In addition, there is a small selection of recipes from the Chinese diaspora in India, Trinidad, Jamaica, Cuba, Singapore, Taiwan, Malaysia, Indonesia, Burma, Vietnam, Macau, Peru, France, and America, reflecting the borrowings of another cuisine. The subject of the diaspora and their experiences with stir-frying is vast and deserves its own study. These singular recipes give you a sense of how the stir-fry, the supreme culinary chameleon, can bring together the tastes of one culture through the ingredients of another. For cooks who feel they cannot stir-fry because they lack Asian ingredients, these resourceful, clever combinations are living proof that with ingenuity the improvisational possibilities are infinite.

Stir-frying can be enjoyed both for its time-honored recipes and its innovative modern ones, and for the promise it offers to create new classics. The Chinese stir-fry is all things: refined, improvisational, adaptable, and inventive. There is an old Cantonese expression, *"Yad wok jao tin ngaai,"* or "one wok runs to the sky's edge," meaning "one who uses the wok becomes master of the cooking world." For centuries the Chinese have carried their woks to all corners of the earth, continuously re-creating stir-fry traditions. Today, the sky's edge extends beyond geographic borders into cultures newly integrated with all manner of popular and ancient ways. Stir-frying's innumerable possibilities for creating simple, nourishing, and wholly satisfying meals that feed the body and nourish the soul await.

Notes to the Reader

Heat levels are very critical for stir-frying. The recipes and information in this book are geared for the home cook using an average residential range. If you are cooking on a powerful range with more than 14,000 BTUs, such as a custom wok stove, a professional range, a powerful gas range, or a portable wok stove, you will need to lower the heat levels called for and decrease the cooking times. Many of the instructions, such as using a flat-bottomed wok, searing meats before stir-frying, or drying vegetables, will not apply to you. These instructions are to help maximize the heat of a wok or skillet when it is being used on a residential stove. Likewise, if you are cooking on a less powerful stove, be it gas or electric, you will need to increase the cooking times by a few minutes.

Stir-frying is a simple cooking technique that has been practiced for hundreds of years by millions of people. That said, it is important to realize that stir-frying requires cooking on high heat. Always exercise caution. If at any time you are uncomfortable or if the cooking is getting out of your control, immediately stop cooking, turn off the heat, and carefully transfer the hot wok or skillet to a cold burner. If you are new to stir-frying, start with an easy recipe, a simple vegetable stir-fry such as Stir-Fried Garlic Spinach (page 202) or Peppery Vegetarian Rice (page 256). With practice, stir-frying will become more natural, and you can advance to a recipe that combines meat and vegetables, and finally to the most challenging recipes of all, those that involve velveting (see Velvet Stir-Fry, page 100) or oil-blanching.

The Recipes

Please read through the entire recipe before cooking. If you are a novice at stir-frying, I encourage you to read all the sidebars, each of which is filled with information, and, in particular, The Best Oil for Stir-Frying (see page 41), Stir-Frying with Proper Heat and Control (see page 52), and Basic Steps for Stir-Frying (see page 54). It is helpful to read the sidebars that focus on specific types of dishes and techniques, such as dry stir-fries, moist stir-fries, simple stir-fries, clear stir-fries, velveting, and fried rice.

Stir-Frying Recipes: Classics and Innovations (pages 47–285) includes all the recipes, organized by food categories: meat, poultry and eggs, fish and shellfish, vegetables and tofu, and rice and noodles. Recipes range in complexity from easy to advanced stir-fries. Many have been adapted from the cooks or chefs I interviewed, and those individuals are credited in each recipe.

Chinese terms are rendered in romanized spellings of their Cantonese pronunciations, except for several words already familiar to readers in romanized Mandarin, such as Beijing, Sichuan, and Guangzhou. I have also followed the convention established in my last two books and used the spelling *wok hay*, for the "breath of the wok," even though the standardized Cantonese spelling is *wok hei*. I have taken this liberty because the spelling *hei* can lead to an incorrect pronunciation for the non-Cantonese speaker. I have chosen the Cantonese dialect in honor of my Cantonese heritage and because of the Cantonese reputation for being masters of the stir-fry.

General Instructions

- The **14-inch flat-bottomed carbon-steel wok is the perfect pan** for stir-frying, but knowing that some cooks may be more comfortable using a skillet I have indicated all the recipes in which a 12-inch stainless-steel skillet can be interchanged with a wok. When a recipe calls for a wok only, it is because when I tested the recipe in a skillet it did not work.

- Throughout the book I call for **preheating the wok or skillet** by heating it until a bead of water vaporizes within 1 to 2 seconds of contact. Occasionally, there are some woks and skillets that the water test doesn't work on. After preheating the pan, the water beads up like a mercury ball, stubbornly refusing to vaporize. In such cases, you will have to experiment with preheating the wok or skillet until the pan is hot but the oil does not smoke once it is added.

- Familiarize yourself with the **food identification photographs** in the Stir-Fry Pantry (see page 31). Shopping can be daunting if you are unaccustomed to selecting Asian ingredients, and these photographs are provided to make the process easier and more enjoyable for you. In many cases, the photograph indicates my favorite brands for condiments and sauces.

- On page 45 is a photograph that shows the various **ways to cut ginger, scallions, and garlic;** I have included it because readers are sometimes unsure of how thick to cut a ginger slice, what "finely shredded" means when it comes to scallions or ginger, or how fine minced garlic should be. There are also specific technique photos throughout the book on how to cut a variety of ingredients.

- **Ginger** is always peeled unless otherwise indicated. See Ginger Essentials on page 42 for more information.

- Unless otherwise indicated, the entire trimmed **scallion** is used whether it is cut into sections, sliced, chopped, or minced.

- All the recipes were tested with **peanut oil**. I feel peanut oil is excellent for stir-frying because of its high smoking point and neutral flavor. I prefer Planters for its quality and availability. If you do not or cannot use a nut-based oil, feel free to use your favorite vegetable oil, but make sure that it has a high smoking point. For more information, see The Best Oil for Stir-Frying on page 41.

- If you cannot find **Shao Hsing rice wine, substitute dry sherry;** the flavor is not identical but it is comparable.

- All **vegetables** should be thoroughly washed in several changes of cold water. Make sure vegetables are dry by air-drying them in a colander for several hours, or use a salad spinner to remove excess water. Vegetables must be moisture-free to prevent stir-fries from becoming soggy. When a vegetable is "thinly sliced," it should be no more than ¼-inch thick. If you are unfamiliar with preparing certain Asian vegetables such as lotus root, see photographs in Handling Asian Vegetables (page 187).

- Whenever **Sichuan peppercorns** are called for in a recipe, they must first be roasted and ground. Put ¼ cup of Sichuan peppercorns in a dry, cold wok and remove any tiny stems. Stir over medium-low heat for 3 to 5 minutes until the peppercorns are very fragrant and slightly smoking. Be careful not to let them burn. Once they're cooled, grind them in a mortar, then store them in a jar.

- When **soy sauce** is called for, I use a thin or light (not to be confused with low-sodium) soy sauce such as Kikkoman. I highly recommend Kikkoman Organic Soy Sauce; the flavor is clean and fresh.

- **Fresh chili peppers** are stemmed and unseeded unless otherwise indicated. Always wear kitchen gloves when handling fresh or dried chilies. Many of the recipes give a range of chilies. If you are sensitive to hot food, it's best to start with a small amount. You can always add more chilies, but once added you cannot take them out. Do not eat whole dried chilies that have been stir-fried.

- **Meat and poultry** should be trimmed of fat. When a recipe calls for cutting either meat or poultry into ¼-inch-thick slices, they should be about 2 inches long and 1 inch wide.

- **Ketchup** is an ingredient that is sometimes called for in Chinese cooking. I have tried many different brands, but in my opinion Heinz has the best flavor.

- When **chicken broth** is called for I know most cooks will use a canned product. I recommend making homemade broth (page 284), which can be frozen in convenient 1-pint containers. Homemade broth will give dishes more depth of flavor, and it is far more economical. I prefer a reduced-sodium broth if using canned.

- Use the amount of **salt** called for in the recipes as a guideline. Ingredients such as soy sauce and chicken broth will affect how much salt is required. Each brand of soy sauce contains a different amount of sodium, and homemade broth will also influence the amount of salt needed.

- It is essential to have a set of **dry and liquid measuring cups.** I find it useful to have two complete sets of **measuring spoons,** one set for measuring dry ingredients and the other for wet. When it comes to liquid measuring cups, a two-quart size is handy for measuring bulky ingredients such as spinach. The eight-ounce Pyrex with its spout is not only indispensable for measuring liquids but is also perfect for swirling sauce ingredients into the wok.

- Throughout this book there are instructions to **maximize the heat in your pan** to prevent a stir-fry from turning into a soggy braise. Maintaining the heat on a residential stove, in particular, is critical to successful stir-frying.

Fresh Ginger, traditional wooden ginger grater, cleaver, and Shanghai bok choy

The
Essential
Kitchen

Wok Envy

Over the last few years, I have taught Chinese cooking throughout the United States and even as far away as Singapore and Bali. No matter the destination, I always have my wok in tow. My wok, with its incredible patina developed from years of cooking, is irreplaceable. In fact, my wok is so valuable to me I never risk packing it in an unlocked check-in piece of luggage. Wherever I go, so goes my wok, hand-carried onto the airplane.

After years of trial and error, I developed a system for squeezing the wok into a standard carry-on suitcase. I have also learned to travel with an exceedingly minimal wardrobe; if I pack my clothes in an even layer to a maximum thickness of two inches, I can just wedge the wok, wrapped in a plastic bag, into the suitcase. The hard metal bowl of the wok works perfectly to protect fragile items. The rest of my belongings fit into the rest of the space. The bag's extra-sturdy zipper has proved essential.

The packing/carrying issue is not, however, my most critical accommodation. That would be the extra thirty minutes beyond the usual check-in time that I need in order to deal with homeland security. If you've never traveled with a wok in your carry-on, trust me, it's an experience: I load the suitcase onto the conveyor belt, and, as it passes through the detection screen, the agent's face tenses. He/she beckons a colleague to help scrutinize my luggage. They reverse the conveyor belt and run the bag back and forth, grimly monitoring the screen, until, finally they call over another TSA agent. I am told to step aside as the hand examination ensues. "It's a wok. I'm a traveling cooking teacher . . ." I start to explain. The agent cuts me off and sternly instructs me to remain silent. Sometimes it's amusing, but it's more than likely alarming because I've been fretting since the night before that this time the agent will actually take my wok from me. As I watch them deconstruct my carefully packed bag, I prepare to argue that, not being a firearm, club, or knife, the wok is not on the list of prohibited flight items. The agent waves a tissue that looks like a fabric softener sheet in his latex-gloved hand over the contents of my bag.

I have had tweezers, mascara, and manicure scissors confiscated, while my three-and-a-half-pound carbon-steel cooking implement clears security. In San Diego once, a surly security agent who had treated me like a criminal burst into a big grin when he finally realized the mystery item was a wok. His demeanor completely changed. "What *is* the secret to making good fried rice?" he wanted to know. As annoyed as I was, I told him leftover cold rice is the key to success—and, of course, stir-frying it in an iron wok.

Naturally given to worry, I am the last person in the world who should be traveling with a controversial item. So why do I do it? At first it was for the same reason I insist on using my wok for guest appearances on television cooking shows: my carbon-steel wok with its fine patina has a natural nonstick surface that is so unsurpassed I have total confidence my stir-fries will cook perfectly on live national television.

When I teach I always demonstrate a stir-fry within the first ten minutes of a class. All it takes is one taste of the intense flavor a stir-fry made in an iron wok imparts, and the seduction begins. The aroma of the food, impeccably seared on the natural nonstick surface, seals the deal. The students' curiosity is teased, and then when I tell them a journalist once likened my wok to an old-time musician's Gibson guitar or a veteran hitter's Louisville Slugger they begin to see the wok as I do, as a living work of art. With its fine ebony finish, my wok has a soul and character unattainable with a nonstick or a stainless-steel pan. There is no need to even mention that Chinese chefs only cook with carbon-steel woks.

I tolerate the inevitable angst of airport security because it is gratifying to see students awaken to the fact that the hippest pan is the one that has been around for over two thousand years. There's nothing quite like seeing students caught in the spell of wok envy.

Grace Young stir-frying red onions for Stir-Fried Curried Beef

A Wok for Every Reason

While woks of numerous shapes and materials are available on the market, not all are well suited to stir-frying. The material out of which a wok is made and its design have enormous effect on a stir-fry's success. Chinese restaurant chefs, for example, exclusively prefer carbon-steel woks because these woks give stir-fries the elusive, smoky caramelized essence prized by Chinese gourmets. Stainless-steel, anodized aluminum, and nonstick woks cannot replicate this coveted taste.

I like a carbon-steel wok for stir-frying not only for the special fragrance and wok taste it gives food, but also because once the pan is seasoned, its natural nonstick-like surface allows meat, poultry, seafood, vegetables, and rice to stir-fry with minimal oil. An added health benefit is that a carbon-steel wok imparts iron into the diet (see Seeking the Iron Tattoo, page 19). No other pan will heat up as quickly or cool down as fast when removed from heat, which is critical in preventing foods from over-cooking once a stir-fry is complete. In addition, a carbon-steel wok, which is inexpensive compared to high-quality Western cookware, will last a lifetime.

The type of stove on which the wok will be used is another critical factor in making your wok choice. The classic round-bottomed wok, originally intended for use on a hearth stove, fit snugly over a hole where the flames could hug the bottom and sides of the wok.

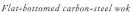

Flat-bottomed carbon-steel wok

A typical Western residential range cannot simulate that intense heat, and consequently, requires a flat-bottomed wok that is specifically designed for a less powerful stove. A wok with a 14-inch diameter is ideal for cooking a standard recipe that serves four using a residential range. In contrast, a 12-inch wok will crowd the food, making it impossible to stir-fry, and a 16-inch wok is too large and, therefore, it is difficult to attain sufficient heat. The following is a selection of my favorite woks and the best stoves to use with them.

Flat-Bottomed Woks

This Westernized carbon-steel wok is the most popular and practical for a residential stove with average power. It has a flared bowl and a 5- to 6-inch-wide base that allows the wok to sit directly on the burner, enabling the pan to get hotter than a round-bottomed wok stabilized on a wok ring. A flat-bottomed wok is essential when stir-frying on an electric range and works even more effectively on a gas range.

The flat-bottomed wok is available in two styles: those with one long wooden handle and a small wooden spool handle, and those with two small metal or wooden spool handles. The first is my favorite style of all-purpose wok. Its heat-resistant long handle, which is comfortable to hold when stir-frying, also makes lifting the wok with one hand easier when transferring food out of the wok. The second style is far less practical: the small handles of metal or wood are attached to the rim of the wok. The metal handles become very hot, and the cook must use pot holders, only adding to the overall cumbersomeness of the endeavor. Also, when the wok has a stir-fry in it, the pan is too heavy to lift with one hand.

Round-Bottomed Woks

The round-bottomed wok with a flared bowl symbolizes the tradition of wok cooking. Designed for optimal efficiency, its round shape concentrates heat in the well and provides ample room in which to stir-fry. In order to prevent a round-bottomed wok from tipping over on a range, it must be supported by a wok ring (see above). An unstable wok is unsafe for cooking. A number of stove manufacturers now make special wok burners with a grate or rack designed to hold a round-bottomed wok. These grates vary in design and practicality and often lift the wok too far from the heat. Use of a round-bottomed wok on an electric range is not recommended because of the difficulty in attaining sufficient heat. Additionally, an electric range responds too slowly to temperature adjustments. A round-bottomed wok is best on a gas range (with at least 12,000 BTUs). It is also excellent on a semi-professional range, a custom-made wok stove, or an outdoor portable wok stove.

The round-bottomed wok is available in three distinct styles:

- Cantonese: The classic carbon-steel wok is easily recognized by its open flared bowl and its two small metal or wooden spool handles. The wok can range in diameter from 10 to 30 inches, but the best size for home use is 14 inches. It is generally factory-made, but hand-hammered pans can be found in wok specialty stores. Its great advantage is that if it is stabilized with a wok ring it frees both hands, allowing the cook to stir-fry with two spatulas, as if tossing a salad, or to use one hand to add ingredients while the other hand stir-fries with a spatula.

- Northern: Also known as the *pao* wok, the Northern wok, so called because it is favored by northern Chinese cooks, is made of carbon steel and has a slightly closed bowl shape and a heat-resistant hollow metal handle. There are modern *pao*-style woks that have been Westernized, made with a single long wooden handle, with the intention that all the cooking is done with the pan set on a wok ring. Traditionally, a *pao* wok was used only by extremely skilled cooks because of the coordination these implements require: while one hand pushes ingredients in the wok with a Chinese metal ladle, the other hand performs the dramatic *pao* action—a circular jerking motion in which ingredients are tossed into the air and caught in the well of the wok. Traditional *pao* woks are impractical for stir-frying on a residential stove, because the wok cannot get sufficiently hot set on a wok ring and the *pao* motion cools down the wok.

- Chinese-Made Cast-Iron Woks: This is a favorite of traditional Cantonese home cooks who sometimes claim this is the best wok for producing stir-fries with the coveted taste of *wok hay* (see *Wok Hay* in the Home Kitchen, page 111). These woks are not widely available; they are found in Chinese wok specialty stores only. They are made in the Cantonese style, with two small metal ear handles and, because they are round bottomed, must be stabilized with a wok ring. The cast iron is thinner and lighter in weight than American-made cast iron and therefore heats much faster. Unlike a carbon-steel wok, which cools quickly, a cast-iron wok retains heat; the moment a stir-fry is finished the food must be removed to prevent overcooking.

Note: I do not recommend American-made cast-iron woks because they take too much time to heat up and to cool down, in addition to being heavy and unwieldy. When stir-frying, it is essential to have a pan that is light enough to lift with one hand without requiring pot holders.

Skillet: The Wok Alternative

A flat-bottomed carbon-steel wok is the pan I recommend for stir-frying. When pressed to stipulate a pan for cooks who prefer not to use a wok, I suggest a 12-inch, heavy-duty stainless-steel skillet. A 12-inch skillet has a much larger flat surface area than the well of a 14-inch wok; consequently, more cooking oil will be necessary when stir-frying to prevent meat, poultry, eggs, fish, shellfish, tofu, rice, and noodles from sticking. Also, a skillet does not have the roominess of a wok; i.e., when stir-frying ingredients with volume or bulkiness, like spinach, noodles, or rice, the food is likely to spill out of a skillet but not a wok. I do not like cast-iron skillets for the same reasons I dislike American-made cast-iron woks.

Stainless-steel skillet

Note: I do not recommend a nonstick wok or skillet. The high heat required for stir-frying damages ordinary nonstick pans. High-quality nonstick pans that can be used on intense heat are far more expensive than a carbon-steel wok. I see no reason to waste money on costly pans when a seasoned wok uses just as little oil as a nonstick pan, yet is far superior at caramelizing and lightly charring ingredients and imbues stir-fries with their distinct flavor and aroma. Last, and perhaps most important, the preheating of an empty wok or skillet (see Stir-Frying with Proper Heat and Control, page 52), essential to successful stir-frying, is generally not recommended for nonstick pans.

Opposite page:
A Chinese-made cast-iron round-bottomed wok with wok ring (top) and carbon-steel round-bottomed wok with wooden handle, also called a Northern wok or modern pao-*style wok (bottom)*

Additional Equipment and Utensils for Stir-Frying

- **Spatula:** I prefer the Chinese metal spatula for stir-frying because its thin, slightly contoured edge is more effective than either a wood or plastic spatula for getting under food such as meat or poultry that can stick. The Chinese spatula also fits the contour of the wok and the shovel-like shape holds more food than a regular spatula. These utensils are available in wok specialty stores and Asian markets. The 14-inch stainless-steel spatula is the most practical for use with a 14-inch wok. If you cannot find a Chinese spatula, a metal pancake spatula will work adequately.

- **Wok Skimmer:** A wide-mesh brass strainer with a flat bamboo handle is extremely practical when oil- or water-blanching (see Velvet Stir-Fry, page 100). Timing is essential when blanching, and a wok skimmer is efficient at quickly gathering up 1 to 2 cups of ingredients in one motion, thus preventing overcooking. The skimmer comes in a variety of sizes, but the most useful has a 6- or 7-inch diameter.

- **Wok Ring:** This inexpensive aluminum or stainless-steel ring is designed to stabilize a round-bottomed wok for cooking. (See photo on page 14.) The wok ring is a Western invention. It looks like a metal "crown" that sits on top of a burner on a residential range. Unfortunately, most wok rings lift the wok too high off the heat and, if the range has average power or is electric, this makes it impossible for the wok to heat sufficiently.

- **Wok Lid:** Wok lids are made of aluminum and come with domed or flat tops. It is advisable to have your wok in hand when purchasing a lid and to test a range of lids until you find the one that fits the most snugly. For a 14-inch wok, the general rule of thumb is a 13-inch lid.

- **Ladle:** Chinese chefs prefer the ladle for stir-frying, but the technique they use requires special coordination that comes with a certain level of expertise not typical of a home cook. As a chef stir-fries, he uses one hand to hold the ladle, bowl side down, to push the food away from him as he almost simultaneously uses his other hand to jerk the wok in a small circular motion so that the food is continually tossed. Chefs also use the ladle to measure and combine sauce ingredients while stir-frying. Occasionally, I have met home cooks who use a ladle to stir-fry, but I find it impractical for home use.

Left to right: pancake spatula, wok skimmer, two styles of wok spatulas in a seasoned flat-bottomed carbon-steel wok, with domed wok lid (top)

- **Deep-Frying Thermometer:** This is an essential cooking tool for velveting (see Velvet Stir-Fry, page 100) and when oil-blanching ingredients prior to stir-frying. When a recipe calls for heating the oil, do not risk guessing the temperature of the oil: use a deep-frying thermometer to ascertain the exact temperature. When testing the temperature of the oil, make sure the tip of the thermometer is not touching the pan.

- **Knife:** It is essential to have a high-quality 8- to 10-inch chef's knife, 7- to 8-inch vegetable cleaver, or 8-inch santoku knife (see Sharp Enough to Stir-Fry, page 18). Before purchasing a knife, test as many as possible to see what feels well balanced in your hand. Make sure the handle has a good comfortable grip, and avoid handles that are slippery. Keep in mind that knives made of superior steel will hold their edge longer, so buy the best knife that you can afford. Follow the manufacturer's instructions for caring for the knife, particularly when it comes to washing and storing it.

- **Knife Sharpener:** All knives, no matter the quality, will eventually become dull from use. If you are inexperienced using a stone and steel, bring your knives to a reputable establishment to have them professionally sharpened. However, know that knives need to be resharpened regularly. There are a number of manual and electric knife sharpeners on the market and they vary in quality. Select a high-quality sharpener that can restore or re-create your desired edge angle.

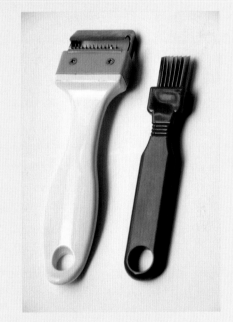

- **Vegetable Cutters:** Julienning carrots and finely shredding scallions can be labor intensive. I recommend two cutlery tools (*bottom photo*) that will save you time and work: the Kinpira Peeler (*left*), excellent for shredding carrots, and the Negi Cutter (*right*), which makes fine scallion shreds. Be careful when using both tools as they are very sharp. See pages 45 and 135 for how to use them.

Sharp Enough to Stir-Fry

My father's knife skills were so exceptional that, in 1999, he was filmed by CBS *Sunday Morning* slicing ginger at the age of eighty-five. Baba didn't disappoint. His steady hands produced slices of ginger so translucent they curled off his razor-sharp cleaver. One of the secrets to his expertise was his weathered sixty-year-old carbon-steel cleaver and his meticulous maintenance of its edge. Professional chefs, trained to sharpen their knives with a stone and hone it with a steel, would have no doubt cringed at his method: my father used an electric knife sharpener, the kind that is attached to a can opener, circa 1960, to hone the blade's edge.

While stir-frying calls for little in the way of culinary equipment beyond an iron wok, the preparation of stir-fry-worthy ingredients requires a professional-quality chef's knife or cleaver. A dull knife makes cutting ¼-inch-thick slices of chicken or fine scallion shreds an irksome chore. Inexperienced cooks who are loath to prepare ingredients for a stir-fry are likely to have never experienced the joys of using a sharp knife.

There are many excellent knives on the market, and the knife that is best for you is a very personal choice based on what feels right to you and what fits your budget. Stir-frying mainly requires cutting vegetables, meat, poultry, fish, and shellfish. As long as the knife is sharp, I have no preference if you use a chef's knife, a cleaver, or a santoku knife. The chef's knife is the great workhorse that is an all-around versatile cutlery tool. There are two kinds of cleavers—the meat and the vegetable—and it is the vegetable cleaver that is the best all-purpose knife for cutting meat or vegetables for stir-frying, with its wide blade useful for scooping up ingredients. A meat cleaver is intended for cutting through heavy bones and is impractical and unnecessary for stir-fry preparations. The third option is the santoku knife, sometimes described as a cross between a cleaver and a chef's knife, that originated in Japan. It has a slightly thinner broad blade that makes it particularly excellent for cutting vegetables. Santoku means "three virtues" or "three uses" and refers to the fact that the knife is well suited to slicing, mincing, and dicing. The knife is often scalloped along both sides of the blade, a design feature that prevents food from sticking. If you are inexperienced using a knife, I suggest taking an introductory cutlery class to learn how to use and maintain your cutlery properly.

Unfortunately, many home cooks find it difficult to master sharpening a knife with a stone and steel. They are unsure of what angle to hold the knife blade to the stone and steel, which makes it easy to damage knives. Worse yet, they then resign themselves to unsafe, inefficient, and imprecise cutting with a dull blade. Nearly every major knife manufacturer offers a variety of simple knife-sharpening systems (manual or electric). I have to confess that I have given up using a stone and steel ever since I started using the Chef'sChoice manual knife sharpener. The system is infinitely simpler, because as you swipe the knife the sharpener automatically sets the knife at the correct angle. It's impressive how straightforward and effortless it makes sharpening a knife—it takes me all of thirty seconds to sharpen a knife with a razor-sharp edge. In my opinion, a quality knife-sharpening system is a small investment you'll never regret.

Cutting ingredients should never be drudgery. Whatever you select from the vast array of high-quality chef's knives and cleavers that are available on the market, be resolute about maintaining the sharp edge: purchase a home knife-sharpening system, have your knife of choice professionally sharpened, or master using a stone and steel. The best knife, and the best knife sharpener, are the ones that work most effectively for you.

Seeking the Iron Tattoo

Well into the second half of the twentieth century, cast-iron cooking pans were treasured not only for their ability to distribute heat evenly, but also as a source of iron in the diet. But as nonstick ease and flawless appearance grew in priority, especially in American cooking, awareness of the dietary potency of cast iron diminished. Today, only the most nutritionally sophisticated of cooks tend to know, or appreciate, the enormous service with which cooking in cast iron or carbon steel can enhance diet and health.

Joyce Leung, a pediatric nutritionist at Harlem Hospital in New York, explains that cooking in such pans is superior even to the use of iron supplements for nutritionally deficient patients. "Iron supplements have to be taken in concentrated doses that may not be wholly assimilated and often cause constipation. Carbon-steel and cast-iron pans, on the other hand, allow the body to absorb iron gently and thoroughly," says Leung. She often has her patients conduct an experiment that illustrates how this cookware leaches iron into food. "I advise my patients to cook mashed potatoes and then to leave them in an iron pot for several days. Afterward, when they turn the potatoes over, they find them tinged a charcoal gray color, evidence I refer to as the 'iron tattoo.' I tell them to lick it up, that it's the best way to get iron."

Many Americans, fastidious about perceived flaws in the coloration of their food, often recoil at the idea of eating anything not "perfect" in appearance. As a result, healthy eating opportunities are often discarded or dismissed. In the case of carbon-steel and cast-iron utensils, the old adage "make a feature of the flaw" is advice worth following.

Most cultures have iron cookware traditions. Their foods, cooked in a carbon-steel or cast-iron pan such as the wok or a skillet, allow the body gently to ingest the iron that has been absorbed through the reaction of the cookware to heat. Nutritionists such as Leung recognize the power of iron cookware to resolve even such severe deficiencies as anemia. And Leung, a vegetarian, should know. She has been cooking in a carbon-steel wok for the past thirty years, and her hemoglobin levels are consistently above normal.

How to Season a Wok

Today's factory-made carbon-steel woks often appear so clean and sparkling that they resemble stainless-steel pans. Do not be fooled by the shiny clean surface. Not only do all new carbon-steel woks have an antirust coating from the factory that must be removed before cooking, but they also must be seasoned, or cured, in order to seal them from rust.

Seasoning a wok is a two-step process: first, the wok must be scoured and rinsed; next, it must be heated to season it. To scrub off the factory coating, I recommend a stainless-steel scouring pad, soapy hot water, and ample elbow grease. It is not likely that you will see the coating's residue unless, after scrubbing, you fill the wok with water and scrutinize the surface: there will be tiny particles floating in the water. Scour the inside of the wok several times and also scour the outside at least once with the sudsy hot water. (Note that this is the last time you will ever use a scouring pad to wash your wok. Once your wok has been scoured and seasoned, you will wash it only with hot water and a Scotch-Brite–type sponge.) Then rinse the wok in hot tap water.

I suggest you open the windows and turn on the exhaust fan before putting the empty rinsed wok on a burner so that the room is well ventilated. Heat the wok over low heat one to two minutes, just until all the water on the surface has evaporated. Depending on how thoroughly you washed off the factory oil, the heated wok is likely to produce a faint smell from the residual coating. Do not be surprised if the metal inside the wok's well begins turning yellow or blue. This color change is a natural part of the process, although some woks do not change color. Now allow the wok to cool.

While there are numerous ways to season a wok, I recommend two methods. **Method I,** my favorite, involves the simple stir-frying of scallions and ginger in peanut oil. Orthodox Chinese cooks will use only Chinese chives, but since these are not widely available, I recommend scallions and ginger, both of which are also traditional and accessible, and are ingredients that similarly "clean" and protect the wok's surface. Heat the wok over high heat until

a bead of water vaporizes within one to two seconds of contact. There is no exact number of minutes that can be given for preheating a wok because stoves vary in power. It can be as few as 10 seconds or less if you have a powerful range, or as much as a minute or two for a weak range. Once the wok is preheated, swirl 2 tablespoons of peanut or vegetable oil into the well and add ½ cup of sliced unpeeled ginger and 1 bunch of scallions, cut into 2-inch pieces (make sure they are not wet). Reduce the heat to medium and slowly stir-fry the mixture for 5 minutes. As the mixture begins to soften, use the back of the metal spatula to press the seasonings around the entire inside surface of the wok, including the upper edges.

Some cooks consider a wok to be seasoned after a few minutes of stir-frying. I prefer to continue the process over medium heat for about 15 more minutes, still pressing the mixture around the entire inside surface. If the mixture becomes dry, add an additional tablespoon or two of oil. Once the scallions and ginger become brown and a little crusty, remove the wok from the heat to a cold burner, and allow the mixture to cool before discarding it. At this point, the wok may or may not be slightly discolored or mottled in the well. The wok should be fragrant with the scent of scallions and ginger.

Finally, wash the wok's entire inside surface under hot tap water *without* liquid dish soap, rubbing with the soft side of a sponge. Then place the rinsed wok on a burner and heat over low heat until there are no longer any visible water droplets, about 1 minute. Remove the wok from the heat to a cold burner. The wok is now seasoned and ready to be used for cooking.

Within a month or two of frequent use, the interior of the wok may begin to resemble a well-used metal roasting pan. This speckled, worn look indicates the inception of your wok's patina—the thin coating that will provide a natural nonstick surface while protecting the wok from rust.

Method II uses the oven as a way of baking the oil into the wok. The heat of the oven gives the wok a much sturdier patina and bypasses the awkward stage when a newly seasoned pan becomes mottled and unevenly discolored. However, that said, this process is challenging. The metal of the wok becomes very hot, the process takes over an hour, and utmost care and attention is required throughout to prevent mishap. Know that you will need to have well-made pot holders or oven mitts and two washcloths that will be ruined. In addition, if the wok has wooden or plastic handles, they must be removed. If the handles are plastic and cannot be removed, do not use this method. If the wok has wood handles that cannot be removed wrap the handles with wet washcloths that are slightly soggy but not dripping. Then completely wrap the washcloths with heavy-duty aluminum foil. Do not touch the wok or unwrap the foil during this process. The metal must be completely cooled before any part of the wok can be touched.

Preheat the oven to 425°F. Open the window and turn the exhaust fan on high. Using a paper towel that has been folded over several times, spread ½ teaspoon peanut or vegetable oil over the entire inside surface of the wok. Put the wok in the oven for 20 minutes. Remove from the oven with pot holders, place on a cold burner, and let cool until warm to the touch, about 10 minutes. Do not remove the foil on the handles as the washcloths get very hot

and it is easy to get a steam burn. Using the same paper towel, carefully spread another ½ teaspoon peanut or vegetable oil over the entire inside surface. Put the wok back into the oven for 20 minutes. Repeat this step one more time for a total of three heatings. The wok will become darker with each baking. After the last baking, allow the wok to cool completely on a cold burner. Then wash the pan's entire inside surface under hot tap water *without* liquid dish soap, rubbing with the soft side of a sponge. Put the rinsed and still wet wok on a burner and heat over low heat until there are no longer any visible water droplets, about 1 minute. Remove the wok from the heat to a cold burner. Do not coat with oil again. When the wok has completely cooled, carefully unwrap the foil. Be careful as the washcloths may still be hot and steamy. Remove the washcloths. The wok is now seasoned and ready to be used for cooking.

Note: If you are seasoning a Chinese-made cast-iron wok, be aware that it will have a light coating of residual metal powder instead of factory oil. Nonetheless, you should scrub and wash a cast-iron wok and season it with the same method used for a carbon-steel wok.

The first step in seasoning a new carbon-steel or cast-iron wok is to scrub off the factory coating with hot, soapy water using a stainless-steel scouring pad.

Then stir-fry scallions and ginger in peanut oil over medium heat. As you stir-fry, use the spatula to press the mixture over the entire interior surface. Some cooks do this for as few as 5 minutes, but I like to stir-fry the scallions and ginger for about 15 minutes, adding another tablespoon or two of oil if the mixture becomes dry.

Once a carbon-steel wok has been seasoned, the more it is used for cooking the faster it will blacken. Be prepared that the wok, after being seasoned with scallions and ginger, will look mottled and discolored for a long time before it finally blackens. The interior of a carbon-steel wok after two years of use (left), a carbon-steel wok after four months of use (center), a carbon-steel wok newly seasoned (right)

Patience to Wok

Given my impatient nature, my love for cooking with a wok is all the more improbable. When I first began stir-frying, I anticipated that my carbon-steel wok would blacken immediately. Not only did the pan fail to turn black, but I found that I had erased the new finish, so bright and stainless-steel-like, only to be left with the discolored markings of what looked like a ruined pan. I was certain I had committed some sort of Chinese culinary sin. What's more, a sticky film covered the surface, which, even after washing, prevented the wok from feeling or looking clean.

The prized patina that blackens a well-cared-for wok (see The Curious Blackening of the Iron Wok, page 26) can require several years to form. The definition of patina in *Webster's* dictionary is "any thin coating or color change resulting from age." During a carbon-steel wok's first dozen uses, after seasoning with scallions and ginger, the well may begin to darken, often turning shades of blue, as if bruising, or sometimes a yellow or orange hue may appear near the well's center that will deepen with cooking. I have also seen woks that barely change their appearance in their first few uses. But then I once encountered a wok that had been used only a few times yet had achieved a beautiful blackness in the well. In other words, there is no predicting how a carbon-steel wok will respond to its virgin use; with cooking, it will tarnish over time, as the layers of cooked fat gradually become infused into the porous metal. Cast-iron woks, by contrast, have more reliable—and graceful—transitions. Their natural gray color steadily deepens until the treasured blackened tone is achieved.

Most Western cooks are accustomed to the untarnished immutability of modern cookware; cultivating the patina of a carbon-steel wok, however, requires unusual patience. In the early stages of its use (what I think of as the adolescent period), the wok's surface grows mottled. With my first wok, I was so unsettled by the splotchy discolorations that by the time I spotted faint corrosion I assumed that it was permanently ruined, and I actually tossed it out. I even repeated my impatient mistake with a second wok. It wasn't until I gave a third wok a try that I decided not to give in to the impulse to second-guess the process. The wok may still have looked damaged to my eyes, but by steadily cooking with it the marred orange pigment eventually attained the tint of diluted tea, and, with time, acquired a beautiful copperish tone. Ultimately, the carbon-steel wok reminded me of one of life's primal lessons: things are not what they appear to be.

Early on, I scrutinized my carbon-steel wok after every use. I was fascinated by any changes in its appearance and, of course, impatient to identify any signs of aging. But monitoring such progress was as pointless as measuring a child's growth every day; the changes are much too subtle. I did discern how intensification of the patina made the stir-frying of meat possible with the use of very little oil, lending a natural nonstick finish to the surface, which gave the meat a delectable sear. The wok grew less susceptible to rusting. One day, no longer obsessing or impatient, I simply realized that my wok had achieved a tough, dark, mahogany patina. It was a culinary victory. In truth, the prized patina of a well-cared-for carbon-steel wok requires time.

Since then I have "broken in" countless new woks; some for myself, others for students and friends. I have acted as a wok doctor, coaching initiates and assessing the health of young woks. When new wok users fret over scratching the patina with a metal spatula or other such details, I remind them that the goal is not physical perfection and that the scratches will fill in with time. The scratches do not affect the taste of the food. Every wok ages differently, just as people do, and it is beautiful to see how the imperfections work themselves out.

Popcorn in a Wok

I recently gave a wok to a friend for her fiftieth birthday. After seasoning it with ginger and scallions and before presenting it to her, I decided to cook with it for a month to fortify its patina. The surface progressed quite nicely, but I wanted it to have special durability before I sent it off, and so I gave it an unusual treatment: I used the wok to make popcorn. A few years ago I discovered that after making popcorn in my wok its patina was darker in color and was also more fortified. As the corn pops, it evenly disperses a light coating of oil around the wok's entire inside surface, which the heat then burns in. Of course, popping corn will not make a new wok suddenly look or behave like a thirty-year-old pan. The traditional way to develop a patina once the wok has been seasoned is to cook regularly with the wok. You cannot replicate the elegance of a truly old wok overnight; however, the popcorn trick will cheat the process a little. If you are content to let your wok slowly age without shortcuts, then use this recipe only if you want perfect popcorn.

To reduce clean up, I wrap the inside of the lid in aluminum foil, since the oil is dispersed not only on the wok's inside surface but also on the lid.

2 tablespoons peanut or vegetable oil

⅓ cup popcorn kernels

Coarse salt

Heat the oil and a few popcorn kernels in a covered 14-inch flat-bottomed wok over medium heat about 1½ minutes or until 1 or 2 kernels pop. Quickly open the lid just enough to add the remaining popcorn. Then cover and reduce the heat to medium-low. If you do not hear constant popping, increase the heat to medium. Shake the wok constantly back and forth on the burner about 1½ minutes or until the kernels stop popping. Salt to taste. Makes 6 cups.

The Curious Blackening of the Iron Wok

The Cantonese consider stir-fries that have been properly cooked in a carbon-steel or cast-iron wok to have *wok hay*, which I translate as the "taste or breath of the wok." This means that the ingredients have been lightly charred to produce a seared concentrated flavor. This prized taste can only come from a well-seasoned wok, and the more blackened the wok, the more apt it is to create *wok hay*.

Robert L. Wolke, a retired chemist and the author of *What Einstein Told His Cook*, explained to me that "the blackness of a well-seasoned wok comes from the high-temperature decomposition—carbonizing—of organic substances, mostly fats. (Some darkening comes also from oxidation of the steel.) A black pan—or any black object—absorbs virtually all the light that is incident upon it, reflecting virtually none. All this absorbed light energy is retained by the black pan as heat rather than being reflected. The pan, therefore, does indeed heat up faster than, for example, a shiny metal pan. A good-absorbing black pan is also good at radiating the heat it has absorbed. It re-radiates almost all of it, heating the food more efficiently than a shiny pan would."

Terry Huey, who grew up in Omaha, Nebraska, working in his family's restaurant, Chu's Chop Suey House, observed first-hand what happens to a wok when it is used to cook 100 to 200 dishes a day: as it ages, the wok physically changes, becoming heavier and the metal thicker. Kian Lam Kho, who writes a Chinese food blog called redcook.net, laments that a stir-fry cooked in a new wok lacks the richness of food cooked in a well-seasoned and long-used one, like the thirty-year-old carbon-steel wok he so cherishes. "The food doesn't taste the same; it's much more delicious stir-fried in my old wok," says Kho.

Tips for Cooking in a Newly Seasoned Wok

A newly seasoned iron wok has a fragile patina that needs to be fortified. The best way to reinforce the patina is to cook with the wok as much as possible. Do not think of your wok only as a pan fit for cooking Asian food. It is equally excellent for sautéing chicken breasts, pan-frying steaks, scrambling eggs, or even popping popcorn (see Popcorn in a Wok, page 25).

Although the versatile wok can be used for more than just stir-frying, avoid boiling, poaching, or steaming in a new wok, because water dissolves and dries out the patina. In fact, for this reason, many traditional cooks have a wok designated only for cooking with water and another separate wok reserved for stir-frying, pan-frying, and deep-frying. Also, avoid cooking with strong acidic ingredients that will break down the patina and impart an off flavor. Even a brief simmering of a sweet-and-sour sauce made with acidic tomatoes and vinegar can ruin a new patina. Once a wok is well seasoned, you can safely cook acidic foods. However, it is wise to make a habit of never leaving acidic food in the wok once the cooking is complete.

A newly seasoned wok is thirsty for fat. Stir-frying coats the wok's pores with a fine film of oil that eventually gives it a sturdy patina and a natural nonstick surface. To accelerate the development of the patina on a new wok, I fry bacon in it or use it to deep-fry. (No more than 6 cups of oil are needed for a 14-inch wok.) After deep-frying, the wok will benefit further if the hot oil is allowed to cool in the pan and as it does soak into the wok's pores.

Washing a Wok

There are two schools of thought on the best way to wash a carbon-steel or cast-iron wok. Some cooks swear that a wok should be washed with hot tap water only. The belief is that if a wok has been cleaned with liquid dish soap, food is more likely to stick, as well as absorb a soapy taste. On the other hand, many cooks believe a little liquid dish soap is necessary for proper cleaning. I follow both systems. I soak my wok in hot water without soap. I then wash the wok with a sponge, and if the sponge happens to have some soap in it I will use it. I have never had any problems with food sticking or tasting off. In fact, if I cook something very fatty such as bacon in the wok, I will first wipe out the cooled pan with paper towels to remove as much fat as possible before washing it in hot soapy water and then rinsing the pan.

After stir-frying, I soak the wok in hot water for as few as 5 minutes or up to an hour. Once the wok has soaked in water, it is easy to wash it with a Scotch-Brite–type sponge. I prefer the soft side of the sponge for washing the inside and the rougher side for stubborn food particles that stick and also to scrub off food debris from the outside of the wok. After washing, if the wok still feels sticky or has any residual food, I do the Wok Facial Scrub (see opposite page), which thoroughly cleans it in addition to giving it a light oil moisturizer. Otherwise, after washing the wok, rinse it under hot tap water. Do not attempt to dry it with paper towels because toweling will not thoroughly dry the metal. Instead, put the rinsed wok on a burner over low heat and dry 1 to 2 minutes or until there are no longer any visible water droplets. Cool the pan before storing it.

Perhaps the most critical advice of all for washing your wok is to protect it from well-meaning friends or family who think your mottled or blackened wok is dirty and requires extra scrubbing. After you have carefully cultivated your wok's patina, there is nothing more painful than finding it stripped to its original state. Should this happen, re-season the pan by simply following the instructions in How to Season a Wok (see page 20). Lastly, if your wok has been neglected and is rusted, treat it as if it were a new wok, using a stainless-steel scouring pad to wash it, and then re-season it. A wok is extremely forgiving and can be re-seasoned countless times.

Note: What not to use: I do not recommend using the hard bamboo brush known as a wok brush for cleaning a wok. This brush is perfect for washing restaurant woks that have tough patinas formed from cooking hundreds of dishes each day, but when used on a residential carbon-steel wok the brush is too harsh and will scratch off the delicate patina. It can be safely used on a Chinese-made cast-iron wok. I also do not use steel wool or any kind of abrasive powder cleanser, and I would never wash a wok in the dishwasher.

Wok Facial Scrub

When food debris or rust resists cleaning, a "facial"-like scrub of the inside surface of your wok will not only clean it, but also rejuvenate the pan. This salt and oil cleaning is especially useful for woks that have been neglected for months or even years and have suffered from lack of use. For neglected pans, after cleaning the wok with salt and oil, the pan can be re-seasoned.

2 teaspoons salt

1 teaspoon peanut or vegetable oil

Heat a 14-inch flat-bottomed wok over high heat until a bead of water vaporizes within 1 to 2 seconds of contact. Remove the wok from the heat. Add salt and peanut or vegetable oil. With 3 paper towels that have been folded multiple times to make a thick pad about 3 x 3 inches, scrub with the salt-oil mixture, being sure as you rub that your hand is protected by the pad (a hot wok is extremely dangerous and can cause serious burns). You will see that the salt and the pad will turn a light shade of brown. The salt crystals gently rub off any food debris or rust that may be on the surface, and the oil acts like a moisturizer to lightly lubricate the surface. Wipe the wok clean. Rinse the wok under hot tap water, rubbing lightly with a soft sponge to remove any remaining salt crystals. Put the rinsed wok on a burner over low heat for 1 to 2 minutes to make sure the pan is totally dry. Cool the pan before storing it.

Storing a Wok

When storing a wok, it is important to put the pan in a place that will protect the patina from becoming scratched. I use my wok so often that I leave it with its lid on the stovetop. I have several other woks that I use less frequently that I store stacked one upon the other in a kitchen cabinet. You can also hang your wok from a pot rack, but if you do not cook in that pan on a regular basis its patina is likely to attract lint or dust. If the wok is used infrequently, it is best to put it in a large paper bag to protect it from dust, then store it in a dry, airy spot such as a kitchen cabinet. Protecting your wok with a paper bag is essential if you live near the seashore or in a damp climate, both of which increase the risk of rust. Some cooks suggest lightly oiling a wok before storing it to enhance the patina. I do not recommend this because the oil can easily become rancid, especially if the wok is not used regularly.

The Stir-Fry Pantry

Vegetables

Bean sprouts *(gna choi)*: There are two varieties of Chinese sprouts: mung bean sprouts, which are more commonly available, and soybean sprouts. The head of a mung bean sprout is the size of a grain of barley, about ¼ inch wide. Choose fat, plump sprouts no more than 2½ inches long. Avoid long, stringy, brown, or limp sprouts, all indications that they are old. Store in the refrigerator's vegetable crisper bin for no more than 1 day.

Bok choy *(bok choi)*: This member of the cabbage family is available in several varieties. The most common variety found in Chinatown is sold in bunches, 8 to 11 inches long, with white stalks and unblemished dark green leaves. Premium bok choy is called *bok choy sum*, or heart of bok choy, and it is more delicate. In addition, there is baby bok choy: it varies in size from 3 inches to 8 inches in length, and it is the choicest. Shanghai bok choy is probably the most widely available baby bok choy, and it is

Left to right: bok choy, baby bok choy, Shanghai bok choy

Fresh and dried chilies, left to right: jalapeño, Thai or bird, dried, Anaheim

recognizable by its overall pale green color and the spoonlike shape of its stems. Choose bok choy with tightly closed buds. Avoid any open flowers, yellow leaves, or stems that are beginning to brown, all signs that the vegetable is past its prime. I prefer bunches that are smaller than 11 inches in length; the bigger bunches tend to be more mature and too fibrous for stir-frying. Bok choy is available all year round but is best in the winter months. Store in the refrigerator's vegetable crisper bin for up to 3 days.

Chayote *(hup cheung gwa)*: Also known as mirliton, this pale green, flat, pear-shaped squash is 5 to 7 inches long and 3½ inches at its widest point. It is in season from fall to spring. Chayote must be peeled before cooking. The best are firm when pressed, with no brown spots. Store in the refrigerator's vegetable crisper bin for up to 1 week.

Chilies, dried red peppers *(laat ziu gon)*: These are 2 to 3 inches long, and should be fragrant and have a sheen. As these peppers age, they lose flavor and aroma. Store in a jar in a cool, dry, dark cupboard.

Chilies, fresh *(laat ziu)*: Three varieties of chili peppers are called for in this book. Red or green varieties can be found for all of them. To reduce the heat, remove the seeds when using any chili pepper. Store in a paper bag in the refrigerator's vegetable crisper bin for about 1 week.

Anaheim: A slender pepper, 5 to 7 inches long, Anaheims are mild to moderately hot.

Jalapeño: This relatively plump pepper is tapered, 2 to 3 inches long, and fiery hot.

Thai or bird chilies: This pepper is thin, 2 to 3 inches long, and fiery hot.

Chinese broccoli *(gai lan)*: Also known as Chinese kale, the individual stalks are most commonly sold year-round in 2-pound bundles, but are best in the winter months. The leaves are dark green and the stalks are 10 to 14 inches long and ½ to ¾ of an inch wide. Tiny pale green and white buds are hidden in the leaves. When selecting Chinese broccoli, never choose broccoli with stalks with dried ends, open flowers, or yellow leaves; these are signs of age. Store in the refrigerator's vegetable crisper bin for up to 5 days.

Chinese eggplant *(ke zee)*: The best eggplants are lavender, firm, and blemish free, with a silky skin. They are 8 to 9 inches long and 2 inches wide. Because they are smaller than the Western variety, they are much more tender, with almost no seeds, and are said to be less bitter. Select smooth, firm-skinned eggplant that are heavy for their size. Store in the refrigerator's vegetable crisper bin for up to 1 week.

Cilantro *(yeem sai)*: Also known as fresh coriander or Chinese parsley, cilantro has delicate leaves and a strong flavor, and is best when sold with its roots. Select green, fresh leaves with thin stems, avoiding yellow, wilted leaves. Wash carefully in several changes of cold water to remove dirt before using. Submerge the roots in a glass of water, cover the leaves with a plastic bag, and store in the refrigerator for up to 5 days.

Edamame *(mou dao)*: Although sometimes available fresh in pods, it is more likely that you'll find shelled edamame in the frozen section of most Chinese markets or health food stores.

Fava beans *(can dou)*: Also called broad beans, these pods are about 8 inches long. Remove the beans from the pods, then skin the beans, because the skins are tough. Choose tightly closed pods. Store in the refrigerator's vegetable crisper bin for up to 1 week.

Left to right: chayote, Chinese eggplant, fuzzy melon, ginger, fava beans. Bottom: water chestnuts, peeled and unpeeled

From top: long beans, lotus root. Center row, from left: Chinese broccoli, yau choi, *snow pea shoots. Bottom: water spinach*

Fuzzy melon *(zeet gwa)*: This green squash with mild flavor ranges in length from 4 to 10 inches long. The most desirable fuzzy melon has very fine prickly hairs. The squash must be peeled before cooking. The best season for them is the summer. Store in the refrigerator's vegetable crisper bin for up to 1 week.

Ginger root: See Ginger Essentials, page 42.

Long beans *(dul gock)*: Also known as yard-long beans, these are available in two varieties: dark green beans and light green beans, and both are best in the summer. The dark beans are crisper, the light less crunchy. Both can be 18 to 30 inches long. Even when farm-fresh, the beans are limp and have tiny brown blemishes. Store in the refrigerator's vegetable crisper bin for up to 5 days.

Lotus root *(leen gnul)*: Lotus root is ivory-colored, about 16 inches long, and has 3 sections (although some markets separate the sections) with little root hairs between each piece. Each section requires careful washing to remove the mud in which it is grown.

Dried and fresh mushrooms, left to right: thick- and thin-capped dried shiitake, fresh enoki, thick- and thin-capped fresh shiitake

Lotus root is in season in September, October, and November, but it is available other times of the year. Never select lotus root that has been wrapped in cellophane or Cryovac packages; you must be able to smell the lotus root to make sure it has a clean smell. Select roots that are heavy, firm, and blemish free. Once the root is cut, rinse it again to make sure all the mud has been removed. Cut off any dark spots. Store in the refrigerator's vegetable crisper bin for up to 5 days.

Mushrooms

Shiitake are available dried and fresh:

Dried *(dung gwoo)*: Also known as Chinese dried mushrooms, or dried winter mushrooms as they are called in Japan, these dried fungi are brownish, gray-black mushrooms and vary greatly in quality. Shiitakes are sold in cellophane packages, in boxes, and in bulk in Chinese grocery stores. Pale, thick mushroom caps with lots of cracks are the most prized and are called *fa gwoo*. The flavor of these mushrooms is robust and concentrated, with an almost meaty taste. They also require 2 to 3 hours more soaking time than the 30 minutes required for thin-capped mushrooms. The thinner caps, which are browner in color, are less flavorful and inexpensive. Store in an airtight jar in a cool, dark, dry cupboard.

Fresh *(seen gwoo)*: Choose mushrooms that are firm, plump, and blemish free. They should have a clean, fresh smell. The hard stems must be removed before cooking. There are two varieties commonly sold: one has a thick, dark-colored cap with a fat stem, the other a thin, tan-colored cap with a skinny stem. They should be placed in a paper bag and stored in the refrigerator's vegetable crisper bin for 1 to 2 days.

Napa cabbage *(wong nga bock)*: Select cabbage

with pale white to yellow crinkly leaves and creamy white stems that are blemish free, with no tiny brown or black spots. Store in the refrigerator's vegetable crisper bin for up to 10 days.

Snow pea shoots *(dau miu)*: From the snow pea, these delicate shoots are a cold-weather vegetable; as the weather warms up, the shoots toughen. The shoots are pale green, with small, delicate leaves, tendrils, and stems. The leaves are matte and the shoots appear slightly limp even when fresh, but should never be yellow. Less desirable is the hothouse variety, available year-round, which has uniform dark green sprouts with no tendrils. Store in the refrigerator's vegetable crisper bin for 2 to 3 days.

Water chestnuts, fresh *(ma tai)*: A dark brown bulblike vegetable, lightly covered in dirt, water chestnuts are about 1½ inches wide and 1 inch thick. They are grown underwater in mud and have a thin skin that must be thoroughly rinsed and peeled. Choose ones that are heavy and firm. Put in a paper bag and store in the refrigerator's vegetable crisper bin for up to 1 week.

Water spinach *(toong sum choi)*: The entire stalk is about 18 inches long and is pale green in color, with slightly darker green leaves. Most of the stalk is made up of a hollow stem with skinny, pointy leaves. Water spinach is sold in big 1½-pound bunches. Store in the refrigerator's vegetable crisper bin for no more than 2 days as it deteriorates quickly.

Yau choi *(yau choi)*: Also known as *choi sum*, this Asian green is recognizable by its slender green stems, its oval green leaves, and slightly mustardy flavor. In the photo on page 34 it may appear to look like Chinese broccoli, but the stems are much thinner and more flexible. Select *yau choi* that has tight buds and blemish-free leaves. Store in the refrigerator's vegetable crisper bin for 3 to 4 days.

Sauces, Condiments, and Wine

Bean sauce *(mien see)*: Also known as ground bean sauce, brown bean sauce, or yellow bean sauce, this condiment is sold in cans and jars. I prefer Koon Chun brand in the 13-ounce jar. It is made from soybeans, salt, wheat flour, sugar, sesame oil, and spices. Store in the refrigerator for several months.

Chili bean sauce *(laat dao zheung)*: Also known as chili bean paste, this is made with soybeans, chilies, and spices. It has a much fuller flavor than chili garlic sauce. Every brand differs slightly, so you must experiment to find the one you prefer. Store in the refrigerator for several months.

Chili garlic sauce *(shoon yong laat ziu zheung)*: Also known as chili garlic paste, this reddish-brown sauce with flecks of red chili is made of chili pepper, salt, rice vinegar, and garlic. Do not confuse this with chili bean sauce, which is more flavorful. Store in the refrigerator for several months.

Fish sauce *(yu lou)*: Richly flavored from the extract of fermented anchovies, this thin sauce is prized in Vietnamese and Southeast Asian cooking. A favorite brand is Viet Huong Three Crabs.

Hoisin sauce *(hoisin zheung)*: This very thick, chocolate-colored sauce is mildly sweet and smoky in flavor. Made from sugar, soybeans, garlic, sesame seeds, chili peppers, and spices, it is sold in cans or jars. I prefer Koon Chun brand, which is available in a 13-ounce jar. Store in the refrigerator for several months.

Oyster sauce *(how yul)*: This thick, brown sauce, also known as oyster-flavored sauce, is used in cooking and as a condiment. Sold in bottles, oyster sauce varies greatly in quality. The brand I like, Lee Kum Kee, has a woman and boy in a small boat pictured on the label. A vegetarian oyster sauce made from mushroom extracts is also available. Store in the refrigerator for up to 1 year.

Top row, left to right: sesame oil, chili oil, Shao Hsing rice wine, dry sherry, rice vinegar, oyster sauce, peanut oil, Chinkiang vinegar, dark soy, soy sauce. Bottom row, left to right: fermented bean curd with chili, bean sauce, hoisin sauce, chili bean sauce, pickled cucumbers, salted soybeans, mango chutney, Pickapeppa Sauce, Matouk's Calypso Sauce

Shao Hsing rice wine *(siu hing ʒul)*: This inexpensive wine is made by fermenting glutinous rice and is available in Chinese liquor stores. My favorite is Pagoda brand. Dry sherry is a very good substitute. Store at room temperature.

Soy sauce *(see yul)*: Also known as thin soy sauce and superior soy sauce, this is the most common soy sauce used in cooking, and is saltier than dark soy sauce and lighter in color. My favorite brand, Kikkoman, carries an organic soy sauce that is excellent.

Dark soy sauce *(low ʒul)*: Also known as black soy sauce, this is blacker, thicker, and richer in color and slightly sweeter in taste than soy sauce because it has been aged longer.

Vinegar *(cho)*: Chinese vinegar is made primarily from glutinous rice. Store at room temperature in a cool, dark, dry cupboard.

Chinkiang vinegar *(zun gong cho)*: Dark and semi-sweet, this vinegar is produced in Eastern China and is slightly similar in taste to balsamic vinegar.

Rice vinegar *(zing mai cho)*: This is a pale, amber-colored vinegar that is mild in flavor.

Wet bean curd, white *(bock fu yu)*: These are beige-colored 1-inch cubes of fermented bean curd in liquid. There is also a variety that comes in a thick red sauce called *nom yu*. Store in the refrigerator for up to 1 year.

Oils

Chili oil *(laat yul)*: Reddish orange in color, this is flavored with dried red chilies. Store in a cool, dark, dry cupboard for up to 6 months, or refrigerate.

Peanut oil *(fa sung yul)*: Its high smoking point makes peanut oil ideal for stir-frying. I prefer Planters for its overall quality. Store in a cool, dark, dry cupboard for up to 6 months, or refrigerate.

Sesame oil *(ma yul)*: Golden brown, fragrant, and aromatic, this seasoning oil is made from toasted or roasted sesame seeds. Choose pure sesame oil rather than one that has been blended with another oil. I prefer Kadoya brand. Store for up to 1 year in the refrigerator.

Fresh Ingredients

Chinese bacon *(lop yuk)*: Drier and harder than Western bacon, this dry-cured pork belly is available in Chinese butcher shops and some Chinese markets. It has an earthy, smoky flavor and comes in a 1-inch-thick slab, never in thin slices. You must ask for it by its Cantonese name, *lop yuk*; do not ask for "Chinese bacon." Store tightly wrapped for up to 2 weeks in the refrigerator, or for up to 2 months in the freezer.

Chinese sausage *(lop chong)*: Made of pork, chicken, pork liver, or duck liver, this dried sweet sausage is sold in Chinese butcher shops, where it generally is found hanging in pairs connected by a thick cord behind the counter. Available extra-lean and "regular," I generally select the extra-lean pork for cooking. The sausages are also sold in Cryovac packages in the refrigerator section of some Chinese grocery stores. Resembling skinny salami, the links are 6 to 7 inches long and about ½ inch wide. Like Chinese bacon, the sausages are very hard and can be difficult to slice if not fresh. Store in the refrigerator.

Fresh Noodles

Broad rice noodles *(haw fun)*: These are sold in long sheets that have been folded to roughly the size of a folded small kitchen towel. They are soft and flexible until they are refrigerated. Do not refrigerate them if you are planning to use them the day of purchase. (If refrigerated, they must be steamed before stir-frying.) Broad rice noodles are sold in Chinese bakeries, in stores that sell fresh tofu, or at the checkout counters of some Chinese grocery stores. Store in a plastic bag for 3 to 4 days in the refrigerator.

Fresh Chinese egg noodles *(dan mein)*: These fat, fresh egg noodles have a golden egg color and are almost the same thickness as spaghetti. They are available cooked and uncooked, and I prefer the uncooked variety. They require only 1 to 3 minutes of boiling. The noodles can be found in the refrigerator section of most Chinese markets. Store for up to 5 days in the refrigerator.

Tofu

Firm tofu *(dul foo)*: This comes in 3-inch squares or in 14-ounce to 1-pound blocks. Fresh tofu should have a clean smell. Store in the refrigerator, changing the water daily, for up to 3 days.

Five-spice tofu *(mmm heung dul foo gawn)*: Also known as spiced tofu, this is pressed tofu flavored with a soy sauce marinade. It has a dry, firm texture and is sold in 3-inch squares or in 8-ounce packages in the refrigerator section in Asian markets. Store

Fresh ingredients, top: Chinese bacon. Left to right: fresh Chinese egg noodles, fresh broad rice noodles, Chinese sausage, five-spice tofu

in the refrigerator. Once the package is opened, use within 3 to 4 days.

Dried Ingredients

Cloud ears *(wun yee)*: Also known as tree ears or as black fungus, these dried fungi are gray-black in color. Cloud ears look like delicate, paper-thin, crinkled, 1-inch leaves. They are sold in plastic bags in Chinese grocery stores; they should be transferred to a jar and stored in a cool, dark, dry cupboard for up to 1 year. Do not confuse these with wood ears, which are much bigger and thicker.

Curry powder *(ga lei)*: A blend of spices such as turmeric, ginger, peppercorns, cumin, coriander, cinnamon, and cloves.

Fermented black beans *(dul see)*: Also known as Chinese dried black beans, or preserved beans, these small beans are fermented with salt and spices, and are a popular seasoning with meat, seafood, and poultry. They are sold in plastic bags or in a small, round, cardboard container. Before using, I like to rinse the beans in several changes of cold water. A favorite brand is Yang Jiang Preserved Beans, which are packaged in a cardboard box. The beans keep indefinitely in an airtight jar in a cool, dark, dry cupboard, or in the refrigerator.

Five-spice powder *(mmm heung fun)*: This combination of ground Chinese cinnamon, cloves, fennel, Sichuan peppercorns, and star anise is sold in plastic bags or in a small jar. Store in an airtight jar in a cool, dark, dry cupboard.

Dried Noodles

Cellophane noodles *(fun see)*: Also known as glass noodles, bean thread noodles, or green bean thread, these are available in a variety of package sizes, from 1.76 to 17.6 ounces. Cellophane noodles are sold in plastic bags in Chinese grocery markets. Store in an airtight jar in a cool, dark, dry cupboard.

Dried ingredients, top, left to right: cloud ears, fermented black beans, Sichuan peppercorns. Bottom, left to right: dried shrimp, cellophane noodles, thin rice stick noodles

Rice sticks, dried *(mai fan)*: Also called vermicelli, these noodles are superfine and very brittle. They come in a big rectangular block in a 1-pound package. Store rice sticks in a sealed plastic bag in a cool, dark, dry cupboard for up to 6 months.

Scallops *(gawn yu chee)*: Dried scallops look like fresh scallops, except for their golden color. They are expensive and very flavorful. Dried scallops are sold in boxes or loose in large bins in grocery stores or herb shops. Broken scallops are less expensive and can be equally flavorful. Choose scallops that are fragrant, golden, and shiny. Store in an airtight jar in a cool, dark, dry cupboard indefinitely.

Shrimp *(ha mai)*: These are ½ to 1 inch long and are very flavorful. Dried shrimp are sold loose in big bins or in plastic packages in Asian markets. Choose bright orange shrimp; avoid shrimp that look flaky. Store in an airtight jar in a cool, dark, dry cupboard for up to 1 year.

Sichuan peppercorns *(fa ʒiu)*: The peppercorns are reddish brown in color and are, in fact, berries. They are sold in plastic bags and have tiny twigs that need to be removed. The peppercorns must first be dry-roasted, then ground before being used for cooking. Store in an airtight jar in a cool, dark, dry cupboard.

The Best Oil for Stir-Frying

The ideal oil for stir-frying is one with a high smoking point because it allows the oil to be heated to a high temperature *without* the fatty acids in the oil breaking down. Reaching the smoking point—the temperature at which the oil will literally begin to smoke—changes the chemical structure of the oil, destroying its nutrients and imparting an unpleasant taste to ingredients. For this reason, the "hot wok cold oil" technique for adding oil to a wok (see Stir-Frying with Proper Heat and Control, page 52) is critical.

Traditionally, the Chinese have preferred peanut oil for stir-frying. Peanuts, or groundnuts, were introduced to China in the sixteenth century when the Chinese discovered they could press the nuts and extract an excellent cooking oil. I prefer peanut oil because it has a high smoking point and is a good balanced medium for stir-frying. If nut allergies are a concern, other oils with high smoking points include grapeseed, rice bran, corn, safflower, and canola oil.

No matter which oil you choose, be certain it is not rancid by first smelling it. The oil should have a clean, fresh scent. To prevent it from turning rancid, store the oil in a tightly sealed container in a dark, cool place or in the refrigerator if it is used infrequently. It will liquefy at room temperature.

Always use fresh oil when stir-frying. Oil that has already been used for deep-fat frying automatically has a lower smoking point and for that reason can present a danger when reheated. While it is a common practice for Chinese home cooks to save oil that has been used for deep-fat frying, filter it, and reuse it for stir-frying, I *do not* recommend this because reused oil can never sear ingredients with the same intensity as fresh oil. In fact, according to Shirley Corriher, author of *Cookwise*, "Never use frying fat twice. Even fat with a high flash point can burst into flame at a dangerously low temperature after just one high-temperature use." The one exception to this rule: I will reuse oil that has been previously used for velveting (see Velvet Stir-Fry, page 100) because that oil has been heated only to 280°F (versus 375°F for deep-fat frying) and has been used at that temperature for no more than 1 minute.

Oils with low smoking points, extra virgin olive oil and roasted sesame oil among them, are too unstable at high temperatures and cannot be used for stir-frying. Rather, add sesame oil to season or flavor a dish at the end of cooking. The apparent anomaly of sesame oil having a smoking point of 410°F on the Bailey's oil chart below has baffled me. The prevailing understanding is that roasted Asian-style sesame oil cannot be used for stir-frying because of its low smoking point. The chart does not specify what kind of sesame oil was tested, nor how it was pressed, treated, or purified. All smoking points depend on the variety of the seed and how the oil was processed.

Approximate Smoke Points for Fresh Home-Use Oils

(Note that these values are for fresh oil and can drop dramatically with a single use.)

Type of Oil	°F	°C
Sunflower	392	200
Corn (refined)	410	210
Olive ("pure")	410	210
Peanut	410	210
Sesame	410	210
Soybean	410	210
Rapeseed*	437	225
Grapeseed	446	230
Cottonseed	450	232
Safflower	450	232
Almond	495	257
Rice Bran	500	260
Avocado	520	271

*Canola oil comes from strains of rapeseed with low erucic acid content.

Source: Daniel Swern (ed.). Bailey's Industrial Oil and Fat Products, 4th ed. *New York: John Wiley and Sons, 1979, as reproduced in Michele Anna Jordan.* The Good Cook's Book of Oil & Vinegar. *Reading, Mass.: Addison-Wesley Publishing Company, 1992.*

GINGER ESSENTIALS

Buy Fresh

Fresh ginger is a rhizome. The more common mature variety has a thin, dry skin and is available year-round. Select ginger that is heavy and firm to the touch, with slightly rough, unwrinkled skin that has a faint sheen. In the spring and summer, young ginger, sometimes called stem ginger, is in season. It is milder in flavor, pale yellow in color, with pink-tipped shoots and a tender skin. Store ginger in the refrigerator's vegetable crisper bin in a brown paper bag for up to 2 weeks.

Ginger as a Tenderizer

Ginger contains a protein-digesting enzyme that tenderizes meat. Some recipes for marinated raw meat or poultry call for minced or shredded ginger in the marinades. The enzyme works even more effectively with heat when cooking.

How to Peel

The easiest way to peel ginger is to scrape the skin off with the edge of a teaspoon (**1**). The spoon easily removes the skin from the nooks and crannies around the knobs.

Sliced: Cut the peeled ginger into coins, about the size of a quarter. To smash sliced ginger to release more flavor, lay the chef's knife flat on the cutting board with the sharp edge facing away from you. Put a slice of ginger under the blade closest to where the blade meets the handle. Grasp the knife handle, place the heel of your free hand on the blade over the slice, and press down firmly until the slice splits but remains intact.

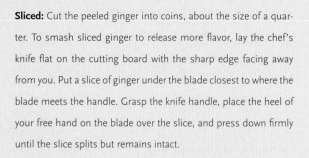

Finely Shredded: Cut the piece of peeled ginger into paper-thin slices (**2**). Stack 2 or 3 slices at a time, then cut the stack into scant $1/8$-inch-wide fine shreds (**3**).

Minced: Cut the piece of peeled ginger into paper-thin slices. Stack 2 or 3 slices at a time, then cut the stack into fine shreds. Cut the shreds crosswise into scant ⅛-inch pieces.

Juice: Grate a small amount of ginger with a traditional Chinese ginger grater (**4**), Microplane, or cheese grater and then squeeze the ginger pulp with your fingers to extract the juice (**5**).

4

5

Note: It is a common mistake to use a cheese grater or Microplane to finely shred or mince ginger. A cheese grater or Microplane can only be used to grate ginger for juice. Grated ginger cannot be substituted for finely shredded or minced; grated ginger is too wet and will immediately spatter when added to hot oil.

Ginger Rice Wine

For many overseas Chinese immigrants, ginger was a precious commodity. When they were fortunate enough to obtain ginger, they would preserve it by cutting the peeled ginger into thick slices, putting the slices in a clean jar, covering them with rice wine, dry sherry, or another liquor, and then sealing the jar. Not only was this an excellent way to store ginger, but it infused the rice wine with an intense ginger flavor that made it more valuable for cooking. Today, ginger is widely available, but if you have more ginger than you can use this is an excellent way to inject ginger essence into your rice wine or sherry. Likewise, the ginger becomes flavored with the rice wine. That said, wine-soaked ginger is less than ideal for stir-frying. Even after towel drying, ginger that has been soaked in liquor will still be moist and will cause spattering when added to hot oil.

Pickled ginger can be found in jars or plastic containers in the refrigerator section of most Asian markets. I prefer "natural" ginger, which has the least amount of preservatives.

GARLIC ESSENTIALS

Buy Fresh

When selecting garlic, look for heads with skin that is wrapped tightly and that has a sheen. Do not purchase garlic that has germinating green shoots, an indication that the head is old. Once the garlic germinates, it loses its sweetness and can even have a bitter taste. If you have cloves with green shoots, remove the shoots before using. Store garlic at room temperature in a breathable open container in a cool, dry spot away from light. If the head is whole, it should keep for a month or two; however, once cloves are removed the storage life shortens.

How to Smash and Peel Cloves

Trim the root end of an unpeeled garlic clove. Lay the chef's knife flat on the cutting board with the sharp edge facing away from you. Put the clove under the blade closest to where the blade meets the handle. Grasp the knife handle, place the heel of your free hand on the blade over the clove and press down firmly until the clove breaks. The peel will split apart and fall off the clove; the clove will be slightly smashed.

How to Mince

Garlic is an essential ingredient in stir-fries. Numerous recipes in this book call for minced garlic, most notably many of the Hakka recipes, which require 2 or 3 tablespoons. If you lack strong knife skills, this amount can be tedious work and enough to discourage you from stir-frying. Understanding this obstacle, I decided to investigate garlic presses, which until now I have always maintained are useless gadgets because while they may save time in the hand-mincing department, they use up that found time in what it takes to clean them.

Some cooks use a mini food processor for mincing, but if you are processing less than ¼ cup of garlic it just splatters in the bowl and ends up only roughly chopped. Worst of all, the bowl turns out to be as difficult to clean as the press! Rösle, a company from Germany, makes a press that easily crushes garlic with the peel, and can be cleaned in only seconds by a rinse under running water. I do not wash it with soap as I use the tool to crush only garlic. The Rösle press is made of heavy-duty stainless steel and weighs nearly 12 ounces. The superior quality of the Rösle is reflected in the price, which is more expensive than other garlic presses, but I have come to the conclusion that it is worth the investment, especially if you are averse to mincing garlic by hand. The press makes mincing a large amount of garlic quick and efficient and also saves your fingers from smelling of garlic.

If a small amount of garlic is called for in a recipe, I still prefer hand-mincing. I smash the garlic clove and then mince the garlic. For large amounts, the convenience and the time-saving attributes of a garlic press are indispensable. Two important facts to keep in mind when using a garlic press: you will not need to use as much pressed garlic as hand-minced and the flavor intensifies as it sits.

According to Robert L. Wolke in *What Einstein Told His Cook 2*, "When garlic is cut into smaller and smaller pieces, or reduced even further by being crushed, more vacuoles are broken open, more alliinase enzyme is released, and more thio-sulfinates are formed, producing a stronger aroma and flavor." **Note:** Preminced garlic packed in oil is available sold in jars. I never purchase this product as the flavor of fresh garlic is far superior.

THE PROPER PREPARATIONS OF GINGER, SCALLIONS, AND GARLIC

Top: minced, finely shredded, and sliced ginger. Middle: minced, finely shredded, chopped, and sliced scallions. Bottom: minced, crushed and sliced garlic

TWO WAYS TO SHRED SCALLIONS

An inexpensive Negi Cutter (see page 17) is the easiest way to make fine scallion shreds. Be careful when using the Negi Cutter as it is extremely sharp. Using a chef's knife or cleaver, trim off the root end and any withered tops. Then pull the shredder through about 2 inches of the white portion of the scallion. Cut off 2 inches of the shredded scallions and continue using the cutter in 2-inch segments.

Using a chef's knife or cleaver, trim off the root end and any withered tops. Cut the scallion into 2-inch-long pieces. Cut each 2-inch segment in half lengthwise. Put the cut side face up and thinly slice into 2-inch-long fine shreds.

The ingredients for Chinese Trinidadian Stir-Fried Shrimp with Rum are prepared and ready to be stir-fried.

Stir-Frying

RECIPES

Classics and Innovations

Stir-Fry

Missing . . . and Lost in Translation

The Chinese word for "stir-fry" in Cantonese is *chau* (sometimes written as *ch'ao*; Chinese American *chow*; Mandarin *chao*). In actuality, the *chau* motion is not a stirring action, but is closer to a tumbling, tossing, or a quick scooping action. The goal is to continuously toss bite-sized ingredients in a small amount of oil in a wok over high heat so that each morsel is constantly exposed to the hot wok's well. The result is a light searing of ingredients that allows them to cook both quickly and uniformly, without burning or charring.

From the first Asian cookbook published in English in America, in 1914, the *Chinese-Japanese Cook Book*, through subsequent books over the next several decades, writers translated *chau* as "fry," "stir constantly," or "stir the mixture continuously." Not until 1945, when Buwei Yang Chao wrote *How to Cook and Eat in Chinese*, did the term "stir-fry" first come into use. Chao describes stir-frying as "blitz cooking." I find the use of "blitz" fascinating because stir-frying does have a rigorous character, a rapid striking action. Chao's description is equally vigorous: "Roughly speaking, *ch'ao* may be defined as a big-fire-shallow-fat-continual-stirring-quick-frying of cut-up material with wet seasonings. We shall call it 'stir-fry' or 'stir' for short. The nearest to this in western cooking is sauté." In contrast to stir-frying, sautéing is the French technique of quick cooking bite-sized or large pieces of food, generally in butter or olive oil, in a large shallow sauté pan over moderately high heat.

After the publication of Chao's book, a few cookbook authors adopted the term "stir-fry," but most continued to write their recipes using a range of action verbs from "fry briskly," "stir and toss," "sauté," "quick fry," to "toss cook." By 1966, *The Thousand Recipe Chinese Cookbook* by Gloria Bley Miller, and in 1968, *The Cooking of China* volume in the Time-Life Foods of the World series both uniformly used the term "stir-frying." Yet, in 1972, Craig Claiborne and Virginia Lee's seminal *The Chinese Cookbook* returned to the terminology of "tossing quickly" and "cook, stirring briskly."

It is easy to imagine that in the years prior to the popularity of television cooking shows, novice Chinese cooks were baffled by the term "stir-fry" and that the word "stir" misled them into thinking it was a circular, stirring action. One of the best explanations of stir-frying comes in the opening chapter of *The Chinese Cookbook* by Claiborne and Lee: "The point of stir-frying is to keep the food moving constantly so that all parts of the dish come in contact with the hottest part of the pan and cook quickly and evenly. This is accomplished by quickly and repeatedly sliding a spoon or spatula down between the food and the pan and turning the food over on itself with a digging and tossing motion." The action is indeed a combination of digging and the continuous flipping of the food over on itself, although the suggestion that a spoon is the correct utensil is odd. Yet, in their recipes Claiborne and Lee curiously never use the term "stir-fry."

Chinese scholars have conflicting views on the origins of stir-frying. In *The Food of China*, author E. N. Anderson speculates that stir-frying was invented in the Han Dynasty (206 B.C.–A.D. 220). "Although it is not directly mentioned in the texts or otherwise, it can be inferred from the great stress on slicing foods thinly and evenly, and the presence of model woks in the archeological record. . . . The wok (the name is the Cantonese pronunciation of *kuo*) is a specialized piece of equipment, perfect for stir-frying and not at all the tool of choice for anything else. The presence of wok models on model Han stoves is thus good evidence for the development of the most distinctively Chinese method of cooking." However, H. T. Huang in *Science and Civilisation in China* states that stir-frying was developed in the Song Dynasty (960–1279). Whether stir-frying began in the Han or the Song dynasty, historians agree that its stature as a refined cooking technique was not realized until the Ming Dynasty (1368–1644). Jacqueline M. Newman, an expert on Chinese cooking, speculates that stir-frying was practiced "by a few in Han times but did not become popular, that is really used until the Ming [dynasty]."

Sadly, while the term "stir-fry" is now part of the American culinary vocabulary, the art of stir-frying remains misunderstood. Indeed, the word partially does suggest the action, but it does not allude to the complexity or refinement of how it is enjoyed by connoisseurs. In Chinese culinary culture stir-frying is revered for its many variations, each offering a distinct taste. There are two main stir-frying categories. The velvet stir-fry (see Velvet Stir-Fry, page 100) is the pinnacle of sophistication and is valued for the extraordinary satiny texture that is achieved when chicken, fish, shellfish, or meat has been marinated in an egg white–cornstarch mixture, then blanched in oil or water before stir-frying. The second category is a simpler style of stir-frying that is divided into three varieties: the first includes "raw stir-fries," such as Cashew Chicken (page 123), in which all the ingredients are raw when added to the wok; the second, "cooked stir-fries," like Singapore Noodles (page 274), have one or more cooked ingredients, such as barbecued pork; and the third, "dry stir-fries" (see Dry Stir-Frying and Moist Stir-Frying, page 121), such as Classic Dry-Fried Pepper and Salt Shrimp (page 166), are distinct for the absence of any liquid ingredients and for the slightly longer stir-frying, which in the recipe mentioned gives the shrimp an almost caramelized, smoky flavor.

In China and in Southeast Asia, street cooks stir-fry what the Cantonese call *siu chau* (see The Simple Stir-Fry, page 201), the quick stir-fry beloved for its home-style taste that is served piping hot and bursting with the heat of the wok. There is also the moist stir-fry, like Ginger Tomato Beef (page 80), characterized by the liberal use of stock or sauce to create a "comfort" stir-fry best enjoyed with plenty of rice to soak up the delicious sauce. And, finally, the quintessential stir-fry is the esteemed *ching chau*, or clear stir-fry (see Stir-Fry Purist's Dish, page 217), the classic treatment of a single ingredient stir-fried in a little oil and minimally seasoned so that nothing mars the true essence of the ingredient. Stir-fried by a master cook, this simple treatment offers the ultimate stir-fry experience, especially when applied to seasonal vegetables vibrant with flavor.

Perhaps it is an unreasonable expectation to hope that the word "stir-fry" might also now connote all the possible different tastes that the technique itself produces. That said, we have come a long way from thinking of it as blitz cooking or the tumble-fry. Now it remains to be seen if the extraordinary subtleties of the "velvet stir-fry," "clear stir-fry," and all the many variations become a part of the American vocabulary.

The Language of Stir-Frying

Stir-frying, more than a technique, represents a cultural way of thinking. The Cantonese, whose expertise in stir-frying is renowned, have adapted the word *chau* (stir-fry) in a number of colloquialisms that cover a range of diverse topics, each of which in some way embodies the soul of the rapid-fire action, the tossing and the flipping that identify the technique.

- *Chau gwoo piu*, or to stir-fry stocks, refers to the process of buying stocks as fast transactions for quick profit.

- *Chau gam*, to stir-fry gold, means to speculate in gold for quick profit.

- *Chau nung* means to lose or get "burned" at real estate or stock speculation. The phrase translates as "burnt stir-fry." A similar expression is *chau waai jo*, stir-fried until (the food) got spoiled—that is, doing something until it is ruined. The opposite, *chau hei*, or stir-fry rising, means to expand, as in profits.

- *Chau lau*, also known as *chau dei chan*, or to stir-fry real estate, as in "flipping" property, refers to the concept of continually turning, i.e., flipping over or making a quick turnover of real estate for financial gain.

- *Chau lang fan*, to stir-fry cold rice, is a derogatory expression for repeating information without adding any significant new content.

- *Chau san* is both a culinary term that describes to stir-fry by breaking up ingredients such as ground meat or rice that tend to clump up, and a term that means to freelance.

- *Chau gaang*, or to stir-fry a work shift, means to work two shifts, day and night, with the connotation of trying to make ends meet.

- *Chau yan*, or to stir-fry a person, is the act of dismissing or firing an employee.

- *Chau yau yu* is both a culinary term that means to stir-fry squid, and is slang for "to be fired." Legend has it that in the old days workers brought their sleeping mats to the workplace. When dismissed from a job, a worker would roll up his or her sleeping mat. A two- or three-inch square of raw squid that has been cut from the body is flat, but after cooking it curls up into a tight cylinder that for some people resembles a rolled sleeping mat.

- *Chau* by itself is also employed as an active verb, as in "I fired him" or "he's fired," and is more commonly used than the full phrase *chau yau yu*.

- *Chau fei* means to stir-fry tickets and is the act of scalping tickets for quick profit.

- *Chau che*, or to stir-fry a car, means an automobile is literally flipped over in a serious accident.

- *Chau ha tsak haai*, or to stir-fry shrimp and to tear crab up into pieces, is a derogatory expression for swearing in a coarse manner.

- *Chau teet*, or to stir-fry iron, is an expression rarely used and was hard labor punishment for serious criminals in the Ming Dynasty.

- *Chau nau*, is to quarrel loudly. *Nau* is often used in Cantonese as a verb meaning to scold.

Stir-Frying with Proper Heat and Control

A gas stove is always preferable to an electric stove for stir-frying because it is easier to control the heat. Regardless of whether you cook in a carbon-steel wok or a stainless-steel skillet, successful stir-frying begins with preheating the pan before adding the cooking oil. The Cantonese call the technique *yeet wok doong yul*, or "hot wok cold oil." The oil is obviously not cold once it touches the hot wok, but there is a sizable difference in temperature between the oil and the wok. The success of this technique lies in this difference. This is the same principle behind preheating a barbecue grill before cooking on it; preheating a grill helps prevent foods from sticking. Pouring oil into a cold wok or skillet and then attempting to heat them simultaneously will, without exception, cause meat, poultry, fish, shellfish, rice, and noodles to stick to the pan.

In an article in *Saveur* magazine titled "Sticky Situations," Shirley Corriher, author of *Cookwise*, explains that preheating a dry pan before adding fat "allows the metal to expand, closing up microscopic nooks and crannies and creating a hot, even surface." According to Corriher, the fat then becomes a "more effective buffer between the pan and the grippy little proteins in the food that you're cooking." Another crucial reason for using the "hot wok cold oil" technique is that it prevents the oil from getting too hot and reaching its smoking point (see The Best Oil for Stir-Frying, page 41). When an oil begins to smoke, it is breaking down, and this results in the destruction of the nutrients in it and its natural flavor.

There is no exact time, as in number of minutes, that can be given for preheating a wok or skillet to the right temperature for stir-frying because stoves vary in power. An electric range or a weak gas range may require a couple of minutes to heat a pan, while a powerful gas range or a semiprofessional range may take only ten seconds or less. My preferred method is to heat a wok or skillet over high heat until a bead of water vaporizes within 1 to 2 seconds of contact. Occasionally I have found that the water test does not work on some woks and skillets. After preheating, the water beads up like a mercury ball, stubbornly refusing to vaporize. In such cases in which the water test cannot be done, you will have to experiment with preheating the wok or skillet until the pan is hot but the oil does not smoke once it is added. If you should add more than one droplet of water to the pan, be sure all the water evaporates before adding the oil. This will prevent dangerous spattering. Once all the water has evaporated, you can immediately swirl in the oil by pouring it in a thin stream in one circular motion around the inside edge of the wok. Then quickly tilt the wok back and forth to allow the oil to cover the entire bottom surface of the wok. If the pan has been correctly heated you will see the oil shimmer upon being added. Then proceed to add the aromatics and begin to stir-fry.

My advice to novice cooks is to turn off the heat on a gas range once the drop of water evaporates and then swirl in the oil. After adding the oil, you can quickly return the heat to high, add the aromatics, and begin stir-frying. For an electric range, leave the heat on and transfer the wok to a cold burner. Swirl in the oil and then return the wok to the hot burner. This brief pause prevents the oil from getting too hot and from smoking if you should be a little slow in adding the ingredients.

Not only must you have a hot wok to produce a great stir-fry, but you must also know how to control the heat. Many novice cooks make the mistake of thinking the pan can never be hot enough. Chinese restaurant chefs cook on stoves with ten to twenty times the power of a residential range, but they have been trained to work safely with intense heat. If, however, you are inexperienced at stir-frying, an overly hot pan means smoking oil and ingredients that will burn upon being added to the wok. For this reason, using a powerful home range, a semiprofessional range, a custom-made wok stove, or an outdoor portable wok stove is not advisable for the inexperienced stir-fry cook. If your stove is extremely powerful (over 16,000 BTUs), I recommend stir-frying at a low heat setting and being prepared to turn off the heat from time to time, as experienced Chinese restaurant chefs do when the temperature gets too hot and threatens to burn the ingredients.

The moment the aromatics are added to the oil in a preheated wok you should hear a sizzling sound that remains steady regardless of whether you are adding meat or vegetables to the wok. Harold McGee, the author of *On Food and Cooking*, cautions that a pan that is not hot enough allows "moisture to accumulate." He explains that if a pan is not sufficiently preheated, "meat stews in its own juices until they boil off, and its surface doesn't brown well." If you are stir-frying beef in a pan that isn't hot enough, you'll see the meat begin to foam as it releases its juices and it will literally turn gray. Even if the wok regains heat, it will be too late to sear the meat. Preheating the wok not only ensures that meat will sear, but also that it retains tenderness and succulence. The disappearance of the sizzle sound means the wok has lost its heat. This will occur if the wok is not preheated sufficiently, if there is too much food in the wok, or if wet ingredients like rinsed but not dried vegetables have been added.

Note: I do not advocate using nonstick woks or skillets for stir-frying (see A Wok for Every Reason, page 13). Furthermore, the instructions above for preheating a pan do not apply to a nonstick wok or skillet. In general, preheating nonstick pans without oil or food already in them is not advisable.

BASIC STEPS FOR STIR-FRYING

This is a general guide for typical stir-fries that are a combination of vegetables and a protein (i.e., meat, poultry, shellfish, or tofu). The technique is slightly altered for simple stir-fries (see page 201) and can vary depending on the cook and the recipe.

Cutting, Marinating, and Measuring Ingredients

Cut the ingredients into uniform bite-sized pieces to ensure even cooking. Marinate the meat or poultry. Measure all the seasonings. Stir-frying requires your full attention; there is no time to be measuring ingredients last minute. Combine the liquid ingredients, preferably in an 8-ounce liquid measuring cup to make swirling the liquids into the wok easier.

Lining Up Ingredients in Order of Use

Put all the prepared ingredients, preferably in the order in which they will be used, next to the stove. It is essential to have your metal spatula within easy reach, and any other tools required, such as the wok lid, wooden chopsticks, colander, wok skimmer, or a deep-fry thermometer handy. Once stir-frying commences, there is no time to be searching for anything.

Preheating the Wok

Heat a 14-inch flat-bottomed carbon-steel wok or 12-inch skillet over high heat until a bead of water vaporizes within 1 to 2 seconds of contact. For more details, see Stir-Frying with Proper Heat and Control, page 52.

Addition of Oil

Swirl in the peanut or vegetable oil in a thin stream, pouring it down the sides of the wok (**1**). Lift the wok and quickly rotate it so that the oil completely coats the well.

Addition of Aromatics

Add the aromatics, such as ginger, garlic, shallots, onions, or scallions, and stir-fry briefly until fragrant. After adding the aromatics, use a Chinese metal spatula or pancake turner (preferable to a wooden spatula because its thinner edge is more effective in getting under the protein that is added next) to stir-fry the ingredients.

Addition of Protein(s) in an Even Layer to Sear

Push the aromatics to the side of the wok, carefully add the protein

(meat, poultry, shellfish, or tofu), and spread it evenly in one layer in the wok (**2**); cook undisturbed 1 minute to allow the protein to begin to sear. Remember not to crowd the wok or skillet with too much food. *Do not stir-fry more than 12 ounces of beef; 1 pound of pork; 1 pound of chicken; 1 pound of duck; 1 pound of shrimp; or 12 ounces of scallops.* The addition of too many ingredients lowers the wok's temperature, causing ingredients to braise rather than stir-fry. After searing, stir-fry the protein, incorporating the aromatics, until it begins to brown and is about three-quarters done. Remove the wok from the heat and using the spatula transfer the meat and aromatics to a plate.

Addition of Dry Vegetables

Return the unwashed wok to the burner, swirl a little more oil into the wok over high heat, and add the vegetables. Make sure vegetables are dried—no water remaining on surface—to prevent stir-fries from becoming soggy. Vegetables, unlike protein, can be stir-fried immediately, without having to be first spread in an even layer in the wok. For more details, see Essentials for Stir-Frying Vegetables and Tofu, page 184.

The Sizzle Means . . .

Throughout the stir-frying process, you should hear a constant sizzling sound. If there is no audible sizzle, it indicates that the wok was not sufficiently heated (see Stir-Frying with Proper Heat and Control, page 52), or that the wok's heat has been reduced by the addition of too many ingredients or wet vegetables. If this happens, your stir-fry has become a braise.

Addition of Liquid Ingredients and Seasonings

When the vegetables are three-quarters done, return the protein and aromatics with any juices that have accumulated on the plate to the wok. These juices intensify the taste of any stir-fry. Swirl in the liquid ingredients in a thin stream along the sides of the wok (**3**). (Pouring all the liquid into the center of the wok will bring down the temperature of the pan.) The liquid adds flavor and also deglazes the pan, loosening and dissolving the browned bits formed during stir-frying. Add any remaining seasonings and sprinkle in dry seasonings like salt and pepper so they are well distributed and do not clump in one spot. Then stir-fry only until the protein is just cooked and the vegetables are crisp-tender.

Serve

Transfer the stir-fry to a platter. A stir-fry should be enjoyed immediately while it is piping hot and exudes the taste of the wok. That said, there are also some stir-fries that are delicious when eaten warm or at room temperature, e.g., Singapore Noodles (page 274) and Spicy Long Beans with Sausage and Mushrooms (page 212).

Stir-Fries

The Longing for the Taste of Home

What is patriotism but love of the good things we ate in our childhood?

—Lin Yutang, *The Importance of Living*

When I was sixteen years old, during the 1970s, my parents allowed me to move to England for the summer to live with my Auntie Helen and Uncle Sam, a physicist who was on sabbatical working at the Rutherford Laboratory in Didcot about thirty minutes from Oxford. During the months leading up to my departure, I anticipated the trip, often trying to imagine the food I was about to discover, the food of another continent and culture. To my great surprise, my first night in England, Auntie Helen greeted me with a Chinese dinner not unlike the one my parents were sitting down to in San Francisco. Every night, in fact, Auntie Helen, an excellent cook, made home-style Cantonese food. And when we went out on little excursions—even when we vacationed in Scotland—Auntie and Uncle were uncannily able to always find the one Chinese restaurant in every town. The owners, clearly unaccustomed to Chinese clientele, greeted us with both elation and amazement, but inevitably would advise us that the food was not worth eating: inauthentic, it catered to Western tastes.

When I finally got a taste of English cooking, I was appalled. Regardless of whether it was fish and chips, bubble and squeak, bangers and mash, or spotted dick, the food was unappealing, nothing at all like the sophisticated fare of today. The meat-heavy diet was fatty and lacked freshness. I came to appreciate just how lucky I was to have Auntie Helen's fine home cooking.

I also realized for the first time the indescribable comfort of eating Chinese home-cooked dishes. Everything, from the sizzle of a stir-fry to the aroma of steaming rice, evoked memory and satisfaction.

Uncle Sam and Auntie Helen had spent the first six months of their sabbatical in Geneva, Switzerland, where Asian fare was nonexistent. By the time they had moved to the small village of Chilton, where we lived, their insatiable craving for Chinese home cooking had only grown. Chilton had no Chinese population or any place to buy Asian ingredients. So, on our occasional trips to London, Auntie Helen stocked up on Chinese staple ingredients: soy sauce, sesame oil, ginger. Yet, even without Chinese vegetables or fresh fish, Auntie Helen managed every day to make simple stir-fries and steamed dishes using the vegetables and meat she found in the local supermarket. Her meals restored my spirit.

My experience of culinary longing during my time in England has been and continues to be replayed by countless Chinese living in the diaspora. Our desire for the foods of childhood and the "taste" of home has brought forth a tenacity and inventiveness exemplified by Chinese immigrants the world over. The Chinese who settled in the Mississippi Delta in the late 1800s, for example, lived without Chinese produce well until the mid-1900s. Rachel Sit Wong of Greenville, Mississippi, recalls her mother's craving for snow peas was so intense that she found a way to approximate the taste by using shelled English pea pods (see The Chinese of the Mississippi Delta, page 96). By coincidence, John Kuok of Auckland,

New Zealand, wrote me that in the 1950s his family moved from Foochow, China, to Delhi, India, where his mother, a wonderful and resourceful cook who made do with what she had, also substituted peeled pea pod shells for snow peas. Worlds apart, these two inventive cooks understood the yearning for the foods of home.

Beginning in the nineteenth century, the Chinese—principally those in the southern provinces of Guangdong and Fujian—left China in record numbers in search of economic opportunities in North America, Australia, Central America, South America, and the Caribbean. Others moved to Mauritius, Madagascar, and South Africa. Previously, Chinese migration had been concentrated in Southeast Asia, with the exception of small explorations in the seventeenth century into Mexico and Peru. This massive migration was spurred by a need for cheap labor in the West and by the political and economic turmoil in China, a situation exacerbated by years of famines, droughts, and epidemics. According to the Chinese diaspora scholar Walton Look Lai, "Seven and a half million Chinese left China (with 6.5 million remaining within the Southeast Asian region)." An estimated 600,000 Chinese immigrated to the Americas for work as contract laborers, with about 45 percent going to Latin America and the Caribbean. Approximately 370,000 immigrated to the United States and Hawaii. By the mid-1800s, Peru had over 100,000 Chinese, and Cuba more than 125,000 Chinese brought in by the Spaniards.

Wherever the Chinese ventured, the vast majority remained faithful to their homeland traditions: they spoke the Chinese language and dressed in native clothes, with the men wearing their hair in the customary queue. Their way of eating was perhaps their most valued devotion. According to Walton Look Lai's *Essays on the Chinese Diaspora in the Caribbean*, a group that left Hong Kong in 1884 on the SS *Diamond* to sail through the Suez Canal for the Caribbean stocked the ship with such foods as "salted eggs and vegetables, turnips, rice, cooking oil, vinegar, soybean sauce, fowl, pigs, and other livestock, as well as Chinese medicine."

Frieda Quon, who was born in the Mississippi Delta, recalls that her parents made the eighteen-day journey by passenger ship from Hong Kong to America in 1940. Quon's mother, utterly unaccustomed to American food, fasted until the ship docked in Hawaii, where she was finally able to order a Chinese meal. Rose Wong, a native of Jamaica, says her mother made the epic journey from China to Jamaica in the 1920s, traveling first by ship to Vancouver, then by rail to Toronto before boarding a banana boat for Kingston, Jamaica. She told her daughter how the Cantonese and Hakka passengers fought each other in the train's minute kitchen in a battle to cook their native foods. Even after living in Jamaica for years, Wong's mother refused to eat anything but Chinese home cooking. "We kids would eat some Jamaican foods, but I remember my mom never got used to living in Jamaica."

Regardless of where the Chinese journeyed, there was always one dish they could rely on: the stir-fry. Its simplicity allowed for adaptability to any circumstance. Without a wok, a stir-fry could be made in a skillet or pot. Without Asian vegetables or ginger, local vegetables could be stir-fried with a little garlic or onions. Even without Chinese condiments like soy sauce, a stir-fry could be stripped bare, using only a minimal amount of oil and bite-sized vegetables, unmarinated meat, poultry, or seafood, and salt. The Chinese preferred such simple stir-fries over local cuisine. My godmother, Wei Gin, told me that in 1942 while living in London during World War II she missed having stir-fried Chinese broccoli (*gai lan*) so

badly that one day she stir-fried cauliflower stems, closed her eyes, and tried to imagine the crisp, bittersweet taste of Chinese broccoli. Worse yet, because of the war, it was impossible to find rice. The only food she could find that was remotely similar in taste was oatmeal.

Sen Pu, a pharmacist from Brattleboro, Vermont, recalls how her family left their native Taiwan for Libya in the early 1960s. She was eight and a half years old. "When we packed our belongings, my mother included a wok. It was as essential to her as a piece of furniture." Tripoli had local vegetables such as carrots, onions, cabbage, spinach, beans, scallions, green peppers, and chili peppers. Chicken, beef, and lamb were available, but the family missed the pork (Muslim culture forbids pork) and peanut oil traditional to their own way of cooking. Pu, unaccustomed to olive oil, remembers reacting to its "terrible" smell, produced when her mother warmed the oil to release its aroma prior to cooking with it.

Eventually, her mother joined with other Taiwanese families stationed in Libya, ordering staples like soy sauce and dry goods from Taiwan. They were shipped by boat once or twice a year, occasionally arriving bug-ridden. In time Pu's family grew their own Chinese vegetables, including bok choy, Chinese green chives, and amaranth. They even experimented with growing ginger, but whenever a visitor came from Taiwan her mother would always request a delivery of fresh ginger. Regardless of how her siblings came to enjoy local Middle Eastern specialties, Pu was grateful that her mother insisted on eating Chinese food every day at home.

Dun Yong, who opened the first Chinese grocery store in Amsterdam, came to Holland from China in the 1930s by working on a steamship shoveling coal. He started his tiny store, called Dun Yong, in 1959, by writing letters to Chinese sailors who worked on

Dutch ships originating in Hong Kong and Singapore, and asking them to bring him Chinese goods: soy sauce, oyster sauce, dried bok choy, dried fish, canned goods, and even fresh ginger. The transaction gave the underpaid sailors a way to earn a little extra money, and the Dutch captains allowed them to stash merchandise in every available space in their living quarters, including the shower room. In the Amsterdam port, Dun would meet the headmen representing the laundry section, the kitchen section, and the machine room, who delivered the goods.

Dun's son Hengko recalls growing up in Amsterdam in the 1950s without access to Chinese vegetables. His father used local vegetables to make his stir-fries. When Hengko's wife, Wai Ming, emigrated from Hong Kong to Holland in the 1970s, she found the family meals unusual. Often they would have two dinners: a Dutch meal cooked by Hengko's mother, who was Dutch, and another prepared by his father with traditional Chinese foods. Wai Ming was happiest when her father-in-law cooked a Cantonese meal of soup, rice, and two dishes—one of them always a stir-fry. As the store grew in size and popularity, Hengko began importing Chinese vegetable seeds from Hong Kong, which he then sold to local Dutch farmers. Their harvests enabled him to supply his store with Asian vegetables. But the one ingredient the farmers could never successfully cultivate, because of Holland's cold climate, was ginger. Decades after his father paid Chinese sailors to fill their quarters with goods, Hengko found himself importing ginger from Brazil and Costa Rica.

Ernest Wing King, a Hakka who was raised in South Africa, recalls that his grandfather left his Hakka (see The Hakka Diaspora, page 102) clan in Mei Xian, China, in 1896 to immigrate to Mauritius. Chinese ingredients were completely unavailable in South Africa. "During World War II, when ships came from Asia en route to South Africa, we'd go to the harbor to beg and borrow for soy sauce," he recalls. The Chinese sailors on those boats also stocked their minute living quarters with Chinese nonperishable ingredients and made a business of selling their goods from port to port. Because cabbage, beans, and peas were the only green vegetables available, King's family grew their own Chinese vegetables from seeds smuggled into the country. His mother had "green fingers" and also knew how to make *hom choi*, the salted mustard greens that are a favorite in Hakka cooking. She also made her own tofu. "My family always ate Chinese food," says King. "We wouldn't eat the boiled potatoes that were the staple of South Africa."

Not only were the Chinese living abroad resourceful in procuring or making their traditional staples, but they also adapted their cooking to local availability. This cross-pollination of cultures was the most radical influence on Chinese cuisine, often resulting in an entire repertoire of nontraditional recipes and the development of Chinese immigrant food. Some recipes are simplifications of classic dishes, while others combine the culinary traditions of two cultures, with intriguing results. These culinary borrowings work particularly well in stir-fries because once the fundamentals of the technique are understood, the improvisational possibilities are infinite.

Growing up in Jamaica, Rose Wong remembers that as a teen in the 1950s she and her girlfriends liked to stir-fry because it was fast cooking. The combining of Chinese foods with Jamaican flavors was fashionable, and a popular ingredient was Pickapeppa, a local hot pepper sauce also known as Jamaican ketchup. They used it in stir-fries such as Chinese Jamaican Stir-Fried Chicken with Chayote (page 133). The combining of a West Indian sauce with dark soy sauce creates a fiery stir-fry that is totally unlike the spicy dishes of China's Sichuan or Hunan provinces. It is also equally different from Wong's mother's traditional Hakka cooking, which is not known for spiciness. Another Chinese Jamaican, Terry Chung Schultze, now living in Toronto, continues the "tradition" she learned in Jamaica of adding dry or moist jerk seasoning to any stir-fry.

Tane Ong Chan, owner of The Wok Shop in San Francisco, who was raised in Albuquerque, New Mexico, during the 1940s, remembers her mother stir-frying Western cabbage with bacon (page 229) because it was impossible to find Napa cabbage, Chinese bacon, and ginger. When noted Chinese cooking authority and cookbook author Florence Lin arrived in New York City in 1947, she craved Stir-Fried Edamame with Pickled Cucumber (page 234). Unable to find the pickled cabbage, she improvised with sauerkraut. While working for UNESCO in Paris in the 1960s, Maejeane Chang substituted pancetta for Yunnan ham when making her stir-fry of bok choy (page 226).

Many Chinese living abroad found that the only way to their economic survival was to open a Chinese restaurant. Having to cater to local tastes, they produced a cross-cultural cuisine that was, more truthfully, a bastardization of Chinese cooking. The most famous of these dishes is chop suey (see Chop Suey, page 236), which originated in the United States, and is now found worldwide.

Tane Ong Chan, whose father opened the Chung King restaurant in 1942 in Albuquerque, remembers customers dousing the chop suey with "bug juice," their name for soy sauce. "In New Mexico cockroaches are black, so I guess they decided soy sauce was the same color. They'd pour 'bug juice' on chop suey like ketchup on French fries," says Chan. The restaurant's Mexican American clientele would also eat fried rice with saltine crackers, which they used in place of tortillas to shovel the fried rice onto their forks. "Then they'd take a bite of the fried rice and a bite of the cracker. It was how everybody ate their fried rice," Chan explained.

In Peru, Belgium, Holland, and Ireland, stir-fries are routinely offered with French fries. I have visited Chinese Jamaican restaurants in New York City, where Cantonese and Jamaican chefs cook side by side, and dishes such as jerk chicken fried rice (page 262) and jerk pork chow mein are served along with traditional Chinese dishes. I have also visited Chinese Indian restaurants where Cantonese chefs use chilies in quantities unheard of in Cantonese cuisine. Stir-fries have triple the amount of sauce typical of a Cantonese stir-fry. The sauciness appeals to the Indian fondness for curry sauces. Rice wine and pork, typically used in Chinese cooking, are forbidden due to Hindu and Muslim dietary laws.

In 1982, Cheuk Kwan, the Chinese Canadian documentary filmmaker, was inspired to create his fifteen-part documentary series on Chinese restaurants around the world while visiting Mombasa, Kenya, where he was served a stir-fry of watermelon beef, prepared by an African chef in a Chinese restaurant owned by a Chinese South African. In Peru, Chinese food is so popular that there are thousands of *chifas*, or Chinese restaurants, throughout the country. The most famous dish, *lomo saltado* (page 92), is a stir-fry of filet mignon slices, *aji amarillo* (a Peruvian chili), garlic, red onions, tomatoes, and cilantro that is served with French fries. Chinese Peruvian fried rice, *arroz chaufa*, is made with cooked rice, scallions, a little shredded egg pancake, and shrimp, chicken, or pork. In China, dark soy sauce is not traditionally used in fried rice, but it is a staple of Chinese Peruvian, Chinese Cuban (Chinese Cuban Fried Rice, page 264), and Chinese Mexican fried rice.

In 1978, Cheung Fook Kwai, who was a young

cook at the time, moved his five children and wife from Hong Kong to the small town of Vaals in Holland. They opened a Chinese restaurant called Azie, serving typical Cantonese dishes such as steamed whole fish with scallions and ginger. "Customers told my father that the food was inedible and that they wanted their money back," recalls daughter Cheung Shuk Ching. "Dutch customers didn't want rice or noodles with their meal, but French fries, even though they're not on the menu. It's not the Chinese way to serve stir-fries with lots of sauce, but our customers always demanded extra sauce, so we learned to cook the food to suit their tastes." The Cheungs also learned that because of the Indonesian connection to the Netherlands, the Dutch expected Chinese food to have an Indonesian flavor. Accordingly, they adapted their stir-fries, adding ingredients such as paprika in sweet-and-sour sauces.

As culinary pioneers, Chinese immigrants used their ingenuity and resourcefulness to re-create that coveted "taste of home" to ease their sense of displacement, to create a community of memory, and to restore some feeling of well-being and wholeness. When my own mother emigrated from China to the United States in 1949, she had no knowledge at all of how to cook; her family's meals in Shanghai had been made by servants. Not only did meat loaf, pot roast, roast chicken, and macaroni and cheese have no appeal to her, but she was possessed of that longing Lin Yutang so eloquently wrote about. She was accustomed to a sense of harmony and freshness in her meals and could find none of it in her new home. Mama learned to cook Chinese dishes by asking her mother-in-law to teach her, by sharing recipes with girlfriends who had also recently moved from China

to America, by clipping recipes from the local Chinese newspaper, and by experimenting in the kitchen to re-create the tastes she missed.

My mother was lucky to have been living in San Francisco, where a wide range of Chinese ingredients and produce was readily available. For most of my childhood I didn't realize there were foods that she missed from her life in China. Mama could barely contain her excitement the day she discovered water spinach being sold in Chinatown. This was in the 1970s, and here was a vegetable she hadn't seen in nearly twenty-five years. That night she stir-fried the water spinach with a little fermented bean curd, and as she tasted the first bite, you could see a new-found contentment cross her countenance; it was as if she had been reunited with a very-long-lost friend.

Today, globalization has made Chinese ingredients more readily available worldwide, and the challenges that faced early Chinese immigrants is less acute. Tastes have also evolved and many young Chinese exposed to different cuisines are no longer as attached to Chinese food as previous generations have been. Still, the pilgrimage to find Chinese ingredients continues in some communities. In America, the most recent wave of Chinese migrant workers comes from Fujian province in southern China. Many have found jobs cooking in Chinese restaurants in unlikely places such as rural Ohio, Kentucky, Tennessee, and Florida, far from any Chinese community. Regularly they take an overnight bus to New York City's Chinatown, where they wire money home, enjoy a Fujianese meal in a local restaurant, and stock up on Chinese ingredients.

Chinese kitchens around the world continue to differ according to the fresh produce and ingredients their unique locations provide. What unites them is the wok. Stir-frying is the common culinary parlance.

The Alchemy of Stir-Frying

Peipei Chang

No matter which Chinese home kitchen you walk into, you will find variations of one particular scene if a stir-fry is about to be made: perhaps a bowl of marinated sliced meat or poultry sits on the counter along with a small dish of chopped chilies or minced garlic, vegetables drain in a colander set on the dish rack, a pile of finely shredded scallions rest on a cutting board. Such a still life invariably quiets me, and I pause to reflect on the beauty of the ordinary. In this simple picture there is nothing of the dramatic, like that of a whole salmon waiting to be poached or a luscious rack of lamb soon to be roasted. Instead, within this image of unremarkable ingredients is the evidence of supreme care. I notice the uniformity with which the vegetables and meat have been cut, the meticulous peeling and slicing of the ginger that has left it paper-thin and translucent. Every simple ingredient has been prepared with exquisite economy.

Peipei Chang

Stir-frying masterfully exemplifies the fine art of making less seem like more. It alchemizes everyday ingredients into delectation. The twentieth-century Chinese philosopher Lin Yutang explained the Chinese philosophy as "a marriage of flavors." "Let the meats and vegetables be combined and 'married,' instead of meeting each other for the first time when served on the table in their respective confirmed bachelorhood and unspoiled virginity, and you will find that each has a fuller personality than you ever dreamed of."

My friend Peipei, who came to New York from Shanghai twenty years ago, taught me her native recipe for stir-frying eggplant (page 228). She begins with a small piece of pork that she dices and then chops with a cleaver to produce a mound of ground pork about the size of a golf ball. She then stirs in a big pinch of finely minced scallions, a teaspoon of soy sauce, and the tiniest amount of minced ginger. Next Peipei stir-fries the pork, breaking up the meat and browning the little bits in the wok and removes the pork to a small plate. She adds the oil, sliced eggplant, and stir-fries with it chopped garlic, infuses it with a shot of rice wine and a dash of sugar and soy sauce, and then returns the pork to the wok. Peipei's secret, she confided, is the garlic, two crushed cloves, added just before she covers the wok and lets it sit off the heat long enough to coax the essence of the fresh garlic into the eggplant. The thick, tender eggplant slices, lightly steeped in garlic and hinting of pork, have a deep, rich flavor that totally belies the simplicity of the vegetable's preparation. Peipei occasionally makes this eggplant dish without meat and enjoys it equally. When I omit the pork, I find that, delicious as it still is, the dish lacks a certain character.

I no longer ponder how the magic works—how one meatball's worth of pork or that tiny pinch of minced ginger can even be detected in the final dish. That is part of the mystery of a well-constructed stir-fry. It is built on layers of flavor and texture, and every ingredient, no matter how seemingly insignificant in quantity, contributes to the alchemy.

Spicy Dry-Fried Beef

Meat

RECIPES

ESSENTIALS FOR STIR-FRYING MEAT AND POULTRY

Buy Fresh

Whenever possible, I purchase naturally raised meat and poultry. It is not always affordable but, fortunately, with stir-frying no more than one pound of meat or poultry is necessary for any recipe. I believe the taste is superior and the extra cost is worth the peace of mind that comes from knowing your food is free of antibiotics and hormones. I also use meat and poultry the day of purchase; fresh ingredients are essential in stir-frying.

Cutting Meat or Poultry

Regardless of whether you are cutting meat or poultry into slices, matchsticks (shreds), or cubes, cut as uniform pieces as possible to ensure even cooking. If the pieces are of various sizes, by the time the bigger ones are just done the smaller pieces will be overcooked. Some cooks find freezing meat or poultry 15 to 30 minutes before cutting it makes it semifirm and, therefore, easier to slice or shred; I find that unnecessary.

Beef

The most tender cut of beef I recommend for stir-frying is flank steak. However, it does have long tough fibers that can be chewy to the point of being inedible if cut incorrectly. To avoid this, when cutting flank steak for stir-fries, it is critical to *cut the meat across the grain*; this cuts the fibers into such small pieces that they become tender. Fortunately, flank steak has a longitudinal grain that is easily identifiable. Always trim and remove all excess fat and gristle from flank steak before cutting.

Slices: Cut the trimmed steak with the grain into roughly 1½- to 2-inch-wide strips (**1**). (The width of flank steak varies, which is why the strips will be roughly 2 inches wide.) One strip at a time, cut the beef across the grain into ¼-inch-thick bite-sized slices. There are two ways to slice the meat into bite-sized slices: it can be cut with a chef's knife or cleaver perpendicular to the cutting board (**2**), or the knife can be held at a 60° angle to make a slant cut (**3**). Some cooks prefer the slant cut because it creates a larger slice that absorbs more seasoning, and with more surface area exposed to heat the meat cooks faster.

Matchsticks: Follow the directions for cutting the beef into slices. Stack several slices and cut across the grain into shreds the size of matchsticks (**4**).

Pork and Lamb

The cuts of pork (shoulder or butt) and lamb (boneless leg of lamb or shoulder) that I recommend for stir-frying do not have tough fibers like beef, so it is unnecessary to cut with the grain in mind. Once trimmed of fat, they can be cut in any direction for slices, matchsticks, or cubes.

Chicken Breast, Skinless, Boneless

Always trim and remove all excess fat from the chicken breast before cutting. Chicken breast has fibers that run along the length of the breast. These fibers are not as tough as beef fibers, but for optimal tenderness, when cutting chicken into bite-sized slices, it is best to *cut the breast across the grain*.

Slices: For small chicken breasts, about 3 inches in width or less, cut across the grain into ¼-inch-thick bite-sized slices. For larger breasts, cut with the grain into 2- to 2½-inch-wide strips. One strip at a time, cut the chicken across the grain into ¼-inch-thick bite-sized slices. Like beef, chicken can be cut into straight perpendicular slices (**5**) or cut at a 60° angle for a slant cut (**6**).

Matchsticks: Follow the directions for cutting the chicken into slices (above). Stack 2 or 3 slices and cut across the grain into shreds the size of matchsticks.

Cubes: Cut skinless, boneless chicken breast or thigh meat into ½- to ¾-inch pieces, depending on the recipe.

Chicken Thighs, Duck Breast, or Legs, Skinless, Boneless: Always trim and remove excess fat from chicken thighs, duck breasts, or legs before cutting. Chicken dark meat and duck meat do not have tough fibers like beef, so it is unnecessary to cut with the grain in mind. Once trimmed of fat, they can be cut in any direction for slices, matchsticks, or cubes.

Bring Meat and Poultry to Room Temperature

Ingredients will stir-fry more evenly if they are removed from the refrigerator and set at room temperature for 10 to 15 minutes before stir-frying. This is especially important for ice-cold meat and poultry that can be seared on the outside but remain raw within.

5

6

Marinate Meat or Poultry

The other essential for tenderness is to marinate meat and poultry before stir-frying (see Marinating: The Key to Flavor and Tenderness, page 79). Simple ingredients like cornstarch, soy sauce, rice wine, oil, garlic, and ginger not only boost flavor but also help meats to caramelize and brown.

Avoid Overfilling the Wok

When stir-frying, do not crowd the wok or skillet with too much meat or poultry. If a wok is overcrowded, the temperature drops, and ingredients begin to braise rather than stir-fry. Beef is likely to turn gray and release foam; pork, lamb, chicken, and duck will also not sear properly. *As a general rule, in a 14-inch wok or a 12-inch skillet do not stir-fry more than 12 ounces of beef; 1 pound of pork; 12 ounces of lamb; 1 pound of chicken; or 1 pound of duck.*

The Sizzle Means . . .

The moment raw meat or poultry is added to a preheated wok there should be a sizzling sound that remains steady throughout stir-frying. If there is no audible sizzle, it indicates that the wok was not sufficiently heated (see Stir-Frying with Proper Heat and Control, page 52), or that the wok's heat has been reduced by crowding the wok with too large a quantity of meat or poultry. If this happens, your stir-fry has become a braise.

Spread the Meat or Poultry in an Even Layer to Sear

Right after adding the meat or poultry to the oil in the preheated wok, spread the pieces into an even layer and do not touch them for 1 minute. The tendency of the home cook is to begin stir-frying the meat or poultry immediately, but this is counterproductive. By not moving the ingredients for the designated time, you are allowing them to sear. Letting meat or poultry cook undisturbed is particularly important when stir-frying on a residential range as these stoves do not produce the ideal amount of heat for stir-frying. If you have a powerful range, the ingredients can be stir-fried immediately. Once the outside surface of the pieces sear, use a Chinese metal spatula or pancake turner (this is preferable to a wooden spatula because its thinner edge is more effective in getting under the meat) and stir-fry as directed in the recipe.

Addition of Liquid Ingredients

Swirl in the liquid ingredients in a thin stream along the sides of the wok. The liquid adds flavor and also deglazes the pan, loosening and dissolving the browned bits of meat and poultry that collect in the wok from stir-frying.

Spicy Dry-Fried Beef

This is a typical Sichuan technique for dry-frying beef (see Dry Stir-Frying and Moist Stir-Frying, page 121). Unlike most meat stir-fries, the beef is not marinated; instead it is stir-fried immediately then cooked for a few minutes longer to intensify the beef flavors and to give give the meat a slightly chewy texture. Even the carrots and celery are stir-fried until they are "dried." The result is a dish that is a little salty, fiery, and peppery, with a touch of sweetness from the vegetables. I advise using only a wok for this stir-fry. The "dry" technique burns the seasonings into a skillet, making it difficult to wash. (See photo, page 64.)

12 ounces lean flank steak

3 tablespoons peanut or vegetable oil

2 cups julienned carrots

1 cup julienned celery

3 small dried red chilies, snipped on one end

2 tablespoons soy sauce

1 tablespoon minced ginger

1 teaspoon minced garlic

2 teaspoons sesame oil

2 scallions, finely shredded

½ teaspoon salt

⅛ teaspoon freshly ground pepper

1. Cut the beef with the grain into 2-inch-wide strips. Cut each strip across the grain into ¼-inch-thick slices, then stack the beef slices and cut across the grain into 2-inch-long matchsticks.

2. Heat a 14-inch flat-bottomed wok over high heat until a bead of water vaporizes within 1 to 2 seconds of contact. Swirl in 1 tablespoon of the peanut oil, add the carrots, celery, and chilies, then, using a metal spatula, stir-fry 1 minute or until the vegetables have absorbed all of the oil. Transfer the vegetables to a plate.

3. Swirl the remaining 2 tablespoons peanut oil into the wok, carefully add the beef, and spread it evenly in one layer in the wok. Cook undisturbed 1 minute, letting the beef begin to sear. Then stir-fry 1 minute, or until the beef starts to foam and release its juices. Continue stir-frying 2 to 3 minutes or until almost all the liquid has evaporated and the oil begins to sizzle. Reduce the heat to medium and continue stir-frying 3 minutes until the beef is well browned, all the liquid has disappeared, and the wok is almost dry. Swirl the soy sauce into the wok and stir-fry 30 seconds or until well combined. Add the ginger and garlic and stir-fry 10 seconds or until the aromatics are fragrant. Add the carrot mixture and stir-fry 30 seconds or until well combined. Add the sesame oil and scallions and sprinkle on the salt and pepper.

Serves 2 to 3 as a main dish with rice or 4 as part of a multicourse meal.

Stir-Fried Ginger Beef

Ginger beef is a benchmark stir-fry by which Chinese cooks are judged. It is a classic "dry stir-fry" (see Dry Stir-Frying and Moist Stir-Frying, page 121) that calls only for oyster sauce and soy sauce, although this recipe stretches that definition by using a little rice wine. I was never satisfied with my attempts at making ginger beef until I experimented using pickled ginger in combination with fresh ginger; the delicate slices of pickled ginger contribute an assertive ginger flavor in addition to a hint of tartness. You'll find pickled ginger in most supermarkets but Asian markets tend to have a wider selection of brands to choose from. I squeeze the ginger with paper towels so it's not so wet when added to the wok. If the pickled ginger slices are in big pieces, roughly chop them so that the flavor is well distributed.

12 ounces lean flank steak

1 tablespoon minced ginger

1½ teaspoons soy sauce

1 teaspoon plus 1 tablespoon Shao Hsing rice wine
   or dry sherry

1 teaspoon cornstarch

¼ teaspoon salt

¼ teaspoon freshly ground pepper

1 teaspoon plus 1 tablespoon peanut
   or vegetable oil

1 tablespoon oyster sauce

¼ cup sliced pickled ginger (about 1 ounce)

4 scallions, halved lengthwise and cut into 2-inch
   sections

1. Cut the beef with the grain into 2-inch-wide strips. Cut each strip across the grain into ¼-inch-thick slices. In a medium bowl combine the beef, ginger, soy sauce, 1 teaspoon of the rice wine, cornstarch, salt, and pepper. Stir to combine. Stir in 1 teaspoon of the oil. In a small bowl combine the oyster sauce and the remaining 1 tablespoon rice wine.

2. Heat a 14-inch flat-bottomed wok or 12-inch skillet over high heat until a bead of water vaporizes within 1 to 2 seconds of contact. Swirl in the remaining 1 tablespoon oil, carefully add the beef, and spread it evenly in one layer in the wok. Cook undisturbed 1 minute, letting the beef begin to sear. Then, using a metal spatula, stir-fry 30 seconds until the beef is lightly browned but not cooked through. Swirl the oyster sauce mixture into the wok, add the pickled ginger and scallions, and stir-fry 30 seconds to 1 minute or until the beef is just cooked through and the pickled ginger is well distributed.

Serves 2 as a main dish with rice or 4 as part of a multicourse meal.

Stir-Fried Cucumber and Pork with Golden Garlic

This is one of the first stir-fries Amy Yip (see A Child of Ten Stir-Fries, page 109) learned to make as a young girl. A classic yin yang stir-fry, it combines cooling, or yin, cucumber with yang ingredients like pork, ginger, and golden fried garlic. Amy told me that she saves time by using English cucumbers because they do not need to be seeded. Before slicing the cucumber she uses a vegetable peeler to peel off thin lengthwise strips, leaving a little green peel on both sides of each strip.

Garlic mellowed by frying is the main seasoning. To fry the garlic, you will need to tilt the saucepan or wok slightly while securely holding the handle in order to check the temperature of the oil on a deep-frying thermometer. Make sure the tip of the thermometer does not touch the pan. The oil used to cook the garlic is used again in the stir-fry to give additional flavor; normally I do not recommend reusing oil after deep-fat frying, but this oil is only heated to 280°F and is removed from the heat within 1 minute. The remaining cooled oil can be stored in a jar. If you use the wok to fry the garlic, it must be washed and dried before using it to stir-fry the pork.

½ cup peanut or vegetable oil

3 tablespoons chopped garlic

12 ounces lean pork shoulder or butt, cut into
    ¼-inch-thick bite-sized slices

1½ teaspoons cornstarch

3 teaspoons soy sauce

¼ teaspoon sugar

¾ teaspoon salt

8 slices ginger, smashed

1 large English cucumber, ends trimmed, halved
    lengthwise, and cut on the diagonal into
    ¼-inch-thick slices (about 3 cups)

1. In a 1-quart saucepan or a 14-inch flat-bottomed wok heat the oil over high heat until the oil registers 280°F on a deep-frying thermometer. Carefully add the garlic. Cook, stirring 30 seconds to 1 minute or until the garlic is light golden. Remove the saucepan from the heat. Remove the garlic with a metal skimmer and put on a plate lined with paper towels. Carefully remove the oil from the wok and reserve. Wash the wok and dry it thoroughly.

2. In a shallow bowl combine the pork, cornstarch, 1½ teaspoons of the soy sauce, sugar, and ¼ teaspoon of the salt. In a small bowl combine the remaining 1½ teaspoons soy sauce and 1 tablespoon cold water.

3. Heat a 14-inch flat-bottomed wok or 12-inch skillet over high heat until a bead of water vaporizes within 1 to 2 seconds of contact. Swirl in 2 tablespoons of the reserved garlic oil, add the ginger slices, then, using a metal spatula, stir-fry 30 seconds or until the ginger is fragrant. Push the ginger to the sides of the wok, carefully add the pork, and spread it evenly in one layer in the wok. Cook undisturbed 1 minute, letting the pork begin to sear. Then stir-fry 1 minute or until the pork is lightly browned but not cooked through. Add the cucumber and stir-fry 30 seconds or until well combined. Sprinkle on the remaining ½ teaspoon salt, swirl the reserved soy sauce mixture into the wok, and stir-fry 1 minute or until the pork is just cooked and the cucumber begins to wilt. Stir in the reserved garlic.

Serves 2 to 3 as a main dish with rice or 4 as part of a multicourse meal.

Stir-Fried Cumin-Scented Beef with Vegetables

Here's a signature Hunan-style robust stir-fry of beef with cauliflower, carrots, and tomatoes, seasoned with cumin, garlic, and red pepper flakes. It is also an example of one of the more advanced stir-frying techniques. Chefs typically practice a technique called jau yau, *or "passing through oil," when bite-sized pieces of meat, poultry, fish, or shellfish are blanched in oil before stir-frying; this process ensures that the ingredients will be more succulent and flavorful. Unfortunately, most restaurants do this badly, which explains why many stir-fries are often sitting in a pool of oil when served. In this case, the beef is blanched in hot oil for 15 seconds and the result is meat that is exceedingly moist and tender. A note of caution: whenever working with hot oil, exercise extra care.*

This is a recipe where I prefer using a wok because it is so well suited for shallow-frying and stir-frying. I have tried shallow-frying in a high-sided 3-quart saucepan, but because of the larger surface area it requires about a cup more oil and the beef sticks to the bottom and sides of the pot. In contrast, the beef never sticks in a carbon-steel or cast-iron wok and the oil only enhances the wok's patina. Make sure the cauliflower florets are bite-sized so they cook in time. I halve or cut larger florets into quarters.

12 ounces lean flank steak

1 tablespoon cornstarch

1 tablespoon soy sauce

2 teaspoons Shao Hsing rice wine or dry sherry

1 tablespoon plus 1½ cups peanut or vegetable oil

1 tablespoon minced garlic

½ teaspoon red pepper flakes

1 cup bite-sized cauliflower florets

½ cup thinly sliced carrots

½ cup grape or cherry tomatoes, halved

¾ teaspoon salt

1 teaspoon ground cumin

½ cup thinly sliced scallions

1. Cut the beef with the grain into 2-inch-wide strips. Cut each strip across the grain into ¼-inch-thick slices. In a medium bowl combine the beef, cornstarch, soy sauce, and rice wine. Stir to combine. Stir in 1 tablespoon of the oil.

2. Heat the remaining 1½ cups oil in a 14-inch flat-bottomed wok over high heat until the oil registers 280°F on a deep-frying thermometer. Carefully add the beef and spread it evenly in one layer in the wok. Cook 15 seconds or until the beef is opaque but is not cooked through. Turn off the heat. Remove the beef with a metal skimmer and put it on a plate lined with paper towels. Carefully remove the oil from the wok and reserve. Wash the wok and dry it thoroughly.

3. Heat the wok over high heat until a bead of water vaporizes within 1 to 2 seconds of contact. Swirl in 1 tablespoon of the reserved oil, add the garlic and red pepper flakes, then, using a metal spatula, stir-fry 20 seconds or until the aromatics are fragrant. Add the cauliflower, carrots, and tomatoes and sprinkle on ¼ teaspoon of the salt. Reduce the heat to medium and stir-fry 2 minutes or until the vegetables are crisp-tender. Add the cumin and stir-fry 5 seconds. Return the beef to the wok, add the scallions, and sprinkle on the remaining ½ teaspoon salt. Increase the heat to high and stir-fry 30 seconds to 1 minute or until the beef is just cooked through.

Serves 2 to 3 as a main dish with rice or 4 as part of a multicourse meal.

Danny Chan

Cantonese-Style Stir-Fried Pork with Chinese Broccoli

Stir-fried pork with Chinese broccoli is a Cantonese favorite, and when I was growing up it was an essential menu item for every restaurant in San Francisco's Chinatown. This recipe comes from Chef Danny Chan who has made this dish thousands of times since he arrived in America in 1966 and began his career as a Chinese chef. All the minute measurements reflect the more complicated cooking style of a professional chef, even in the home kitchen.

12 ounces lean pork shoulder or butt, cut into
   ¼-inch-thick bite-sized slices
2½ teaspoons cornstarch
4 teaspoons soy sauce
1 teaspoon Shao Hsing rice wine or dry sherry
1 teaspoon minced plus 1 teaspoon sliced garlic
1 teaspoon plus 2 tablespoons peanut
   or vegetable oil
2 teaspoons oyster sauce
1¼ teaspoons sesame oil
⅛ teaspoon freshly ground pepper
4 tablespoons chicken broth
2 teaspoons dark soy sauce
6 medium stalks Chinese broccoli (about 8 ounces)
2 teaspoons finely shredded ginger
4 medium fresh water chestnuts, peeled and sliced
   (about ½ cup)
½ cup drained canned straw mushrooms
½ cup 1-inch red bell pepper squares
8 snow peas, strings removed

1. In a medium bowl combine the pork, 2 teaspoons of the cornstarch, 2 teaspoons of the soy sauce, rice wine, the 1 teaspoon minced garlic, 1 teaspoon of the peanut oil, 1 teaspoon of the oyster sauce, ¼ teaspoon of the sesame oil, and pepper. In a small bowl combine 3 tablespoons of the chicken broth, dark soy sauce, and the remaining 2 teaspoons soy sauce and 1 teaspoon oyster sauce. In a separate small bowl combine the remaining 1 tablespoon chicken broth, 1 teaspoon sesame oil, and ½ teaspoon cornstarch.

2. In a 3-quart saucepan bring 1½ quarts water to a boil over high heat. Add the broccoli stalks and cook, stirring, 2 minutes or until the broccoli is just crisp-tender. Drain the broccoli in a colander, shaking well to remove excess water.

3. Heat a 14-inch flat-bottomed wok or 12-inch skillet over high heat until a bead of water vaporizes within 1 to 2 seconds of contact. Swirl in the remaining 2 tablespoons peanut oil, add the ginger and the remaining 1 teaspoon sliced garlic, then, using a metal spatula, stir-fry 10 seconds or until the aromatics are fragrant. Push the aromatics to the sides of the wok, then carefully add the pork and spread it evenly in one layer in the wok. Cook undisturbed 1 minute, letting the pork begin to sear. Then stir-fry 1 minute, or until the pork is lightly browned but not cooked through. Add the water chestnuts, mushrooms, bell peppers, and snow peas and stir-fry 1 minute or until the snow peas are bright green. Swirl the dark soy sauce mixture into the wok and stir-fry 30 seconds or until well combined. Restir the cornstarch mixture, swirl it into the wok, and stir-fry 15 to 30 seconds or until the pork is just cooked. Put the broccoli on a serving platter and spoon the pork mixture over the broccoli.

Serves 2 as a main dish with rice or 4 as part of a multicourse meal.

Chinese Jamaican Stir-Fried Beef and Carrots

When Rose Wong was growing up in Jamaica in the 1950s, it was fashionable to cook dishes that combined Chinese and Jamaican ingredients. Stir-fried beef and carrots was a recipe she and her girlfriends loved to make. The cooking method is extremely simple, with a minimum of ingredients used to marinate the beef, and yet the combination of a West Indian sauce with soy sauce creates a fiery stir-fry vastly different from the spicy dishes of China's Sichuan or Hunan provinces. Wong remembers her mother was unwilling to try this new style of cooking, preferring to eat only traditional Hakka Chinese dishes.

Today Rose lives in San Francisco, and this stir-fry is a favorite with her family. The key ingredient is a tablespoon of Matouk's Calypso Sauce, a piquant pepper sauce made primarily from pickled Scotch bonnet chilies. The sauce is found in West Indian markets and can also be ordered from Kalustyan's (see Sources, page 287). Be sure to ask for Calypso Sauce as Matouk's makes several different pepper sauces. For slightly tamer tastes, I suggest starting with 2 teaspoons of the sauce. Rose prefers to cut the beef into matchsticks, but you can also just cut it into ¼-inch-thick bite-sized slices.

12 ounces lean flank steak

1 tablespoon soy sauce

1½ teaspoons cornstarch

¾ teaspoon salt

2 teaspoons plus 2 tablespoons peanut
   or vegetable oil

3 cups julienned carrots

⅔ cup thinly sliced onions

2 to 3 teaspoons Matouk's Calypso Sauce

1. Cut the beef with the grain into 2-inch-wide strips. Cut each strip across the grain into ¼-inch-thick slices, then stack the beef slices and cut across the grain into 2-inch-long matchsticks. In a medium bowl combine the beef, soy sauce, cornstarch, and ¼ teaspoon of the salt. Stir to combine. Stir in 2 teaspoons of the oil.

2. Heat a 14-inch flat-bottomed wok or 12-inch skillet over high heat until a bead of water vaporizes within 1 to 2 seconds of contact. Swirl in 1 tablespoon of the oil, add the carrots, then, using a metal spatula, stir-fry 1 minute or until the carrots just begin to wilt. Add the onions and stir-fry 1 minute or until all the oil is absorbed and the onions begin to turn light brown. Transfer the vegetables to a plate.

3. Swirl the remaining 1 tablespoon oil into the wok, carefully add the beef, and spread it evenly in one layer. Cook undisturbed 1 minute, letting the beef begin to sear. Stir-fry the beef 15 seconds or until just combined. Add the carrot mixture and Calypso Sauce, sprinkle on the remaining ½ teaspoon salt, and stir-fry 1 minute or until the beef is just cooked through.

Serves 2 to 3 as a main dish with rice or 4 as part of a multicourse meal.

Marinating: The Key to Flavor and Tenderness

While fresh ingredients are the foundation for delicious stir-fries, marinades are the secret for making meat and poultry dishes sing with flavor and tenderness. Marinades typically are made with cornstarch, rice wine (or dry sherry), soy sauce, and sometimes oil (see below), in addition to other seasonings such as salt, pepper, sugar, ginger, or garlic. Marinades enhance flavor and tenderize meat and poultry (the moderate acidity of rice wine or dry sherry breaks down muscle fiber), and they promote the browning, even caramelizing, of ingredients. Regardless of the ability of marinades to tenderize, great care must always be taken to cut beef or chicken correctly across the grain (see Essentials for Stir-Frying Meat and Poultry, page 66); if the meat or poultry is cut incorrectly, it will be tough, dry, or chewy even after marinating.

You will see the occasional marinade for meat and poultry stir-fries that includes a small amount of peanut, vegetable, or sesame oil. The oil contributes moisture and juiciness to leaner cuts of meat and poultry, thereby boosting flavor. Coating bite-sized food morsels in oil prevents clumping and allows ingredients to be stir-fried more evenly. The thin film of oil also prevents ingredients from sticking to the wok or skillet when stir-fried.

Marinating beef, pork, lamb, chicken, and duck for stir-fries can require as little as a few minutes, but in general 5 minutes should be allowed. Contrast this with a Western-style roast or a thick steak that needs to sit for hours if not overnight in order for the marinade to penetrate. Marinades infuse bite-sized morsels quickly, whether cut as thin as a ¼-inch-thick slice or as thick as a ¾-inch cube. In fact, when a marinade made with soy sauce marinates for more than 45 minutes, the flavor of the soy sauce can become overpowering, and the dish may become too salty.

It is interesting to observe that in the nineteenth and twentieth centuries Chinese home cooks who immigrated to countries that did not have basic Chinese staples, such as soy sauce or rice wine, often had to simplify or omit the step of marinating meat and poultry. As a result, these stir-fries do not have the complex layers of flavor found in more traditional recipes.

Note: Cornstarch is a key ingredient in marinating and velveting (see Velvet Stir-Fry, page 100) meat, poultry, fish, and shellfish. Always stir the mixture until the cornstarch is totally dissolved and no clumps are visible. Substitutions for those with corn allergies are tapioca starch and potato flour. Both are available in most Asian markets.

Stir-Fried Ginger Tomato Beef

When I was a child, my mother would often make this dish. A few winters ago, I was frustrated to find unripe but costly tomatoes in the market. Since my mom's recipe calls for tomatoes that are blanched and peeled, I decided to try making the recipe with peeled canned tomatoes. To my shock, the dish was even tastier. The quality of the canned tomatoes was far superior to tasteless winter tomatoes, and the tomato juices contributed even more flavor. This is saucier than most stir-fries and guarantees that more rice will be eaten.

12 ounces lean flank steak

2 tablespoons minced ginger

1 tablespoon soy sauce

2 tablespoons Shao Hsing rice wine or dry sherry

2 teaspoons cornstarch

¾ teaspoon sugar

½ teaspoon salt

¼ teaspoon freshly ground pepper

3 teaspoons sesame oil

1 teaspoon dark soy sauce

1 tablespoon peanut or vegetable oil

One 14.5-ounce can whole peeled tomatoes in juice

4 scallions, halved lengthwise and cut into 2-inch
   sections

1. Cut the beef with the grain into 2-inch-wide strips. Cut each strip across the grain into ¼-inch-thick slices. In a medium bowl combine the beef, ginger, soy sauce, 1 tablespoon of the rice wine, cornstarch, ¼ teaspoon of the sugar, salt, and pepper. Stir to combine. Stir in 1 teaspoon of the sesame oil. In a small bowl combine the dark soy sauce, the remaining 1 tablespoon rice wine, and the remaining 2 teaspoons sesame oil.

2. Heat a 14-inch flat-bottomed wok or 12-inch skillet over high heat until a bead of water vaporizes within 1 to 2 seconds of contact. Swirl in the peanut oil, carefully add the beef, and spread it evenly in one layer in the wok. Cook undisturbed 1 minute, letting the beef begin to sear. Then, using a metal spatula, stir-fry 1 minute, or until the beef is lightly browned but not cooked through. Transfer the beef to a plate.

3. Add the tomatoes with their juice to the wok, sprinkle on the remaining ½ teaspoon sugar, and bring to a boil, breaking each tomato into two or three pieces with the spatula. Swirl the dark soy sauce mixture into the wok. Return the beef with any juices that have accumulated to the wok, add the scallions, and stir-fry 1 minute or until the beef is just cooked through and the sauce is slightly thickened.

Serves 2 as a main dish with rice or 4 as part of a multicourse meal.

Minced Pork in Lettuce Cups

There are countless versions of this elegant stir-fry, a favorite served at Chinese banquets. Interestingly, the original was made with minced squab. Over time the recipe has "modernized" and now duck, chicken, and pork are often used in place of the squab. This dish is about the enjoyment of ingredients playing off one another; every bite should bring a burst of contrasting textures and flavors. All of the ingredients, from the mushrooms, carrots, and water chestnuts to the pork, have a slightly different level of sweetness and texture, each punctuated by the heat of the fresh chili.

The fresh water chestnuts here add a wonderful crispness. Their thin, chocolate-colored skin is often covered in mud, and they will need to be first rinsed in water, then peeled with a paring knife as you would an apple before chopping it. If fresh water chestnuts are not available, substitute jicama or an Asian pear that has been peeled. Canned water chestnuts are mealy and starchy and are not a good substitute.

8 medium dried shiitake mushrooms

8 ounces ground pork

1 teaspoon soy sauce

1 teaspoon plus 1 tablespoon Shao Hsing rice wine
   or dry sherry

½ teaspoon cornstarch

½ teaspoon sugar

1 teaspoon sesame oil

2 tablespoons peanut or vegetable oil

2 teaspoons minced garlic

1 teaspoon minced jalapeño chili, with seeds

8 fresh water chestnuts, peeled and chopped
   (about 1 cup)

½ cup ¼-inch diced carrots

½ cup thinly sliced scallions

½ teaspoon salt

⅛ teaspoon ground white pepper

16 Bibb or Boston lettuce leaves

Hoisin sauce

1. In a medium shallow bowl soak the mushrooms in ¾ cup cold water for 30 minutes or until softened. Drain and squeeze dry, reserving the soaking liquid for stocks. Cut off the stems and chop the mushrooms to make about ½ cup.

2. In a medium bowl combine the pork, soy sauce, 1 teaspoon of the rice wine, cornstarch, and sugar. Stir to combine. Stir in the sesame oil.

3. Heat a 14-inch flat-bottomed wok or 12-inch skillet over high heat until a bead of water vaporizes within 1 to 2 seconds of contact. Swirl in 1 tablespoon of the peanut oil, carefully add the pork, and spread it evenly in one layer in the wok. Cook undisturbed 1 minute, letting the pork begin to sear. Then, using a metal spatula, stir-fry the pork, breaking it up, until slightly pink, about 30 seconds. Transfer the pork to a plate.

4. Swirl the remaining 1 tablespoon peanut oil into the wok. Add the garlic and chili and stir-fry 10 seconds or until the aromatics are fragrant. Add the water chestnuts, carrots, and mushrooms and stir-fry 1 minute or until well combined. Add the scallions, sprinkle on the salt, pepper, and the remaining 1 tablespoon rice wine, and stir-fry 30 seconds or until the scallions are bright green. Return the pork with any juices that have accumulated to the wok and stir-fry 1 to 2 minutes or until the pork is just cooked

through. Serve with the lettuce leaves: have diners put 2 or 3 tablespoons of the filling in a lettuce leaf, fold the leaf over, and eat like a taco. Some cooks serve the cups with a small dollop of hoisin sauce.

Serves 4 as part of a multicourse meal.

Hot Pepper Beef

This is a recipe I recommend for cooks who have limited access to Asian ingredients. The sauce has a wonderful balance of savory, spicy, mellow, and sweet flavors. Probably the most "exotic" ingredient is hoisin sauce. My favorite brand has always been Koon Chun, but Kikkoman now produces a good hoisin sauce. If your stove has average power, you'll notice that 12 ounces of beef is the ideal amount to stir-fry. I sometimes use a combination of red and green bell peppers as pictured.

12 ounces lean flank steak

2 teaspoons minced garlic

2 teaspoons soy sauce

2 teaspoons cornstarch

1 teaspoon plus 1 tablespoon Shao Hsing rice wine
   or dry sherry

¾ teaspoon salt

⅛ teaspoon freshly ground pepper

1 teaspoon sesame oil

1 tablespoon ketchup

2 tablespoons hoisin sauce

2 tablespoons peanut or vegetable oil

½ cup thinly sliced red onions

3 slices ginger, smashed

½ teaspoon red pepper flakes

1 large green bell pepper, cut into ¼-inch-wide strips
   (about 2 cups)

1. Cut the beef with the grain into 2-inch-wide strips. Cut each strip across the grain into ¼-inch-thick slices. In a medium bowl combine the beef, garlic, soy sauce, cornstarch, 1 teaspoon of the rice wine, ¼ teaspoon of the salt, pepper, and 2 teaspoons cold water. Stir to combine. Stir in the sesame oil. In a separate small bowl combine the ketchup, hoisin sauce, and the remaining 1 tablespoon rice wine. Stir to combine.

2. Heat a 14-inch flat-bottomed wok or 12-inch skillet over high heat until a bead of water vaporizes within 1 to 2 seconds of contact. Swirl in 1 tablespoon of the peanut oil, carefully add the beef, and spread it evenly in one layer in the wok. Cook undisturbed 1 minute, letting the beef begin to sear. Then, using a metal spatula, stir-fry 1 minute, or until the beef is lightly browned but not cooked through. Transfer the beef to a plate.

3. Swirl the remaining 1 tablespoon peanut oil into the wok, add the red onions, ginger slices, and red pepper flakes, and stir-fry 10 seconds or until the aromatics are fragrant. Add the bell pepper and stir-fry 30 seconds or until well combined. Return the beef with any juices that have accumulated to the wok, sprinkle on the remaining ½ teaspoon salt, swirl the ketchup mixture into the wok, and stir-fry about 30 seconds to 1 minute or until the beef is just cooked through.

Serves 2 to 3 as a main dish with rice or 4 as part of a multicourse meal.

Stir-Fried Curried Beef

Here's a popular, easy-to-make beef stir-fry that is perfect for cold weather. I am fond of this recipe because it requires a trip to the market for only the beef and the tomato. All the other ingredients are staples. It takes no time to make this, yet it is a satisfying and comforting meal when served with plenty of rice. Of course, it's often hopeless finding a tomato worth eating in the winter, in which case halved grape tomatoes make an excellent substitute.

12 ounces lean flank steak

1 tablespoon finely shredded ginger

1½ teaspoons soy sauce

1¼ teaspoons cornstarch

1 teaspoon plus 1 tablespoon Shao Hsing rice wine
   or dry sherry

¾ teaspoon salt

¼ teaspoon freshly ground pepper

1 teaspoon plus 1 tablespoon peanut
   or vegetable oil

⅓ cup chicken broth

1 teaspoon dark soy sauce

1 cup thinly sliced red onions

1 tablespoon minced garlic

1 tablespoon curry powder

1 medium ripe tomato, cut into thin wedges

¾ cup frozen peas, defrosted

¼ teaspoon sugar

1. Cut the beef with the grain into 2-inch-wide strips. Cut each strip across the grain into ¼-inch-thick slices. In a medium bowl combine the beef, ginger, soy sauce, cornstarch, 1 teaspoon of the rice wine, ¼ teaspoon of the salt, and pepper. Stir to combine. Stir in 1 teaspoon of the oil. In a small bowl combine the broth, dark soy sauce, and the remaining 1 tablespoon rice wine.

2. Heat a 14-inch flat-bottomed wok or 12-inch skillet over high heat until a bead of water vaporizes within 1 to 2 seconds of contact. Swirl in the remaining 1 tablespoon oil, add the red onions and garlic, then, using a metal spatula, stir-fry 30 seconds or until the onion is wilted. Push the onion mixture to the sides of the wok, carefully add the beef, and spread it evenly in one layer in the wok. Cook undisturbed 1 minute, letting the beef begin to sear. Sprinkle on the curry powder, then stir-fry 30 seconds, or until the beef is lightly browned but not cooked through. Add the tomato and peas, sprinkle on the sugar and the remaining ½ teaspoon salt, and stir-fry 30 seconds or until well combined. Swirl the broth mixture into the wok and stir-fry 30 seconds to 1 minute or until the beef is just cooked through.

Serves 2 to 3 as a main dish with rice or 4 as part of a multicourse meal.

Stir-Fried Beef and Broccoli

Although broccoli is available all year, I like to make this dish in the autumn when broccoli appears in our local farmers' market. Young broccoli has slender stalks with florets that are almost bluish green in color. Halve or quarter large florets so that all of the pieces match in size to ensure that they cook in the same amount of time. I blanch broccoli to shorten the stir-frying time.

12 ounces lean flank steak

1 tablespoon minced ginger

2 teaspoons soy sauce

2 teaspoons plus 1 tablespoon Shao Hsing rice wine
    or dry sherry

1½ teaspoons cornstarch

½ teaspoon salt

⅛ teaspoon freshly ground pepper

1 teaspoon sesame oil

2 tablespoons chicken broth

2 tablespoons oyster sauce

2 teaspoons dark soy sauce

12 ounces broccoli florets and stems, cut into
    ¼-inch-thick slices (about 5 cups)

2 tablespoons peanut or vegetable oil

1 tablespoon minced garlic

1 tablespoon fermented black beans, rinsed
    and mashed

¾ cup thinly sliced onions

1. Cut the beef with the grain into 2-inch-wide strips. Cut each strip across the grain into ¼-inch-thick slices. In a medium bowl combine the beef, ginger, soy sauce, 2 teaspoons of the rice wine, cornstarch, salt, and pepper. Stir to combine. Stir in the sesame oil. In a small bowl combine the chicken broth, oyster sauce, dark soy sauce, and the remaining 1 tablespoon rice wine.

2. In a 1½-quart saucepan bring 1 quart water to a boil over high heat. Add the broccoli and cook, stirring 1 minute or until the broccoli is bright green and the water almost returns to a boil. Drain in a colander, shaking out excess water.

3. Heat a 14-inch flat-bottomed wok or 12-inch skillet over high heat until a bead of water vaporizes within 1 to 2 seconds of contact. Swirl in 1 tablespoon of the peanut oil, add the garlic and black beans, then, using a metal spatula, stir-fry 10 seconds or until the aromatics are fragrant. Push the garlic mixture to the sides of the wok, carefully add the beef, and spread it evenly in one layer in the wok. Cook undisturbed 1 minute, letting the beef begin to sear. Then stir-fry 1 minute, or until the beef is lightly browned but not cooked through. Transfer the beef to a plate.

4. Swirl the remaining 1 tablespoon peanut oil into the wok, add the onions, and stir-fry about 30 seconds or until the onions are just translucent. Add the broccoli and stir-fry 15 seconds or until just combined with the onions. Return the beef with any juices that have accumulated to the wok. Swirl the oyster sauce mixture into the wok and stir-fry about 30 seconds or until the beef is just cooked through.

Serves 2 to 3 as a main dish with rice or 4 as part of a multicourse meal.

Stir-Fried Mongolian Lamb with Scallions

Northern Chinese in Inner Mongolia and Beijing are fond of stir-frying lamb. This recipe uses the classic combination of lamb with scallions—the scallions are said to harmonize with the gamy taste of lamb. Shredding the scallions can be labor intensive. I have an inexpensive scallion shredder that makes this a quick chore, see page 45. Otherwise I use a cleaver or chef's knife to cut the scallions into shreds. The lamb is seasoned with garlic, two kinds of soy sauce, hoisin sauce, sesame oil, rice wine, and a little rice vinegar, and has the perfect balance of flavors, with no one ingredient dominating. The Sichuan peppercorns are not traditionally used in northern Chinese cooking, but they accent the lamb nicely. The recipe calls for boneless leg of lamb, but you can also use lamb shoulder.

12 ounces lean boneless leg of lamb, cut into
　　¼-inch-thick bite-sized slices

1 tablespoon minced garlic

2 tablespoons Shao Hsing rice wine or dry sherry

1 teaspoon dark soy sauce

¾ teaspoon roasted and ground Sichuan pepper-
　　corns (see page 6)

½ teaspoon cornstarch

¼ teaspoon salt

¼ teaspoon sugar

1 teaspoon sesame oil

1 tablespoon hoisin sauce

1 tablespoon rice vinegar

1 tablespoon soy sauce

2 tablespoons peanut or vegetable oil

1 bunch scallions, finely shredded (about 3 cups)

1. In a medium bowl combine the lamb, garlic, 1 tablespoon of the rice wine, dark soy sauce, ground Sichuan peppercorns, cornstarch, salt, and sugar. Stir to combine. Stir in the sesame oil. In a small bowl combine the hoisin sauce, rice vinegar, soy sauce, and the remaining 1 tablespoon rice wine.

2. Heat a 14-inch flat-bottomed wok or 12-inch skillet over high heat until a bead of water vaporizes within 1 to 2 seconds of contact. Swirl in the peanut oil, carefully add the lamb, and spread it evenly in one layer in the wok. Cook undisturbed 1 minute, letting the lamb begin to sear. Then, using a metal spatula, stir-fry 1 minute, or until the lamb begins to brown but is not cooked through. Add the scallions and stir-fry about 10 seconds or until just combined. Swirl the hoisin sauce mixture into the wok and stir-fry 30 seconds to 1 minute or until the lamb is just cooked.

Serves 2 as a main dish with rice or 4 as part of a multicourse meal.

Chinese Peruvian Stir-Fried Filet Mignon ❧ *Lomo Saltado*

The first time I tasted lomo saltado *was at Red Egg, a sophisticated Chinese Peruvian restaurant in New York City's Chinatown. The restaurant is owned by Darren Wan whose grandfather emigrated from Guangzhou, China, to Peru in the 1930s. The dish was indescribably delectable: the meat, tender and succulent, was lightly spiced with fragrant chili heat and refreshed by onions and tomatoes that were barely cooked—then so unexpected served over French fries. When Wan brought me into the restaurant's kitchen to watch the chef cook the dish I was surprised to discover filet mignon was used— no wonder the beef was so tender even without being marinated!*

The Chinese began immigrating to Peru in the nineteenth century, and by the mid-1800s, there were over 100,000 Chinese living in Peru. The popularity of Chinese cooking in Peru has resulted in thousands of chifas, *or Chinese restaurants, throughout the country.* Lomo saltado *is so popular with Peruvians that many make the dish at home.*

A few months later in San Ramon, California, I met Luis Li, a native of Peru, whose father emigrated from Guangzhou to Peru in the 1920s. Luis kindly showed me how to prepare lomo saltado *for the home cook. He explained to me there are many different varieties of the* aji *chili, but he prefers* aji amarillo, *a moderately hot, fruity chili native to Peru. He buys the chilies frozen in a local Mexican store, or he uses* aji mixto, *which comes in a 15-ounce jar. Li used 1 tablespoon of the frozen chilies and the dish was delicious but wildly hot. In the recipe I've given a range for cooks with tamer tastes. The Union Square farmers' market in New York City carries a variety of* aji *chilies in the summer. Li feels there is no*

substitute for *aji, but because this chili is so difficult to find, I have substituted one thinly sliced Thai chili, with seeds, in its place with very good results. Of course, the flavor of the dish will be superior if you are able to find* aji amarillo.

Li also explained to me that he misses the incredible selection of potatoes available in Peru. He is not fond of American potatoes and prefers frozen potatoes from Peru. I call for a russet potato since frozen Peruvian potatoes are not an option in most markets. These potatoes are incredible because they are twice fried. There are apparently many ways to cook lomo saltado, *including with and without sauce. Li prefers his without sauce and he mixes the French fries into the stir-fry just before serving. Timing is critical for this stir-fry. A minute too long and the beef will be overcooked. The moment it is done, transfer the beef out of the wok so it does not continue to cook.*

12 ounces russet potatoes, peeled and cut into
    sticks 3 inches long by ³⁄₈ inch wide (about
    2 cups)

12 ounces lean filet mignon

2 teaspoons soy sauce

2 teaspoons red wine vinegar

3 cups plus 2 tablespoons peanut or vegetable oil

1 tablespoon minced garlic

³⁄₄ teaspoon salt

¹⁄₄ teaspoon freshly ground pepper

1 small red onion, cut into thin wedges (about
    1 cup)

1 medium ripe tomato, cut into thin wedges

¹⁄₄ teaspoon sugar

1 to 3 teaspoons *aji amarillo* chili, seeded and cut
    into scant ¹⁄₄-inch-thick slices

2 tablespoons chopped cilantro

1. Pat the potatoes dry with paper towels. Line two large plates with several sheets of paper towels. Cut the beef with the grain in half. Cut each half with the grain in half so that you have a total of 4 quarters. Cut each quarter section across the grain into ¼-inch-thick bite-sized slices. In a small bowl combine the soy sauce and vinegar.

2. In a 2-quart saucepan heat the 3 cups oil over medium-high heat until the oil registers 300°F on a deep-frying thermometer, making sure the tip of the thermometer does not touch the pan. Carefully add the potatoes and fry 3 minutes or until they are tender. Remove the pan from the heat. Carefully remove the potatoes with a metal skimmer and drain on one of the paper towel–lined plates. Then discard the oil-soaked paper towels (because the potatoes sometimes will stick to the towels).

3. Reheat the same oil in the saucepan over medium-high heat until the temperature reaches 360°F. Carefully add the same potatoes to the oil and fry until light golden, about 2 to 3 minutes. Carefully remove the potatoes with a metal skimmer and drain on the second prepared plate. Then discard the oil-soaked paper towels. Let the hot oil cool before discarding.

4. Heat a 14-inch flat-bottomed wok or 12-inch skillet over high heat until a bead of water vaporizes within 1 to 2 seconds of contact. Swirl in the remaining 2 tablespoons oil, carefully add the beef, and spread it evenly in one layer in the wok. Cook undisturbed 1 minute, letting the beef begin to sear. Sprinkle on the garlic, salt, and pepper. Then, using a metal spatula, stir-fry 30 seconds, until the beef is lightly browned but not cooked through. Add the red onions and tomatoes and stir-fry 30 seconds or until the tomatoes begins to soften. Swirl the soy sauce mixture into the wok, sprinkle on the sugar and chilies, and stir-fry 30 seconds or until well combined. Add the cilantro and fried potatoes and stir-fry several seconds until the ingredients are combined and the beef is just cooked.

Serves 2 to 3 as a main dish or 4 as part of a multicourse meal.

Luis Li stir-fries outdoors on a portable stove.

Stir-Fried Hoisin Pork with Peppers

When marinating meat or poultry for stir-frying, typically the meat is simply combined with a little cornstarch, rice wine, soy sauce, and possibly oil. Aromatics such as ginger or garlic are added during the stir-fry process so that the heat releases their flavor. However, some cooks prefer to marinate the meat with the aromatics, as in this recipe; the idea is that the scallions, garlic, and ginger infuse the meat with more flavor. This option also makes the dish easier to cook because the aromatics don't need to be stir-fried separately.

12 ounces lean pork shoulder or butt, cut into
　　¼-inch-thick bite-sized slices

¼ cup minced plus ¼ cup finely shredded
　　scallions

3 tablespoons hoisin sauce

1 tablespoon minced garlic

2 teaspoons Shao Hsing rice wine or dry sherry

1 teaspoon minced ginger

1 teaspoon soy sauce

⅛ teaspoon plus ¼ teaspoon salt

⅛ teaspoon ground white pepper

2 teaspoons sesame oil

2 tablespoons peanut or vegetable oil

1 large red bell pepper, cut into ¼-inch-wide strips
　　(about 2 cups)

½ cup thinly sliced carrots

2 teaspoons rice vinegar

1. In a medium bowl combine the pork, the ¼ cup minced scallions, hoisin sauce, garlic, rice wine, ginger, soy sauce, ⅛ teaspoon of the salt, and pepper. Stir to combine. Stir in the sesame oil.

2. Heat a 14-inch flat-bottomed wok or 12-inch skillet over high heat until a bead of water vaporizes within 1 to 2 seconds of contact. Swirl in 1 tablespoon of the peanut oil, carefully add the pork, and spread it evenly in one layer in the wok. Cook undisturbed 1 minute, letting the pork begin to sear. Then, using a metal spatula, stir-fry 1 minute or until the pork is lightly browned but not cooked through. Transfer the pork to a plate.

3. Swirl the remaining 1 tablespoon peanut oil into the wok, add the bell peppers and carrots, sprinkle on the remaining ¼ teaspoon salt, and stir-fry 1 minute or until the bell peppers begin to soften. Return the pork with any juices that have accumulated to the wok. Add the remaining ¼ cup shredded scallions and rice vinegar and stir-fry 1 to 2 minutes or until the pork is just cooked through.

Serves 2 to 3 as a main dish with rice or 4 as part of a multicourse meal.

Sichuan Pork with Peppers and Peanuts

This spicy classic from Sichuan couldn't be easier to make. The pork is marinated in egg white to tenderize the meat, but it does not change the texture to the extent it would be if the meat were truly velveted (see Velvet Stir-Fry, page 100) and blanched in oil or water. Occasionally I make this with chili garlic sauce, but I prefer chili bean sauce; the difference is chili bean sauce is made with soybeans and has greater depth of flavor.

1 pound lean pork shoulder or butt, cut into
    ¾-inch cubes
1 tablespoon egg white, lightly beaten
3 tablespoons Shao Hsing rice wine or dry sherry
2 teaspoons cornstarch
2 teaspoons minced plus 1 tablespoon thinly
    sliced garlic
½ teaspoon sugar
1 teaspoon salt
½ teaspoon ground white pepper
1 tablespoon soy sauce
2 teaspoons Chinkiang or balsamic vinegar
2 tablespoons peanut or vegetable oil
½ cup diced red onions
2 teaspoons chili bean sauce
1 large red bell pepper, cut into 1-inch squares
½ cup unsalted roasted peanuts

1. In a medium bowl combine the pork, egg white, 1 tablespoon of the rice wine, cornstarch, the 2 teaspoons minced garlic, sugar, ½ teaspoon of the salt, and ¼ teaspoon of the pepper. Stir to combine. In a small bowl combine the soy sauce, vinegar, and the remaining 2 tablespoons rice wine.

2. Heat a 14-inch flat-bottomed wok or 12-inch skillet over high heat until a bead of water vaporizes within 1 to 2 seconds of contact. Swirl in 1 tablespoon of the oil, add the red onions and the remaining 1 tablespoon sliced garlic, then, using a metal spatula, stir-fry 1 minute or until the onion wilts. Push the onion mixture to the sides of the wok, carefully add the pork, and spread it evenly in one layer in the wok. Cook undisturbed 1 minute, letting the pork begin to sear. Add the chili bean sauce and stir-fry 2 minutes or until the pork is lightly browned but not cooked through. Transfer the pork to a plate.

3. Swirl the remaining 1 tablespoon oil into the wok. Add the bell peppers, sprinkle on the remaining ½ teaspoon salt and ¼ teaspoon pepper, reduce the heat to medium, and stir-fry 1 to 2 minutes or until the bell peppers begin to soften. Return the pork with any juices that have accumulated to the wok, increase the heat to high, swirl the rice wine mixture into the wok, and stir-fry 1 to 2 minutes or until the pork is just cooked through. Stir in the peanuts.

Serves 2 to 3 as a main dish with rice or 4 as part of a multicourse meal.

Ellen J. Fong's family was one of only two Chinese families in the small town of Ruleville, Mississippi, during the 1930s and '40s. Ellen's mother and siblings ran the typical Chinese-owned family grocery store that served black sharecroppers. Ruleville had no Chinatown, or Chinese restaurants, and in order to buy Chinese ingredients they had to travel to Greenville, forty-seven miles away, to Joe Gow Nue, the only store in the entire state that carried Chinese groceries. Once a year Ellen's family traveled to Greenville to visit her father's grave site in Mississippi's only Chinese cemetery. The family was so poor they had to depend on the kindness of a customer with a car to drive them. Those excursions unfailingly included a stop at Joe Gow Nue, where the family would stock up on their yearly supply of Chinese dry goods.

Ellen's family's general store carried such staples as salted meat, molasses, eggs, and the vegetables favored by their black clientele: rutabagas, cabbage, turnips, and collard greens. A nickel's worth of cigarettes or fifteen cents' worth of salted meat was a typical purchase. When root vegetables grew too old to sell, Ellen's mother would cut them into thin half-moon slices and stir-fry them with onions and a little beef, or she would make a stir-fry of turnip greens with Southern salted pork. Even without ginger or scallions, Ellen's mother was able to make simple stir-fries delicious. "It was about survival," says Ellen. "We had nothing else to eat. If we couldn't sell it, we'd eat it." She remembers her family stir-fried with a frying pan or pot on a woodstove in the winter and a kerosene stove in the summer. "Woks were not available, so we cooked with whatever was available and cheap."

Chinese ingredients were, of course, a luxury. Sometimes the family was lucky enough to secure a little ginger, brought in from San Francisco or Los Angeles. More than likely, however, it would be ruined from freezer storage before they could use it. Without Chinese vegetables, they made do with whatever they had. Some families even made stir-fries with American pumpkin.

Rachel Sit Wong, who grew up in Greenville, Mississippi, remembers how her mother, Sit Jeu Shee, saved shelled English pea pods. "She'd take the empty pod and bend it at the stem end, then peel away the tough inner membrane. After splitting the pod into two pieces, she'd stir-fry the handful of peeled pods with a little beef and garlic. This was her way of making a dish that reminded her of the taste of snow peas." Rachel's mom, who left China for America in 1918, always yearned for Chineses vegetables. She also craved the taste of lotus root, the Chinese starchy vegetable beloved for its delicate, crunchy texture and mildly sweet flavor. She once surprised the family by making a stir-fry of beef with thinly sliced white potatoes, having "perfected the timing so precisely that, to our amazement, the potato had a crispness reminiscent of lotus root without tasting raw," Rachel recalls.

Years later, when the family was able to obtain seeds for Chinese vegetables, they grew their own winter melons, bitter melons, Chinese long beans, and luffa squash. "We saved the seeds from the vegetables, dried them, and planted them again." When ginger finally became available, Rachel's family, like many others, peeled the root and placed it in a jar filled with bourbon or sherry. Stored in the refrigerator, the coveted ginger would not only last for months, but it would also benefit in flavor from the infusion of liquor.

Many of the Chinese who migrated from south-ern China beginning in the 1870s came to the Mississippi Delta as farm laborers, settling anywhere from Memphis to Vicksburg. John Chan, a descendant who grew up in Greenville, Mississippi, recalls that when his uncle George Long visited China, he was struck by how much Guangdong province in southern China resembled the Mississippi Delta. "My uncle said it was hot, hot, hot, with the sun beating down on the fields and the air filled with mosquitoes. The land was rich, dark, and had the same black soil that was so perfect for growing cotton. Seeing this made him speculate that this similarity might have been why the Chinese gravitated to Mississippi."

By 1900, there were about 240 Chinese living along the Delta; by 1960, there were more than 1,200, most operating grocery stores that served impoverished black laborers. The children grew up speaking English with a Southern drawl and Cantonese with a Southern lilt. Managing the grocery stores was grueling work seven days a week, fourteen hours or more a day, requiring everyone to pitch in simply to eke out a living. Mary Ann Wong, who grew up in Clarksdale, Mississippi, recalls her father opening their store at five every morning in time to sell thirty cents' worth of lunch meat, a Moon Pie, and RC Cola to each of the sharecroppers who came in before they hopped on the truck headed for the cotton fields. "I only remember my father working; he never took a vacation or ate in a restaurant."

By the 1940s and '50s, nearly every small town in Mississippi, and in neighboring states like Tennessee, Arkansas, and Louisiana, seemed to have a Chinese-run grocery store. Facing tremendous prejudice, the Chinese community remained close-knit. For weddings, birth celebrations, and other important occasions, anywhere from 500 to 1,000 guests would convene from across the state. A simple Chinese banquet would be prepared by a group of six to eight men. The feast would include such dishes as stir-fried shrimp and celery, soy sauce chicken, barbecued pork, and bird's nest soup. The food was cooked in giant woks set on top of makeshift metal drums, following a long tradition in China in which cooks would come to homes with everything from woks to tables and chairs to cater a banquet. The principal difference was that, in the South, these men were not professional cooks, but simply members of the Chinese community who volunteered their services. This labor of love, this expression of solidarity from one of the most unique chapters of the Chinese diaspora, lasted until the opening of the first Chinese restaurants in the region in the early 1960s.

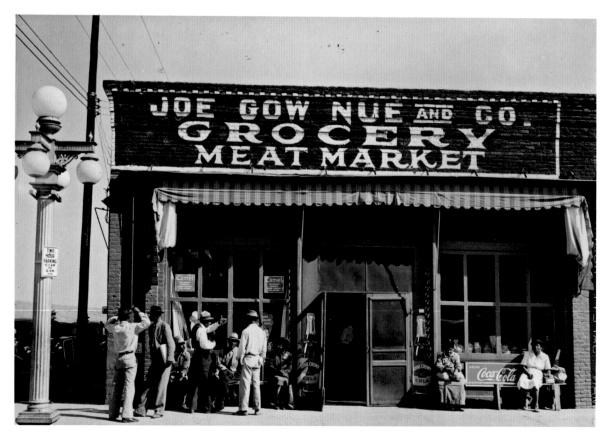

Joe Gow Nue market in Greenville, Mississippi, circa 1930. This was the first Chinese market in Mississippi, carrying a variety of Chinese staple ingredients, teapots, chopsticks, and vases, in addition to American canned goods, lard, sugar, and meat. In the 1940s, the store started a garden and grew Chinese vegetables like bok choy, Chinese broccoli (gai lan), and long beans. During this period the market served as a gathering place for the Chinese. (Photograph courtesy of the Mississippi Department of Archives and History)

Hong Kong–Style Silky Stir-Fried Minced Beef

Ever since I tasted stir-fried minced beef in Hong Kong I have been curious to know how it is made. The flavor is so rich and sumptuous that it seems more like a decadent meat sauce than a stir-fry. Chef Danny Chan hand-minces the beef rather than using ground beef, which has an inferior texture and taste. But the real key is in adding an egg beaten with two egg yolks right after the beef is briefly stir-fried. This is not a dish to eat every day but is well worth it as an occasional treat.

8 ounces lean flank steak

2 teaspoons minced garlic

1 teaspoon soy sauce

2 teaspoons oyster sauce

1 teaspoon plus 2 tablespoons peanut
    or vegetable oil

1½ teaspoons cornstarch

1 teaspoon plus 1 tablespoon Shao Hsing rice wine
    or dry sherry

¼ teaspoon sesame oil

⅛ teaspoon freshly ground pepper

3 tablespoons chicken broth

1 teaspoon dark soy sauce

1 whole large egg

2 large egg yolks

½ cup chopped onions

½ teaspoon salt

½ cup frozen peas

2 tablespoons chopped scallions

1. Cut the beef with the grain into 2-inch-wide strips. Cut each strip across the grain into ¼-inch-thick slices. Stack the beef slices and cut into 2-inch-long matchsticks. Then cut the matchsticks into a scant ¼-inch dice. When all the beef has been diced, roughly chop it for a minute. You should have about 1 cup. In a medium bowl combine the beef, 1 teaspoon of the garlic, soy sauce, 1 teaspoon of the oyster sauce, 1 teaspoon of the peanut oil, 1 teaspoon of the cornstarch, 1 teaspoon of the rice wine, sesame oil, and pepper. Stir to combine.

2. In a small bowl combine the broth and the remaining 1 tablespoon rice wine. In a separate bowl combine the dark soy sauce, the remaining 1 teaspoon oyster sauce and ½ teaspoon cornstarch, and 1 tablespoon cold water. In a another small bowl beat the whole egg and the egg yolks until just combined.

3. Heat a 14-inch flat-bottomed wok or 12-inch skillet over high heat until a bead of water vaporizes within 1 to 2 seconds of contact. Swirl in the remaining 2 tablespoons peanut oil, add the onions and remaining 1 teaspoon garlic, then, using a metal spatula, stir-fry 10 seconds or until the aromatics are fragrant. Push the aromatics to the sides of the wok, carefully add the beef, and spread it evenly in one layer in the wok. Sprinkle on the salt. Cook undisturbed 30 seconds. Add the peas and stir-fry 1 minute or until the beef is still slightly pink. Swirl the broth mixture into the wok and stir-fry 1 minute or until the beef is no longer pink. Swirl the dark soy sauce mixture into the wok and stir-fry 30 seconds or until slightly thickened. Spread the beef mixture evenly in one layer in the wok. Pour the egg mixture over the beef. Reduce the heat to low and cook 45 seconds or until the eggs are not quite set. Add the chopped scallions and stir-fry 10 seconds or until the mixture is just combined and the eggs are no longer runny.

Serves 2 as a main dish with rice or 4 as part of a multicourse meal.

Velvet Stir-Fry: Luscious and Light

The Chinese revere foods prepared with the silky, smooth texture known by the Cantonese as *waat*. No other cooking technique produces such light, delicate, tender succulence, hence the culinary term "velveting" in English. This style of stir-frying, popular with chefs, is most typically accomplished by briefly marinating bite-sized pieces of beef, pork, chicken, fish, shrimp, or scallops in a standard combination of egg white, cornstarch, and a little water or rice wine. The marinated morsels are then blanched in oil or water and thoroughly drained in a colander before being stir-fried. Ingredients that have been marinated in the egg white–cornstarch mixture can also be stir-fried without first being oil- or water-blanched. This abbreviated process will tenderize ingredients, but the finished texture will not be nearly as smooth or as silky.

Chef Yong Soon of Toronto, Canada, says the egg white–cornstarch mixture is the perfect vehicle for protecting meat, poultry (especially chicken breast), fish, or shellfish from drying out. "Once absorbed into the meat, it helps the meat retain moisture and achieve a unique state of tenderness. The egg white–cornstarch mixture also encases the ingredient, thereby sealing in the succulence and preventing toughness." Interestingly, when eaten, velveted ingredients betray no hint of the coating that has rendered them so tender.

There are two variations on the velveting recipe that are less typical. In the first variation, a whole egg is combined with the cornstarch and water, and occasionally a little rice wine is added. This is traditionally used only for beef, pork, and dark meat chicken. According to Chef Richard Chen of Wing Lei restaurant in Las Vegas, the yolk provides another binding agent to protect the meat's moisture. The second variation combines the cornstarch with cold water only, no egg, and can be used with meat, poultry, or shellfish.

According to Shirley Cheng, professor in culinary arts at the Culinary Institute of America, "the purpose of velveting is only to create tenderness and should not be confused with marinating to add flavor." Accordingly, except for a little rice wine, seasonings are never added to the egg white–cornstarch mixture. Flavor is added later, either during stir-frying or with the sauce. The velveting process accentuates the natural succulence and essence of an ingredient, making freshness of ingredients a requirement. For velveting, never use meat, poultry, fish, or shellfish that has been previously frozen because the texture will be inferior. The exception is frozen shrimp that has been defrosted, but fresh is always preferable.

Velveting is a technique more commonly practiced in professional kitchens. For home cooks, it is an advanced method to master and more complicated because it requires the additional step of oil- or water-blanching. After coating the ingredients in the egg white–cornstarch mixture, many chefs are known to toss the coated pieces in a tiny amount of oil to prevent them from clumping together and sticking to the wok. The ingredients are then blanched in oil that has been heated to 280°F on a deep-frying thermometer. This technique, called *jau yau*, or "passing through oil," makes foods firmer and richer. Alternatively, the ingredients can be blanched in simmering water to which a small spoonful of oil has been added, creating a finer, softer, less oily texture. I think velveting is worth the extra effort because the texture it produces is so unbelievably tender. However, I recommend water-blanching for the home cook because it is less complicated and dangerous than oil-blanching, it reduces the amount of oil necessary for stir-frying, and foods taste less fatty because velveting is, in fact, an extraordinary low-fat cooking technique. If you want to velvet ingredients, here are a few tips to ensure success:

- **Drain Shrimp and Scallops**

  After rinsing shrimp and scallops in a colander, shake out water before combining with the egg white–cornstarch mixture. Excess water dilutes the effectiveness of the coating.

- **Combine Cornstarch Until Dissolved**

  When adding the cornstarch to the meat, poultry, fish, or shellfish, stir the mixture until the cornstarch is totally dissolved and no clumps are visible.

- **Use Only 2 Tablespoons of Egg White**

  Use about 2 tablespoons of egg white for 1 pound of meat, poultry, fish, or shellfish. If too much egg white is used, it will not be absorbed. To measure 2 tablespoons, it is easier if you beat the egg white with a fork just enough to break the gel.

- **Shake Out Excess Water Thoroughly**

  After the velveted ingredients have been water-blanched, have a colander ready in the sink, drain the pieces in the colander, and thoroughly shake out any water before proceeding to the next step of stir-frying. Any excess moisture will create extra spattering from the hot oil when the pieces are added to the wok, in addition to turning your stir-fry into a braise.

- **Use a Deep-Frying Thermometer for Oil-Blanching**

  For oil-blanching, it is essential to use a deep-frying thermom-eter so that you know precisely when the oil reaches 280°F. Remember, for an accurate reading, the tip of the thermom-eter should never touch the hot pan.

- **Exercise Care When Handling Hot Oil or Water**

  Whether water- or oil-blanching, it is important to exercise care when adding or removing ingredients to and from the hot liquid. I use a dry wok skimmer or slotted metal spoon to quickly but carefully transfer the marinated ingredients, without splashing, into the dangerously hot liquid. Use the same utensil to carefully remove the ingredients.

- **Velveted Ingredients Should Never Be Browned**

  Ingredients that have been velveted should never be stir-fried to the point of being seared or browned. The reason for this is that water- or oil-blanching partially cooks the velveted ingre-dients. A brief stir-frying, without any browning, is all that is needed to complete the cooking, i.e., stir-fried velveted chicken breast remains white.

- **Soak Cooking Tools in Sudsy Hot Water**

  Be advised that the wok skimmer or slotted spoon and the pot used for blanching the egg white–cornstarch mixture often has a sticky film. Remember to soak both in sudsy hot water to make them easier to wash.

  Note: For specific recipes that use the velveting technique, see Velvet Chicken with Asparagus (page 128); Hoisin Explosion Chicken (page 114); Hong Kong–Style Mango Ginger Chicken (page 124); Fujianese-Style Stir-Fried Fish with Peppers (page 176); Velvet Orange Scallops (page 157), Stir-Fried Crystal Shrimp (page 160).

The Hakka Diaspora

The story of the Chinese diaspora is incomplete without mention of the Hakka, often called the gypsies of China. Approximately one thousand years ago, the nomadic Hakka were driven out of northern China by civil unrest, famines, floods, and invaders who forced them to migrate to the south. They settled finally in what are the present-day provinces of Guangdong, Fujian, and Jiangxi. The Cantonese, who already occupied the prime farm plots in Guangdong, forced the Hakka to eke out their living in the outskirts and mountain villages. The name "Hakka," which means "guest family," connotes their lack of status.

In the mid-nineteenth century, Hakka villages were destroyed as a result of civil wars with the Cantonese. An estimated twenty thousand died from famine and disease in addition to those who perished when the natural disasters plaguing southern China left the Hakka impotent in the face of a failing economy. Small groups of Hakka had begun fleeing China in the early 1800s, but by 1866 the Hakka, who played a significant role in the failed Taiping Rebellion against the Qing (Manchu) government, found themselves desperate to make a mass exodus. While a majority moved to Southeast Asia and Taiwan, thousands of others signed up for work as contract laborers in Hawaii, the Caribbean, South America, North America, and in such distant places as Madagascar, Mauritius, Pakistan, and India.

The resilience of the Hakka revealed itself in the close-knit communities they formed wherever they settled. They continued to speak their own dialect of Chinese and to maintain their cooking traditions, a peasant-style cuisine known for its use of uncomplicated and earthy foods. The nomadic nature of the Hakka life demanded simple, flexible dishes that could be cooked in makeshift situations. Salt was used to preserve foods that would otherwise spoil without refrigeration. Preserved and pickled ingredients, such as fermented black beans, salted fish, dried shrimp, and salted or pickled mustard greens, were stock items valued for their flavor intensity.

Living abroad, the Hakka often lacked basic staples, but they managed to make do with local ingredients. Rose Wong, a Hakka who grew up in Jamaica, recalls her mother salting eggs, turnips, fish, mustard greens, and limes (a substitute for lemons), just as she had done in China. Salted ingredients were essential for a peasant population that often lost critical salt due to manual labor.

Hakka food expert Linda Lau Anusasananan explains: "The original Hakka cuisine was born out of their hardworking lifestyle. The women had little time after long days in the fields, so their cooking had to be quick and easy. Because of their historical need for a portable kitchen, they filled their pantries with preserved, salted, or dried ingredients to endure travel and time. Seasonings such as soy sauce, rice wine, fermented rice, fermented black beans, preserved vegetables, cured meat, ginger, and garlic endow some of the dishes with robust savory flavors. Yet, there are many dishes that the Hakka and Cantonese share. Hakka is sometimes considered a country cousin of Cantonese cuisines. For centuries they lived side by side in the same province, Guangdong. Even abroad, they lived together. Some dishes that often appear on Cantonese menus would be equally at home in a Hakka meal." Some famous Hakka dishes are salt baked chicken, braised pork belly, and steamed pork cake with salted fish.

Hakka stir-fries are noted for their simplicity, with an emphasis on vegetables. Several outstanding recipes are included in this collection: Stir-Fried Cilantro with Bean Sprouts and Shrimp (page 224), a Hakka dish from China, combines a bunch of cilantro with bean sprouts, carrots, and just a small amount of shrimp seasoned with garlic and ginger; Hakka-Style Stir-Fried Cabbage and Egg (page 204) is made by a native Chinese Indonesian but traces its origins to China and exemplifies the modesty with which a dish can be prepared, using only a pound of Napa cabbage stir-fried with one egg and a generous amount of garlic. And, finally, Chinese Jamaican Stir-Fried Chicken with Chayote (page 133) and Chinese Jamaican Stir-Fried Beef and Carrots (page 78) both reflect the culinary cross-pollination of Jamaican and Hakka cooking traditions.

A Culinary Remembrance: From China to the Caribbean

Winnie Lee Lum

In 1930, eighteen-year-old Wei Hon Ming made the arduous journey from Hong Kong to Jamaica. Chinese immigration to the Caribbean and Central and South America had escalated after 1882 with the passage of the Exclusion Act of 1882, barring the Chinese from entering the United States. Additionally, the civil unrest and dire economic conditions in China had forced many of Wei's Hakka (see The Hakka Diaspora, opposite page) relatives and friends to seek a better life abroad. His father had immigrated to Jamaica in 1913 and his mother in 1918. (The Exclusion Act was not repealed until 1943.)

Wei traveled eighteen days by steamer ship from Hong Kong via Shanghai and Kobe, Japan, then crossed the Pacific Ocean to Vancouver, Canada. In his autobiography Wei described the living conditions: "We stayed on the bottom of the ship like a prison camp 50 to 100 passengers in a large compartment, it is hot and smell bad, food was poor, but you can buy your lunch specially from Chinese sailors or stewards if you have money." From Vancouver, Wei traveled by train to Montreal, in what he described as "hot and shaky, five days journey was terrible." The train stopped for one night in Montreal, where Wei boarded a banana ship for Jamaica. Upon arriving in Jamaica, he was reunited with his mother and father.

In Jamaica, Wei became known as Lincoln Williams, the family name changed by the local postmistress. (She subsequently gave each family member his or her given name.) Three years later, Lincoln Williams's nineteen-year-old picture bride, Chin Nuk Hee, made a similar journey from Hong Kong to Jamaica, voyaging by ship to Vancouver, then boarding a train bound for San Francisco, then another bound for Miami, and finally a ship to Jamaica. Like the three soon-to-be family members before her, she was traumatized and homesick by the time she arrived in the Caribbean.

Winnie Lee Lum

The Williamses lived in the small town of Petersfield, about 140 miles west of Kingston, where they were the only Chinese family. Like other Chinese in Jamaica, they ran a general store, selling grocery and dry goods, with a rum bar. Chin Nuk Hee was renamed Nancy Williams. Eventually, Lincoln Williams became one of the first Chinese to own a sugar plantation and to venture into farming.

Williams's family found that one way to stave off the longing to return to China was to cook traditional Chinese meals. "My mom planted Chinese vegetables, knew how to make *hom yu* (salted dried fish) and *hom choi* (salted mustard greens), sprouted her own bean sprouts, sewed all the children's clothes, and could knit and crochet as well," recalls Lincoln and Nancy's daughter, Winnie Lee Lum. Nancy Williams raised seven children and was hardworking and resourceful. She maintained her culinary traditions by preparing Chinese food for her family's every meal, re-creating the same robust Hakka dishes she grew up eating in China with preserved ingredients such as *hom choi* stir-fried with pork. Hakka cooking shares many similarities to Cantonese dishes, so Williams also prepared steamed fish, stir-fried chicken with Chinese mushrooms, and steamed pork with salted fish. The dishes were often simplified variations of traditional recipes, using fewer seasonings since some Chinese ingredients were not available. Jamaica had only basic Chinese staples, such as soy sauce, fermented black beans, oyster sauce, and bean sauce. Williams's earliest dishes were stir-fries of such local vegetables as cabbage, carrots, or sweet bell pepper with garlic. Eventually, by growing her own Chinese vegetables, Nancy Williams was able to add bok choy, long beans, and bitter melon to her repertoire.

Winnie Lee Lum moved to Trinidad in 1966, where her husband Tony Lee Lum was born and raised. Tony Lee Lum's grandfather, the legendary John Lee Lum, was one of the first successful Chinese entrepreneurs of Trinidad, having left Guangdong province in China in 1870 for the California Gold Rush. For several years he worked in California, and then in Canada on the Trans-Pacific Railroad before moving to Brazil, British Guiana, and finally settling in Trinidad in 1880. Lee Lum opened a general store that ultimately grew into an empire of twenty stores around Trinidad. He was one of the first to begin oil exploration in Trinidad and had major holdings in cocoa estates.

Upon arriving in Trinidad, Winnie Lee Lum was surprised to discover the predominance of Cantonese-style cooking in Trinidad even though there was a mix of Cantonese and Hakka populations on the island. After growing up in Jamaica, where the Chinese population was almost entirely Hakka, Winnie Lee Lum found the Chinese restaurants in Trinidad more sophisticated, their chefs often recruited from China. A few even served dim sum, which was not available in Jamaica.

The Chinese had been established in Trinidad since 1806, longer than in Jamaica, where they had settled in 1854. Winnie Lee Lum found the Chinese in Trinidad to be more "Westernized" and more integrated into the Indian and Creole cultures there. "Compared to Tony, I felt more Chinese. My parents were first-generation Chinese, but his Cantonese parents were third generation and that much more removed from Chinese culture. They had a Creole cook who prepared mostly Trinidadian food. My mother-in-law did teach her how to make a few Chinese dishes," explains Winnie Lee Lum.

In contrast to her husband's family, she continued the Hakka culinary traditions she had learned from her family. Today, over forty years later, she still prepares traditional Hakka food daily and continues the old-fashioned Hakka traditions of salting mustard greens and salt-drying fish, just as her mother taught her. Winnie Lee Lum's family likes to frequent the fine local Cantonese-style restaurants on the island and she herself occasionally prepares a Trinidadian meal of callaloo or curry. Her style of cooking has also evolved, absorbing some of the local flavors of Trinidad.

Winnie Lee Lum is the author of *Caribbean Chinese Cooking* and has been teaching Chinese cooking classes for more than twenty-five years. One of her specialties is Chinese Trinidadian Stir-Fried Shrimp with Rum (page 180). She has adopted the local custom of "washing" shrimp with lime juice before cooking to remove its fishiness. The fresh local jumbo shrimp are then stir-fried in garlic and ginger with Jamaican dark rum and ketchup. She considers Chinese Jamaican food less spicy than Chinese Trinidadian. "In Trinidad, we like stir-fries with a little heat from Scotch bonnet peppers," she explains. These are essential in her Chinese Trinidadian Chicken with Mango Chutney (page 116), along with *shandon beni* leaves, a local herb that tastes like cilantro. Typically, Chinese Trini restaurants have hot pepper sauces and sometimes even ketchup on the table. "Chinese food in Trinidad reflects the Creole and Indian influences. Just like the people of Trinidad, it can be a mix of everything."

Stir-Fried Chicken with Pineapple and Peppers

Poultry
and Egg

RECIPES

A Child of Ten Stir-Fries: A Hong Kong Story

Amy Yip

When Amy Yip was ten years old, her mother became ill after giving birth to her seventh child and was confined to bed for a year. The entire household's cooking chores then fell to Amy and her thirteen-year-old brother, Sam.

"Each day after coming home from school, after we did our homework, my mom gave us money to shop for food," Yip recalls. "Other children in the neighborhood also had to do the family shopping, so we all went to the market together. We were poor and had to hunt for the best bargains. In our family with nine people, there were never any leftovers."

During the 1960s, Yip's family lived in an apartment building in Hong Kong with a communal kitchen shared by three or four families on the same floor. There were four cooking stations in the large room. Each station had two burners: one for soup and the other intended for stir-frying. Yip and her brother could look over the shoulders of more experienced cooks and copy what they saw. "My mom didn't know how to cook so she couldn't teach us. Everyone seemed to know how to stir-fry pork and cucumbers [page 73], a popular home-style dish.

Amy Yip

Cucumbers were always cheap," says Yip. Through trial and error, Yip learned how to avoid such mistakes as adding water when stir-frying cucumbers (which makes them too soft) and covering cucumbers as they cook (they have a much better texture if they remain uncovered during stir-frying). The communal kitchen's cooks also taught Yip how to remove the bitterness from a cucumber: cut off each tip and rub the exposed ends with one of the tips until a white liquid is released. Then rinse. To this day, she does this.

Each night, Yip and her brother prepared three dishes for dinner: a soup, a pan-fried fish, and a stir-fry with a big pot of rice. They learned how to make substantial meals out of scarce materials. "Sometimes we would blanch a small piece of pork for five minutes in a pot of water just to give the 'broth' a little meat flavor, before adding the rest of the soup ingredients. Then we'd slice the blanched pork and stir-fry it with vegetables. In this way we could get two dishes out of one piece of pork. Making stir-fries was the best way to stretch a small amount of meat. We learned to make do with what we had and to make everything work. This is the Chinese way."

Stir-Fried Chicken with Pineapple and Peppers

This dish is a specialty of Amy Yip (see A Child of Ten Stir-Fries, page 109) who came up with the idea in an effort to help her son gain weight. The "original" recipe called for marinating the chicken in egg white, but Amy decided to do just the opposite: add an egg yolk.

Most stir-fries are made with bite-sized pieces of meat or vegetables, but this calls for fairly large pieces of boneless chicken thigh meat. I have also prepared this with chicken breast with excellent results. To do that, first separate the chicken supreme (which is about ½ inch thick) from the breast and cut it in half crosswise. Then cut the chicken breast crosswise into ½-inch-thick large slices.

The chicken is first pan-fried over high heat before it is stir-fried. When I saw Amy adding 4 teaspoons of sugar, I thought the chicken would be super-sweet, but the sugar is mellowed by the other ingredients. This is best cooked with a wok because the sugar can really burn into a skillet. You'll notice that as you transfer the stir-fry to a platter there's no sauce; wait a minute or two and an incredible sauce suddenly pools in the plate. (See photo, page 106.)

1 pound skinless, boneless chicken thigh or breast, cut crosswise into ½-inch-thick large slices

1½ teaspoons cornstarch

1 large egg yolk

4 teaspoons sugar

1 teaspoon soy sauce

1 teaspoon dark soy sauce

½ teaspoon salt

1 tablespoon peanut or vegetable oil

1½ cups ½-inch cubed fresh pineapple

½ cup julienned red bell peppers

½ cup thinly sliced scallions

1. In a medium bowl combine the chicken, cornstarch, egg yolk, 2 teaspoons of the sugar, soy sauce, dark soy sauce, and ¼ teaspoon of the salt. Stir to combine. Marinate the chicken uncovered 15 minutes. Using a slotted spoon, transfer the chicken to a separate bowl, shaking off the excess marinade over the first bowl. You should have about 2 to 3 teaspoons reserved marinade.

2. Heat a 14-inch flat-bottomed wok over high heat until a bead of water vaporizes within 1 to 2 seconds of contact. Swirl in the oil, carefully add the chicken, and spread it evenly in one layer in the wok. Pan-fry undisturbed 1½ minutes, letting the chicken begin to sear. Then, using a metal spatula, turn the chicken slices over and pan-fry undisturbed 1½ minutes, letting the chicken brown. Reduce the heat to medium and stir-fry the chicken 2 minutes or until the chicken is dark golden brown. Add the pineapple, bell peppers, scallions, and the reserved marinade and sprinkle on the remaining 2 teaspoons sugar and ¼ teaspoon salt, and stir-fry 1 to 2 minutes or until the chicken is just cooked through and the bell peppers are crisp-tender.

Serves 3 as a main dish with rice or 4 as part of a multicourse meal.

Wok Hay in the Home Kitchen

In China, the superiority of the Cantonese at stir-frying is legendary. The Cantonese consider a stir-fry to be perfect when the ingredients possess a concentrated flavor invigorated with an elusive aroma and taste borne of the wok. While the stir-frying technique is found throughout China, only the Cantonese have a special term—*wok hay* (the standardized Cantonese spelling is *wok hei*)—which I call "the breath of a wok" to describe this superior essence. Blessed with a wealth of produce and seafood year-round, the Cantonese recognized that when fresh ingredients are stir-fried quickly in an iron wok over intense heat, a dish requires only a minimum of seasonings to accentuate the natural character of the ingredients. Such stir-fries, bursting with vitality and a hint of caramelization, possess a life force. It is no wonder the English translation for *hay* (*hei;* Mandarin *qi*) is "energy" or "breath."

Many connoisseurs of Chinese cooking believe that *wok hay* can be achieved only by Chinese restaurant chefs whose commercial wok stoves produce a blazing heat with about ten to twenty times the power of home ranges. But curls of smoky heat wafting from a stir-fry and food that burns in the mouth are not the only indicators that a dish possesses *wok hay*. Certainly a hot wok is preferable for achieving *wok hay*, but a home-cooked stir-fry has commensurate sterling qualities when the ingredients are seasonal and fresh. No matter how great the power of a stove, if the ingredients are not inherently flavorful there is no taste or essence to accentuate through stir-frying. For that reason I generally prefer a home-cooked stir-fry to those offered in Chinese restaurants.

While there are exceptions, there are several reasons for the overall mediocrity of Chinese restaurants in America. Monosodium glutamate is routinely used to artificially boost flavor and camouflage ingredients lacking in freshness or quality. It is also a common practice in Chinese restaurants to oil-blanch meat, poultry, fish, shellfish, and sometimes even vegetables before stir-frying, to tenderize and infuse the ingredients with flavor. Oil-blanching means stir-fries are greasier, and when poorly executed, as is often the case, the stir-fry is served sitting in a shallow pool of oil. The problems are compounded by the inferior cooking oil common to Chinese restaurants and the practice of reusing oil. Restaurants are also vulnerable to the unpredictability of business; if patronage is unexpectedly slow, chefs are often forced to use ingredients past their prime. And restaurants often operate with such small margins of profit that it is next to impossible for the average Chinese restaurant ever to use organic ingredients or produce from a local farmers' market.

In the home kitchen, oil-blanching is rarely practiced. Without oil-blanching, stir-fries are not only healthier, but also offer the true flavor of the ingredients unmasked by the heaviness of excessive oil. So even though the heat produced from an average home range is not nearly as fierce as that created with a restaurant wok range, the glory of a home-cooked stir-fry is its purity of flavor. It is the care and effort a home cook can exercise by shopping locally and selecting quality ingredients in season that elevate a dish.

The fleeting *wok hay*—the heat, vitality, and fragrance—that comes from stir-frying in a wok begins to dissipate the moment it leaves the sizzling pan. A stir-fry, therefore, must be enjoyed immediately. When I was a child, my father insisted that everyone be seated at the dinner table before he would even begin to stir-fry. When I think of a stir-fry, it is that excitement and anticipation of the aroma that foretold the taste of *wok hay* that I recall. Nothing compares to the enviable pleasure of eating a perfectly prepared home-cooked stir-fry.

Kung Pao Chicken

Of the many versions of kung pao chicken that I've eaten, this is one of my favorites. The dark, rich sauce clings to the chicken and peppers, with just an undertone of heat and aromatic flavor from the chilies and Sichuan peppercorns. For the dried chili peppers, use kitchen scissors to snip ¼-inch from one end to release the seeds during cooking. Use 4 chilies for mild heat and 8 or more for maximum heat. If you cannot find unsalted roasted peanuts, buy raw peanuts in the shell, shell them, remove the skins, and dry stir-fry them in a dry wok over medium heat for a few minutes until light golden.

1 pound boneless, skinless chicken thigh or breast, cut into ¾-inch cubes

2 tablespoons minced ginger

1 tablespoon minced garlic

2½ teaspoons cornstarch

1 teaspoon soy sauce

1 teaspoon plus 1 tablespoon Shao Hsing rice wine or dry sherry

2 teaspoons sugar

¾ teaspoon salt

2 tablespoons chicken broth

1 tablespoon Chinkiang or balsamic vinegar

1 teaspoon dark soy sauce

1 teaspoon sesame oil

2 tablespoons peanut or vegetable oil

4 to 8 dried red chili peppers, snipped on one end

½ teaspoon roasted and ground Sichuan peppercorns (see page 6)

1 large red bell pepper, cut into 1-inch squares

¾ cup unsalted roasted peanuts

½ cup minced scallions

1. In a medium bowl combine the chicken, ginger, garlic, cornstarch, soy sauce, 1 teaspoon of the rice wine, 1 teaspoon of the sugar, ½ teaspoon of the salt, and 1 teaspoon cold water. Stir to combine. In a small bowl combine the broth, vinegar, dark soy sauce, sesame oil, and the remaining 1 tablespoon rice wine.

2. Heat a 14-inch flat-bottomed wok or 12-inch skillet over high heat until a bead of water vaporizes within 1 to 2 seconds of contact. Swirl in 1 tablespoon of the peanut oil, add the chilies and ground Sichuan peppercorns, then, using a metal spatula, stir-fry 15 seconds or until the chilies just begin to smoke. Push the chili mixture to the sides of the wok, carefully add the chicken, and spread it evenly in one layer in the wok. Cook undisturbed 1 minute, letting the chicken begin to sear. Then stir-fry 1 minute or until the chicken is lightly browned but not cooked through.

3. Swirl the remaining 1 tablespoon peanut oil into the wok. Add the bell peppers and stir-fry 1 minute or until the peppers begin to soften. Swirl the broth mixture into the wok and stir-fry 1 minute or until the chicken is just cooked through. Add the peanuts and scallions, sprinkle on the remaining 1 teaspoon sugar and ¼ teaspoon salt, and stir-fry 30 seconds or until the scallions are bright green.

Serves 2 to 3 as a main dish with rice or 4 as part of a multicourse meal.

Hoisin Explosion Chicken

There are many versions of this classic recipe that combines ingredients from the far corners of China: the hoisin sauce is a northern condiment, the spicy red pepper flakes are from the west, and the rice wine is an eastern staple. Here the velveting technique (see Velvet Stir-Fry, page 100) is used with chicken for a full-flavored, robust stir-fry laced with heat. In addition to the egg white, cornstarch, rice wine, and salt, a little water helps to further tenderize the chicken.

12 ounces boneless, skinless chicken breast, cut into ¼-inch-thick bite-sized slices

1 tablespoon egg white, lightly beaten

2 teaspoons cornstarch

1½ teaspoons plus 1 tablespoon Shao Hsing rice wine or dry sherry

1 teaspoon salt

3 tablespoons hoisin sauce

1 teaspoon soy sauce

2 tablespoons peanut or vegetable oil

1 tablespoon minced ginger

1 tablespoon minced garlic

½ teaspoon red pepper flakes

1 medium green bell pepper, cut into ¼-inch-wide strips (about 1½ cups)

One 8-ounce can sliced bamboo shoots, rinsed and drained

1. In a medium bowl combine the chicken, egg white, cornstarch, 1½ teaspoons of the rice wine, ½ teaspoon of the salt, and 1½ teaspoons cold water. Stir until the cornstarch is totally dissolved and no clumps are visible. Put the chicken uncovered in the refrigerator for 30 minutes. In a small bowl combine the hoisin sauce, soy sauce, and the remaining 1 tablespoon rice wine.

2. In a 2-quart saucepan bring 1 quart water to a boil over high heat. Add 1 tablespoon of the oil to the boiling water. Reduce the heat to low. When the water is barely simmering, carefully add the chicken, gently stirring it so that the pieces do not clump together. Cook 1 minute or until the chicken just turns opaque but is not cooked through. Carefully drain the chicken in a colander, shaking the colander to remove excess water.

3. Heat a 14-inch flat-bottomed wok or 12-inch skillet over high heat until a bead of water vaporizes within 1 to 2 seconds of contact. Swirl in the remaining 1 tablespoon oil, add the ginger, garlic, and red pepper flakes, then, using a metal spatula, stir-fry 10 seconds or until the aromatics are fragrant. Add the bell peppers, sprinkle on the remaining ½ teaspoon salt, and stir-fry 30 seconds or until the peppers are bright green. Add the chicken and the bamboo shoots. Swirl the hoisin sauce mixture into the wok, and stir-fry 1 to 2 minutes or until the chicken is just cooked through.

Serves 2 to 3 as a main dish with rice or 4 as part of a multicourse meal.

Chinese Trinidadian Chicken with Mango Chutney

Winnie Lee Lum (see A Culinary Remembrance, page 103) learned to make this stir-fry shortly after she moved to Trinidad over forty years ago. The mango chutney combined with the two kinds of soy sauce gives the chicken a dark, rich flavor with layers of fruitiness and heat. If you're unaccustomed to cooking with Scotch bonnet peppers, start with the smaller amount called for as the chilies have very intense heat. Lee Lum says hot pepper sauce can be used as a substitute. In Trinidad, there is a wide selection of hot pepper sauces. Using Tabasco, ½ to 1 teaspoon, is another option. Lee Lum finishes the dish with chopped shandon beni *leaves, a local herb that tastes like cilantro. My favorite mango chutney is Major Grey's. If the chutney has any big pieces of fruit or ginger, chop them up so that the flavors blend.*

1 pound skinless, boneless chicken thigh or breast, cut into ¼-inch-thick bite-sized slices

2 teaspoons soy sauce

½ teaspoon salt

¼ teaspoon freshly ground pepper

3 tablespoons mango chutney

2 teaspoons dark soy sauce

¼ to ½ teaspoon minced Scotch bonnet peppers, without the seeds

2 tablespoons peanut or vegetable oil

1 teaspoon minced ginger

1 teaspoon minced garlic

1 small onion, cut into ¼-inch-wide wedges

3 tablespoons chopped cilantro

1. In a medium bowl combine the chicken, soy sauce, salt, and pepper. Stir to combine. In a small bowl combine the mango chutney, dark soy sauce, and Scotch bonnet peppers.

2. Heat a 14-inch flat-bottomed wok or 12-inch skillet over high heat until a bead of water vaporizes within 1 to 2 seconds of contact. Swirl in 1 tablespoon of the oil, add the ginger, garlic, and onions, and stir-fry 30 seconds or until the onions have just wilted. Push the onion mixture to the sides of the wok, swirl in the remaining 1 tablespoon oil, carefully add the chicken, and spread it evenly in one layer in the wok. Cook undisturbed for 1 minute, letting the chicken begin to sear. Then, using a metal spatula, stir-fry 1 minute, or until the chicken is browned on all sides but not cooked through. Add the mango chutney mixture and stir-fry 1 to 2 minutes or until the chicken is just cooked through. Stir in the cilantro.

Serves 2 to 3 as a main dish with rice or 4 as part of a multicourse meal.

Macanese Stir-Fried Chicken

Macanese cuisine is one of the most unusual examples of the cross-pollination of Chinese cuisine with another culture. In the sixteenth-century, Portuguese traders settled in the Macau Peninsula, just thirty-seven miles southwest of Hong Kong. Its melting pot cuisine reflects a mixture of Portuguese, Southern Chinese, Southeast Asian, European, and even Indian cooking traditions. This has been one of my favorite stir-fries ever since I first sampled Macanese cuisine on a trip to Macau in 1988.

1 pound boneless, skinless chicken thigh or breast, cut into ¼-inch-thick bite-sized slices

2 tablespoons minced garlic

2 teaspoons cornstarch

1 teaspoon soy sauce

1 teaspoon plus 1 tablespoon Shao Hsing rice wine or dry sherry

½ teaspoon sugar

⅓ cup canned coconut milk

¼ cup chicken broth

2 tablespoons Chinkiang or balsamic vinegar

2 teaspoons dark soy sauce

2 tablespoons peanut or vegetable oil

¾ cup thinly sliced shallots

4 ounces chouriço, or dry-cured smoked Spanish chorizo, cut into ¼-inch dice

1 teaspoon turmeric

1 teaspoon sweet paprika

1 cup diced ripe tomatoes

¾ teaspoon salt

1. In a medium bowl combine the chicken, garlic, cornstarch, soy sauce, 1 teaspoon of the rice wine, sugar, and 1 teaspoon cold water. Stir to combine. In a small bowl combine the coconut milk, broth, vinegar, dark soy sauce, and the remaining 1 tablespoon rice wine.

2. Heat a 14-inch flat-bottomed wok or 12-inch skillet over high heat until a bead of water vaporizes within 1 to 2 seconds of contact. Swirl in the oil, add the shallots and chouriço, then, using a metal spatula, stir-fry 30 seconds or until the shallots just wilt. Push the shallot mixture to the sides of the wok, carefully add the chicken, and spread it evenly in one layer in the wok. Cook undisturbed 1 minute, letting the chicken begin to sear. Sprinkle on the turmeric and paprika and stir-fry 1 minute or until the chicken is lightly browned but not cooked through. Add the tomatoes and stir-fry for 30 seconds or until the tomatoes begin to soften. Swirl the broth mixture into the wok, sprinkle on the salt, and stir-fry 1 to 2 minutes or until the chicken is just cooked through and the sauce is slightly thickened.

Serves 2 to 3 as a main dish with rice or 4 as part of a multicourse meal.

Spicy Orange Chicken

One ripe tomato, an orange, and a chicken breast, combined with basic staples become a sumptuous meal through the genius of stir-frying. Spicy orange chicken is a great recipe to make when I'm pressed for time, yet still want to cook something special. The chicken is intensely aromatic from the ginger, Sichuan peppercorns, and orange zest, with just a hint of heat from the chili bean sauce. It has everything I want in one dish, including a beautiful presentation.

1 pound skinless, boneless chicken breast, cut into
    ¼-inch-thick bite-sized slices

2 tablespoons finely shredded ginger

2 tablespoons Shao Hsing rice wine or dry sherry

2 teaspoons soy sauce

1½ teaspoons cornstarch

¾ teaspoon sugar

¼ teaspoon ground white pepper

¼ teaspoon roasted and ground Sichuan pepper-
    corns (see page 6)

¼ cup chicken broth

2 teaspoons rice vinegar

2 tablespoons peanut or vegetable oil

Zest of 1 orange

1 teaspoon chili bean sauce

1 medium ripe tomato, cut into thin wedges, or
    1 cup grape tomatoes, halved (about 5 ounces)

½ cup thinly sliced scallions

¾ teaspoon salt

1. In a medium bowl combine the chicken, 1 tablespoon of the ginger, 1 tablespoon of the rice wine, soy sauce, 1 teaspoon of the cornstarch, sugar, white pepper, and ground Sichuan peppercorns. Stir to combine. In a small bowl combine the broth, rice vinegar, and the remaining 1 tablespoon rice wine and ½ teaspoon cornstarch.

2. Heat a 14-inch flat-bottomed wok or 12-inch skillet over high heat until a bead of water vaporizes within 1 to 2 seconds of contact. Swirl in the oil, add the remaining 1 tablespoon ginger, then, using a metal spatula, stir-fry 10 seconds or until the ginger is fragrant. Push the ginger to the sides of the wok, carefully add the chicken, and spread it evenly in one layer in the wok. Cook undisturbed 1 minute, letting the chicken begin to sear. Add the orange zest and chili bean sauce. Then stir-fry 1 minute, or until the chicken is lightly browned but not cooked through. Add the tomatoes and stir-fry 30 seconds or until just combined. Restir the broth mixture and swirl it into the wok. Add the scallions, sprinkle on the salt, and stir-fry 1 minute or until the chicken is cooked through.

Serves 2 to 3 as a main dish with rice or 4 as part of a multicourse meal.

Five-Spice Chicken with Sugar Snaps

Marinating chicken with five-spice powder is an ingenious way to effortlessly infuse a stir-fry with robust flavors. The spice mixture combines ground Sichuan peppercorns, star anise, fennel, cinnamon, and cloves. For the best results when marinating the chicken, be sure to thoroughly mix in all the seasonings as the five-spice powder has a tendency to clump. Dark soy sauce brings out the rich tones of this dish but if you cannot find it, regular soy sauce can be used in its place.

1 pound skinless, boneless chicken thigh, cut into ¼-inch-thick bite-sized slices

2 tablespoons minced ginger

3 teaspoons dark soy sauce

2 teaspoons honey

1 teaspoon cornstarch

1 teaspoon Shao Hsing rice wine or dry sherry

½ teaspoon five-spice powder

1 teaspoon sesame oil

¼ cup chicken broth

2 teaspoons ketchup

2 tablespoons peanut or vegetable oil

2 ½ cups sugar snap peas, strings removed (about 8 ounces)

¾ teaspoon salt

1. In a medium bowl combine the chicken, minced ginger, 2 teaspoons of the dark soy sauce, honey, cornstarch, rice wine, and five-spice powder. Stir in the sesame oil. Stir to combine. In a small bowl combine the broth, ketchup, and the remaining 1 teaspoon dark soy sauce.

2. Heat a 14-inch flat-bottomed wok or 12-inch skillet over high heat until a bead of water vaporizes within 1 to 2 seconds of contact. Swirl in 1 tablespoon of the peanut oil, carefully add the chicken, and spread it evenly in one layer in the wok. Cook undisturbed 1 minute, letting the chicken begin to sear. Then, using a metal spatula, stir-fry 1 minute, or until the chicken is browned on all sides but not cooked through. Transfer the chicken to a plate.

3. Swirl the remaining 1 tablespoon peanut oil into the wok. Add the sugar snaps and stir-fry 1 minute or until the sugar snaps are bright green. Return the chicken and any juices that have accumulated to the wok. Swirl the broth mixture into the wok, sprinkle on the salt, and stir-fry 1 to 2 minutes or until the chicken is cooked through.

Serves 2 to 3 as a main dish with rice or 4 as part of a multicourse meal.

Dry Stir-Frying and Moist Stir-Frying

Dry stir-frying, *gon chau*, is a slight variation on the stir-fry technique that uses oil to stir-fry but deliberately omits stock, sauce, or liquid of any kind. According to Chef Yong Soon of Toronto, Canada, the only exception to the dry rule is an occasional use of soy sauce or oyster sauce. Not every cook is such a purist. Some add stocks, rice wine, or sauces in limited amounts to a dry stir-fry but use the heat of the wok to evaporate the excess moisture and concentrate the flavor. The purpose of a dry stir-fry is to intensify the flavor and to impart a slightly toasty, caramelized taste and a firmer texture. An example of such a dish is Beef Chow Fun (page 269), which is also known as dry stir-fried beef with broad rice noodles. A *gon chau* sometimes requires an extra minute or two of stir-frying. In the famous Dry-Fried Sichuan Beans (page 233), the vegetables are stir-fried over low to medium-low heat slowly until they are wilted, wrinkled, and perfect for absorbing the seasonings. While most chefs today first deep-fry the beans before briefly stir-frying them to save time, the traditional recipe calls for the beans to be only dry stir-fried with minimal oil. Chef Yong Soon explains that when dry stir-frying, a lid is never used as it might introduce unnecessary moisture through condensation. Another rule according to Chef Chow Chung of Chow Chung Restaurant in Hong Kong is the prohibition of salt in a dry stir-fry, but there are exceptions to this, too.

Sup chau is just the opposite of *gon chau*. *Sup chau* can be translated as a moist or wet stir-fry, but a more exact definition is that the stir-fry uses liquid in the form of stocks, rice wine, water, or a mixture of sauce ingredients to enhance the stir-fry. According to the Chinese Cuisine Training Institute in Hong Kong, the *sup chau* technique "allows the dish to have a shiny presentation and gives a silky mouthfeel. It is a stir-fry finished with a gravy." In the case of Chicken Chow Fun (page 276), for example, the addition of a small amount of broth and rice wine is necessary for creating a dish in which the noodles and chicken are bathed in sauce, in sharp contrast to beef chow fun, the classic dry stir-fry.

Not all *sup chau* stir-fries, however, have "gravy." When stir-frying clams or crabs, a little liquid is necessary for briefly steaming the shellfish in a covered wok before being stir-fried to completion. Singapore Noodles (page 274) uses a combination of broth, soy sauce, and rice wine to cook the rice noodles until they are tender, but there is no visible sauce in the final dish. A moist stir-fry might also begin as a dry stir-fry and then evolve in the last few minutes of cooking by the addition of a few spoonfuls of liquid. The most common *sup chau* calls for adding broth or rice wine with seasonings, often with a little cornstarch, swirled into the wok at the end of the cooking, to produce a delectable sauce that intermingles with the stir-fry's natural juices. Chinese food that has been Westernized often comes swimming in sauce. A genuine moist stir-fry, as the cooking authority Kenneth Lo advised, "usually contains a small amount of sauce, but never too much."

Note: A common misconception is that a stir-fry, any stir-fry, should have a sufficient amount of sauce for spooning over the rice. Dishes such as chop suey were created in part to satisfy the Western diner's expectation of a stir-fry with gravylike sauce. In fact, many Chinese stir-fries are intended to have only enough sauce to cling to the main ingredients. In China, it is common to eat stir-fries with plain rice, without sauce, and without the expectation of sauce.

Cashew Chicken

In America, cashew chicken is one of the most beloved dishes served in Chinese restaurants. Sadly it is often "Westernized," with deep-fried pieces of chicken in a heavy gravy. A true Cantonese cashew chicken should be seasoned with ginger, stir-fried with fresh sugar snaps, carrots, and celery, all in a light sauce that barely clings to the chicken. Look for fresh cashews of the best quality. I often buy unroasted cashews and dry stir-fry them in a dry skillet or wok over medium heat a few minutes, shaking the pan frequently until they are just light golden. For a richer tasting sauce use dark soy sauce in place of regular soy sauce with the broth. The virtues of a "simple" stir-fry (see page 201) are demonstrated in this easy-to-make recipe.

1 pound skinless, boneless chicken thigh, cut into
   ½-inch cubes

1 tablespoon minced garlic

2 teaspoons soy sauce

1½ teaspoons cornstarch

1 teaspoon plus 2 tablespoons Shao Hsing rice wine
   or dry sherry

¾ teaspoon salt

⅛ teaspoon sugar

¼ cup chicken broth

2 tablespoons peanut or vegetable oil

2 tablespoons minced ginger

½ cup sugar snap peas, strings removed

½ cup thinly sliced carrots

½ cup thinly sliced celery

½ cup unsalted roasted cashews

1. In a medium bowl combine the chicken, garlic, 1 teaspoon of the soy sauce, 1 teaspoon of the cornstarch, 1 teaspoon of the rice wine, ½ teaspoon of the salt, and sugar. Stir to combine. In a small bowl combine the broth, the remaining 1 teaspoon soy sauce, 2 tablespoons rice wine, and ½ teaspoon cornstarch.

2. Heat a 14-inch flat-bottomed wok or 12-inch skillet over high heat until a bead of water vaporizes within 1 to 2 seconds of contact. Swirl in 1 tablespoon of the oil, add the ginger, then, using a metal spatula, stir-fry 10 seconds or until the ginger is fragrant. Push the ginger to the sides of the wok, carefully add the chicken, and spread it evenly in one layer in the wok. Cook undisturbed 1 minute, letting the chicken begin to sear. Stir-fry 1 minute, or until the chicken is lightly browned but not cooked through.

3. Swirl the remaining 1 tablespoon oil into the wok, add the sugar snaps, carrots, celery, and cashews, and sprinkle on the remaining ¼ teaspoon salt. Stir-fry 1 minute or until the sugar snaps are bright green. Restir the broth mixture, swirl it into the wok, and stir-fry 1 minute or until the chicken is just cooked through.

Serves 2 to 3 as a main course with rice or 4 as part of a multicourse meal.

Hong Kong–Style Mango Ginger Chicken

One of the great pleasures when visiting Hong Kong is to enjoy the fragrant perfume of mangoes, which are flown in from Thailand and the Philippines, in the local fruit stalls. Years ago I had a stir-fried mango and chicken dish in Hong Kong that was so memorable I was determined to replicate the recipe. Here is my version. The green bell pepper, onion, and mango make a refreshing balance to the chicken, which is flavored with ginger, garlic, and red pepper flakes. I prefer the ataulfo mango, known for its buttery, delicate sweetness. I cut the slices about ¼ inch thick. If the slices are too thin, the mango will fall apart. Do not overcook it; the mango here needs only to be added at the end. The chicken in this recipe is velveted to ensure that it remains moist and succulent (see Velvet Stir-Fry, page 100).

12 ounces skinless, boneless chicken breast, cut into ¼-inch-thick bite-sized slices

2 tablespoons egg white, lightly beaten

2¼ teaspoons cornstarch

4 teaspoons Shao Hsing rice wine or dry sherry

¾ teaspoon salt

2 teaspoons plus 2 tablespoons peanut or vegetable oil

⅓ cup chicken broth

2 teaspoons soy sauce

¼ teaspoon red pepper flakes

1 tablespoon minced ginger

2 teaspoons minced garlic

1 medium green bell pepper, julienned

½ cup thinly sliced red onions

1 ripe mango, peeled and cut into ¼-inch-thick slices (about ¾ cup)

1. In a medium bowl combine the chicken, egg white, 2 teaspoons of the cornstarch, 2 teaspoons of the rice wine, and ¼ teaspoon of the salt. Stir until the cornstarch is totally dissolved and no clumps are visible. Add 2 teaspoons of the oil and stir to combine. Put the chicken uncovered in the refrigerator for 30 minutes. In a small bowl combine the broth, soy sauce, red pepper flakes, the remaining 2 teaspoons rice wine, and ¼ teaspoon cornstarch.

2. In a 2-quart saucepan bring 1 quart water to a boil over high heat. Add 1 tablespoon of the oil to the boiling water. Reduce the heat to low. When the water is barely simmering, carefully add the chicken, gently stirring it so that the pieces do not clump together. Cook 1 minute or until the chicken just turns opaque but is not cooked through. Carefully drain the chicken in a colander, shaking the colander to remove any excess water.

3. Heat a 14-inch flat-bottomed wok or 12-inch skillet over high heat until a bead of water vaporizes within 1 to 2 seconds of contact. Swirl the remaining 1 tablespoon oil into the wok, add the ginger and garlic, then, using a metal spatula, stir-fry 10 seconds or until the aromatics are fragrant. Add the bell peppers and red onions and stir-fry 1 minute or until the bell peppers are almost crisp-tender. Add the chicken and sprinkle on the remaining ½ teaspoon salt. Restir the broth mixture, swirl it into the wok, and stir-fry 1 minute or until the chicken is just cooked through. Stir in the mango.

Serves 2 to 3 as a main dish with rice or 4 as part of a multicourse meal.

Stir-Fried Eggs with Velvet Shrimp

Velvet shrimp radically transform stir-fried eggs into a sophisticated dish. The shrimp are not velveted in the true sense of the technique (see Velvet Stir-Fry, page 100) because they are not blanched in oil or water. Nonetheless, the light egg white–cornstarch marinade gives the shrimp the "crisp" silky texture revered by Chinese food devotees. I take the teaspoon of egg white needed for the marinade from one of the eggs rather than break open a fifth egg. After refrigerating the marinated shrimp, be sure to let them stand at room temperature for 15 minutes before stir-frying; if the shrimp are ice cold, they will not be cooked by the time the eggs are just set. I prefer to stir-fry these eggs in a wok. If you want to use a skillet, it may require another tablespoon of oil to prevent the eggs from sticking.

4 ounces small shrimp, peeled, deveined, and
    patted dry

4 large eggs, 1 teaspoon egg white reserved

½ teaspoon cornstarch

2½ teaspoons Shao Hsing rice wine or dry sherry

⅛ plus ¼ teaspoon salt

1 teaspoon plus 2 tablespoons peanut
    or vegetable oil

⅛ teaspoon ground white pepper

⅓ cup chopped scallions

1 tablespoon minced ginger

⅓ cup frozen peas, defrosted

1. In a medium bowl combine the shrimp, the 1 teaspoon egg white, cornstarch, ½ teaspoon of the rice wine, and ⅛ teaspoon of the salt. Stir until the cornstarch has dissolved. Stir in 1 teaspoon of the oil. Put the shrimp uncovered in the refrigerator for 15 minutes. Bring the shrimp to room temperature for 15 minutes. In a medium bowl beat the eggs, pepper, and the remaining 2 teaspoons rice wine and ¼ teaspoon salt.

2. Heat a 14-inch flat-bottomed wok or 12-inch skillet over high heat until a bead of water vaporizes within 1 to 2 seconds of contact. Swirl in the remaining 2 tablespoons oil, add the scallions and ginger, then, using a metal spatula, stir-fry 10 seconds or until the aromatics are fragrant. Add the shrimp and stir-fry 1 minute or until the shrimp begins to turn color but is not cooked through. Add the peas, swirl the egg mixture into the wok, and stir-fry 1 minute or until the shrimp is cooked through and the eggs are just set but still moist. Do not overcook.

Serves 2 as a main dish with rice or 4 as part of a multicourse meal.

Velvet Chicken with Asparagus

The technique of velveting (see Velvet Stir-Fry, page 100) is most impressive when applied to chicken breast. This is one of the most refined stir-fries. The flavors are deliberately mild and subtle so that the textures of the main ingredients can be better appreciated: the chicken breast is silky-smooth, with extraordinary succulence, and the asparagus is crisp-tender. When the broth and rice wine mixture is swirled in at the end of the stir-fry, it creates a classic Chinese "sauce" that barely clings to the chicken and asparagus.

1 pound medium asparagus, trimmed and cut into
    2-inch pieces (about 3 cups)

1 pound skinless, boneless chicken breast, cut into
    ¼-inch-thick bite-sized slices

2 tablespoons egg white, lightly beaten

1 tablespoon plus ¼ teaspoon cornstarch

2 teaspoons plus 1 tablespoon Shao Hsing rice wine
    or dry sherry

1 teaspoon salt

3 tablespoons peanut or vegetable oil

⅓ cup chicken broth

¼ teaspoon ground white pepper

1 tablespoon minced ginger

2 teaspoons minced garlic

1. In a 2-quart saucepan bring 1 quart water to a boil over high heat. Add the asparagus and cook, stirring, 1 minute or until the asparagus is bright green and the water has almost returned to a boil. Use a skimmer to transfer the asparagus to a colander, reserving the pot of water. Shake well to remove excess water. Transfer the asparagus to a bowl.

2. In a medium bowl combine the chicken, egg white, 1 tablespoon of the cornstarch, 2 teaspoons of the rice wine, and ¾ teaspoon of the salt. Stir until the cornstarch is totally dissolved and no clumps are visible. Add 1 tablespoon of the oil and stir to combine. Put the chicken uncovered in the refrigerator for 30 minutes. In a small bowl combine the broth, white pepper, and the remaining 1 tablespoon rice wine and ¼ teaspoon cornstarch.

3. Return the water to a boil over high heat. Add 1 tablespoon of the oil to the boiling water. Reduce the heat to low. When the water is barely simmering, carefully add the chicken, gently stirring it so that the pieces do not clump together. Cook 1 minute or until the chicken just turns opaque but is not cooked through. Carefully drain the chicken in a colander, shaking the colander to remove any excess water.

4. Heat a 14-inch flat-bottomed wok or 12-inch skillet over high heat until a bead of water vaporizes within 1 to 2 seconds of contact. Swirl the remaining 1 tablespoon oil into the wok, add the ginger and garlic, then, using a metal spatula, stir-fry 10 seconds or until the aromatics are fragrant. Add the asparagus, sprinkle on the remaining ¼ teaspoon salt, and stir-fry 30 seconds or until the asparagus is almost crisp-tender. Add the chicken. Restir the broth mixture, swirl it into the wok, and stir-fry 30 seconds to 1 minute or until the chicken is just cooked through and the sauce lightly coats the chicken.

Serves 2 to 3 as a main dish with rice or 4 as part of a multicourse meal.

Singapore-Style Duck with Chinese Celery

I learned the recipe for this amazing, succulent duck stir-fry from Julie Tay (see Cooks of Two Cultures, page 165), a Chinese Singaporean who teaches cooking at Ai Center in New York City's Chinatown. It calls for salted soybeans, a Malaysian ingredient. Tay used Yeo brand, which comes in a 15.9-ounce jar; it can be a difficult ingredient to find. She advises you can substitute Chinese bean sauce. I find the results are comparable if you reduce the amount of bean sauce to a tablespoon since it is a saltier product; the bean sauce also does not need to be mashed. I recommend using a wok for this recipe as the soybeans will burn into a skillet.

Chinese five-spice tofu is available in Asian markets in the refrigerator section or in specialty tofu shops in Chinatown. You can substitute baked tofu found in health food stores, but the texture is grittier and not as smooth and dry as the Chinese five-spice tofu. I tested this recipe with White Wave Baked Tofu Oriental Style—be sure the tofu is patted dry with paper towels before cooking.

In New York's Chinatown, whole duck legs are inexpensive and available. I use kitchen shears to remove the duck skin, which isn't as easy to remove as chicken skin. Tay advises that chicken legs can be substituted. You can also substitute regular celery, but Chinese celery has concentrated flavor that has no equal, and because the stalks are very fine it takes less time to julienne the vegetable.

Singaporeans love their chilies. When Tay made this for me, she used 2 Anaheim chilies, cut into ½-inch-thick slices. I've given a range for the chilies for those who like heat but may not be able to take the true Singaporean fire. You can also reduce the heat by seeding the chilies. This recipe has a sauce deliberately not thickened by cornstarch.

12 ounces boneless, skinless duck or chicken legs, cut into ¼-inch-thick bite-sized slices

2 teaspoons plus 1 tablespoon soy sauce

2 teaspoons rice vinegar

½ teaspoon cornstarch

½ teaspoon sesame oil

1 teaspoon Shao Hsing rice wine or dry sherry

⅛ teaspoon salt

⅛ teaspoon freshly ground pepper

⅛ teaspoon five-spice powder

⅛ teaspoon sugar

⅓ cup chicken broth

2 tablespoons peanut or vegetable oil

1 cup julienned five-spice tofu (1 square)

2 tablespoons finely shredded ginger

2 tablespoons chopped shallots

2 tablespoons drained salted soybeans, lightly mashed, or 1 tablespoon bean sauce

1½ cups julienned Chinese celery or regular celery

1 to 2 Anaheim chilies, cut into ½-inch-thick slices, with seeds (about ¼ to ½ cup)

1. In a medium bowl combine the duck, 2 teaspoons of the soy sauce, 1 teaspoon of the rice vinegar, cornstarch, sesame oil, ½ teaspoon of the rice wine, salt, pepper, five-spice powder, and sugar. Stir to combine. In a small bowl combine the broth and the remaining 1 tablespoon soy sauce, 1 teaspoon rice vinegar, and ½ teaspoon rice wine.

2. Heat a 14-inch flat-bottomed wok over high heat until a bead of water vaporizes within 1 to 2 seconds of contact. Swirl in 1 tablespoon of the peanut oil, carefully add the tofu, reduce the heat to medium, then, using a metal spatula, stir-fry 1 minute or until lightly browned. Transfer the tofu to a plate.

3. Swirl the remaining 1 tablespoon peanut oil into the wok. Add the ginger and shallots and stir-fry, still over medium heat, 1 minute or until the mixture just begins to brown. Add the mashed soybeans and stir-fry 5 seconds or until just combined. Add the duck, increase the heat to high, and stir-fry 2 minutes or until the duck is no longer pink but not cooked through. Add the celery and chilies and stir-fry 1 minute or until the celery just begins to wilt. Return the tofu to the wok and stir-fry 1 minute or until well combined. Swirl the sauce mixture into the wok, cover, and cook 1 minute. Uncover and stir-fry 10 seconds or until the duck is just cooked through.

Serves 2 to 3 as a main dish with rice or 4 as part of a multicourse meal.

Chinese Jamaican Stir-Fried Chicken with Chayote

Chayote is a slightly flat pear-shaped squash, also known as mirliton, that the Chinese call Buddha's hand. Chayote is native to South America and Jamaica, where Rose Wong remembers eating it stir-fried with chicken and flavored with Pickapeppa Sauce, also known as Jamaican ketchup. It is sold in West Indian markets and also at Kalustyan's (see Sources, page 287).

12 ounces skinless, boneless chicken thigh, cut into
　　¾-inch cubes
2 teaspoons dark soy sauce
2 teaspoons minced garlic
½ teaspoon cornstarch
¾ teaspoon salt
1 teaspoon plus 2 tablespoons peanut
　　or vegetable oil
2 tablespoons Pickapeppa Sauce
1 tablespoon ketchup
2 medium or 1 large chayote (about 14 ounces)
⅓ cup thinly sliced yellow onions

1. In a medium bowl combine the chicken, soy sauce, garlic, cornstarch, and ¼ teaspoon of the salt. Stir to combine. Stir in 1 teaspoon of the oil. In a small bowl combine the Pickapeppa Sauce and ketchup.

2. Peel the chayote. Halve and remove the flat, pale seed (if there is one). Quarter the chayote lengthwise and cut crosswise into ¼-inch-thick slices.

3. Heat a 14-inch flat-bottomed wok over high heat until a bead of water vaporizes within 1 to 2 seconds of contact. Swirl in 1 tablespoon of the oil, add the chicken, and spread it evenly in one layer in the wok. Cook undisturbed 1 minute, letting the chicken begin to sear. Then, using a metal spatula, stir-fry 1 minute, or until the chicken is lightly browned but not cooked through. Add the onions and stir-fry 1 minute or until well combined. Transfer the mixture to a plate.

4. Swirl the remaining 1 tablespoon oil into the wok. Add ¼ teaspoon of the salt and the chayote, and stir-fry 30 seconds or until well combined. Add 2 tablespoons cold water, cover, and cook 5 seconds. Uncover and stir-fry a few seconds. Cover and cook 1 to 2 minutes or until the chayote is just crisp-tender and almost all the liquid has evaporated. Return the chicken with any juices that have accumulated to the wok, add the Pickapeppa Sauce mixture, sprinkle on the remaining ¼ teaspoon salt, and stir-fry 1 minute or until the chicken is just cooked through.

Serves 2 to 3 as a main dish with rice or 4 as part of a multicourse meal.

Rose Wong

Stir-Fried Chicken with Carrots and Mushrooms

I was intrigued the moment my friend George Chew mentioned that his daughter's babysitter Jackie Chong used to make a stir-fry that was so tasty it was the only way he could get Alexandra to eat carrots. This is a comfort stir-fry that melds the sweetness of carrots with shiitake mushrooms and a little chicken. The simplicity of this stir-fry is reminiscent of Hakka-style cooking, so it did not surprise me to learn that Jackie is originally from Ipoh, Malaysia, and is Hakka. Jackie has a clever way of julienning the carrots: she cuts the carrot into big ¼-inch-thick diagonal slices, about 3 inches long, then stacks a few slices at a time and cuts them into julienned pieces. Or you can use the handy Kinpira Peeler. I prefer using a wok rather than a skillet to stir-fry this dish.

12 medium dried shiitake mushrooms

8 ounces skinless, boneless chicken thigh, cut into
    ¼-inch-thick bite-sized slices

1 tablespoon soy sauce

2½ teaspoons cornstarch

2 tablespoons peanut or vegetable oil

1 tablespoon minced garlic

3 cups julienned carrots (about 12 ounces)

1 teaspoon sugar

½ teaspoon salt

⅓ cup boiling water

1 tablespoon dark soy sauce

1. In a medium bowl soak the mushrooms in ⅔ cup cold water 30 minutes or until softened. Drain and squeeze dry. (Reserve soaking liquid for stocks if desired.) Cut off the stems and thinly slice the caps to make about 1 cup.

2. In a medium bowl combine the chicken, soy sauce, and cornstarch. Stir to combine.

3. Heat a 14-inch flat-bottomed wok over high heat until a bead of water vaporizes within 1 to 2 seconds of contact. Swirl in the oil, add the garlic, then, using a metal spatula, stir-fry 10 seconds or until the garlic is fragrant. Push the garlic to the sides of the wok, carefully add the chicken, and spread it evenly in one layer in the wok. Cook undisturbed 1 minute, letting the chicken begin to sear. Add the mushrooms and stir-fry 30 seconds or until well combined. Add the carrots and stir-fry 2 minutes or until the carrots just begin to wilt. Sprinkle on the sugar and salt and stir-fry 5 seconds until just combined. Swirl the boiling water into the wok and stir-fry 1 minute or until well combined. Add the dark soy sauce and stir-fry 1 minute or until the chicken is just cooked through.

Serves 2 to 3 as a main dish with rice or 4 as part of a multicourse meal.

TWO WAYS TO JULIENNE CARROTS

To julienne carrots by hand, choose a fat carrot that is at least 1½ inches in diameter. Cut the peeled carrot into scant ¼-inch-thick diagonal slices. Stack 2 or 3 slices and cut lengthwise into scant ¼-inch-thick julienne.

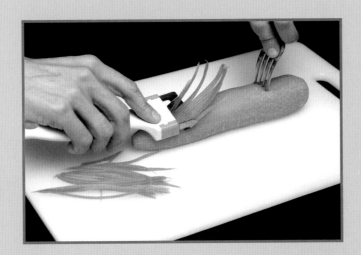

A Kinpira Peeler (see page 17) is a fantastic tool for making julienned carrots. Be careful when using the peeler as it is extremely sharp. First, use a chef's knife to cut a thin slice from one side of a peeled fat (at least 1½ inches in diameter) carrot to create a flat surface. Rest the carrot on the cut side so the carrot won't roll on the cutting board. Spear the carrot on the root end with a fork. Holding the fork firmly with one hand, use the other hand to pull the Kinpira Peeler along the length of the carrot to make long strands. Then cut the strands into 2- to 3-inch lengths. Repeat the action. Note that once you have julienned about half the carrot it will become more and more difficult to cut long strands. I usually start a new carrot and use the partially shredded remains for something else. The Kinpira-cut are thinner than hand-cut julienne.

Vinegar-Glazed Chicken

This is a typical Hunan family-style stir-fry. Traditionally the dish is made with dried red chilies, but this recipe has been simplified with the use of red pepper flakes. The Chinkiang vinegar has great depth of flavor and contributes to the sauce's mellow, rich taste; balsamic vinegar is an excellent substitute. If you are cooking in a new wok, after the stir-fry is finished transfer it immediately to a platter—acidic ingredients like vinegar will destroy a wok's new patina.

1 pound boneless, skinless chicken thigh, cut into
    ¼-inch-thick bite-sized slices

4 teaspoons dark soy sauce

2 teaspoons soy sauce

2 teaspoons Shao Hsing rice wine or dry sherry

1 teaspoon sugar

1 teaspoon cornstarch

¼ teaspoon roasted and ground Sichuan pepper-
    corns (see page 6)

½ teaspoon salt

2 teaspoons sesame oil

2 tablespoons peanut or vegetable oil

6 scallions, halved lengthwise and cut into
    2-inch pieces

1 tablespoon minced ginger

1 tablespoon minced garlic

¼ teaspoon red pepper flakes

2 tablespoons Chinkiang or balsamic vinegar

1. In a medium bowl combine the chicken, 2 teaspoons of the dark soy sauce, 1 teaspoon of the soy sauce, 1 teaspoon of the rice wine, sugar, cornstarch, ground Sichuan peppercorns, and salt. Stir to combine. In a small bowl combine the sesame oil and the remaining 2 teaspoons dark soy sauce, 1 teaspoon soy sauce, and 1 teaspoon rice wine.

2. Heat a 14-inch flat-bottomed wok or 12-inch skillet over high heat until a bead of water vaporizes within 1 to 2 seconds of contact. Swirl in the peanut oil, add the scallions, ginger, garlic, and red pepper flakes, then, using a metal spatula, stir-fry 10 seconds or until the aromatics are fragrant. Push the aromatics to the sides of the wok, carefully add the chicken, and spread it evenly in one layer in the wok. Cook undisturbed 1 minute, letting the chicken begin to sear. Then stir-fry 1 minute or until the chicken is lightly browned but not cooked through. Swirl the soy sauce mixture into the wok and stir-fry 1 minute, or until the chicken is well glazed with the soy sauce. Swirl in the vinegar and stir-fry 30 seconds or until the chicken is just cooked through.

Serves 2 as a main dish with rice or 4 as part of a multicourse meal.

Stir-Fried Chicken with Black Bean Sauce

There are many versions of this classic Cantonese home-style stir-fry. Fermented black beans are the key to any black bean sauce. Whole soybeans that have been preserved in salt and ginger are a staple of every Chinese kitchen. Just a small spoonful is needed to lend its alluring, pungent taste and aroma to a stir-fry. I like to rinse the beans and then mash them with a fork to release their full flavor, but some cooks prefer them whole.

1 pound skinless, boneless chicken thigh or breast, cut into ¾-inch cubes

2 teaspoons cornstarch

1 teaspoon plus 1 tablespoon Shao Hsing rice wine or dry sherry

2 teaspoons soy sauce

¾ teaspoon salt

1 teaspoon plus 1 tablespoon peanut or vegetable oil

1 tablespoon fermented black beans, rinsed

2 teaspoons minced garlic

2 teaspoons minced ginger

1 teaspoon dark soy sauce

⅓ cup chicken broth

1 small red onion, cut into thin wedges (about ¾ cup)

¼ teaspoon red pepper flakes

1 cup thinly sliced carrots

1 scallion, finely shredded

1. In a medium bowl combine the chicken, cornstarch, 1 teaspoon of the rice wine, soy sauce, and ½ teaspoon of the salt. Stir in 1 teaspoon of the oil. Stir to combine. In a small bowl mash the fermented black beans with the garlic, ginger, and dark soy sauce. In another small bowl combine the broth and the remaining 1 tablespoon rice wine.

2. Heat a 14-inch flat-bottomed wok or 12-inch skillet over high heat until a bead of water vaporizes within 1 to 2 seconds of contact. Swirl in the remaining 1 tablespoon oil, add the red onion and red pepper flakes, then, using a metal spatula, stir-fry 30 seconds or until the onions begin to wilt. Push the onions to the sides of the wok, carefully add the chicken, and spread it evenly in one layer in the wok. Cook undisturbed for 1 minute, letting the chicken begin to sear. Stir-fry 1 minute or until the chicken is lightly browned but not cooked through. Add the carrots and black bean mixture, and stir-fry 30 seconds or until fragrant. Swirl the broth mixture into the wok, sprinkle on the remaining ¼ teaspoon salt, and stir-fry 1 to 2 minutes or until the chicken is cooked through. Stir in the shredded scallions.

Serves 2 to 3 as a main course with rice or 4 as part of a multicourse meal.

Stir-Fried Eggs with Tomatoes

Fresh eggs are an ideal food for stir-frying. Whenever possible I buy free-range eggs from the farmers' market. Fresh eggs partnered with farm-ripe produce are sublime. In the summer, ripe tomatoes are superb stir-fried with eggs and seasoned with shallots, garlic, and cilantro—a quick, simple meal guaranteed to satisfy.

4 large eggs
¼ cup chopped cilantro
1 tablespoon sesame oil
½ teaspoon salt
⅛ teaspoon freshly ground pepper
2 tablespoons peanut or vegetable oil
2 teaspoons minced garlic
2 tablespoons chopped shallots
2 medium ripe tomatoes, diced (about 8 ounces)
2 teaspoons Shao Hsing rice wine or dry sherry
¼ teaspoon sugar

1. In a medium bowl beat together the eggs, cilantro, sesame oil, salt, and pepper.

2. Heat a 14-inch flat-bottomed wok or 12-inch skillet over high heat until a bead of water vaporizes within 1 to 2 seconds of contact. Swirl in the peanut oil, add the garlic and shallots, then, using a metal spatula, stir-fry 30 seconds or until the shallots are translucent. Add the tomatoes and rice wine, sprinkle on the sugar, and stir-fry 1 minute or until the tomatoes are just softened. Swirl the egg mixture into the wok and stir-fry 1 minute or until the eggs are just set but still moist. Do not overcook.

Serves 2 as a main dish with rice or 4 as part of a multicourse meal.

The Yin and Yang of Stir-Frying

Chinese culinary philosophy is based on the Taoist belief that foods are either yin, yang, or neutral. Yang foods are said to be warming, drying, and invigorating to the body; yin foods are the opposite: cooling, damp, and soothing. Some classic yang foods are lamb, chicken, walnuts, ginger, red bell peppers, and scallions. Examples of yin foods include bean sprouts, cucumber, crabs, tofu, clams, water chestnuts, bamboo shoots, and lettuce. White rice, eggs, and Chinese long beans are classified as neutral foods.

The yin-yang system of eating is extremely complex and is expressed on many different levels. Summer and spring are yang, a time when more yin foods are eaten to cool the body. Fall and winter are yin and are seasons when the body craves the invigorating nature of yang foods.

In traditional Chinese cooking, emphasis is placed on achieving balance by combining yin and yang ingredients in the same dish. Thus, some of the classic stir-fry combinations are revered not only because they are delicious but also because these timeless marriages of ingredients represent for the Chinese a way of eating that creates a harmonious state of well-being. Examples are Chinese broccoli with ginger; bean sprouts with yellow chives; clams with fermented black bean sauce; chicken with mangoes; and beef with bok choy.

Cooking methods are also classified as yin (steaming, boiling, and poaching) or yang (stir-frying, pan-frying, and deep-fat frying). A simple yin-yang meal would be a stir-fry served with rice, a neutral food, and a clear vegetable soup or herbal soup for optimal balance. For traditional cooks, a meal of multiple dishes deepens the interpretation of complementary opposites. Such meals would combine stir-fried, pan-fried, or deep-fried dishes with steamed, boiled, or poached dishes (all served with rice), and again a simple soup to create the ultimate yin-yang harmony. The notion of yin-yang culinary symmetry enriches the meaning of a "balanced diet."

Chinese Burmese Chili Chicken

Irene Khin Wong, owner of Saffron 59 Catering in New York City and a native of Myanmar (formerly Burma), taught me this recipe, one of her signature dishes. Wong's parents were both born in Myanmar but her father's family was originally from Guangzhou, China. Wong remembers as children she and her siblings loved Burmese food, but because her paternal grandmother lived with the family they mainly prepared traditional Cantonese stir-fries; her father and grandmother did not eat chilies, nor did they enjoy the spices typical of Burmese cooking.

This recipe reflects the fusion of Chinese, Burmese, and Indian cuisines. The paprika, cumin, and chili powder are Indian spices that were incorporated into Burmese cooking, creating layers of lush flavor—a great counterpoint to the mild heat from the fresh chili in this stir-fry. At first bite the heat level is mild but it gradually builds as you eat. Wong says instead of chili powder she sometimes uses ⅛ to ¼ teaspoon cayenne.

She also prefers dark meat but you can use chicken breast. The chicken is cut into large, thick slices the same way it is for Stir-Fried Chicken with Pineapple and Peppers (see page 110). This recipe requires a wok. I tried cooking it in a skillet and the spices burned.

1 pound skinless, boneless chicken thigh or breast, cut crosswise into ½-inch-thick large slices

2 tablespoons peanut or vegetable oil

1½ teaspoons cornstarch

¾ teaspoon salt

½ teaspoon freshly ground pepper

2 teaspoons sweet paprika

1 teaspoon ground cumin

1 small yellow onion, quartered and cut into ¾-inch chunks

2 teaspoons minced ginger

2 teaspoons minced garlic

1 medium red bell pepper, cut into 1-inch squares (about 1⅓ cups)

1 medium green bell pepper, cut into 1-inch squares (about 1⅓ cups)

2 tablespoons fish sauce

1 Anaheim chili, cut into scant ½-inch-thick slices, with seeds (about ¼ cup)

1 medium zucchini, halved lengthwise and cut into scant ½-inch-thick slices (about 1½ cups)

½ teaspoon chili powder

1. In a medium bowl combine the chicken, 1 tablespoon of the oil, 1 teaspoon of the cornstarch, ½ teaspoon of the salt, and pepper. Stir to combine. In a small bowl combine the remaining ½ teaspoon cornstarch and ⅓ cup cold water. In another small bowl combine the paprika and cumin.

2. Heat a 14-inch flat-bottomed wok over high heat until a bead of water vaporizes within 1 to 2 seconds of contact. Swirl in the remaining 1 tablespoon oil, add the onions, then, using a metal spatula, stir-fry 30 seconds or until the onions begin to wilt. Push the onions to the sides of the wok, carefully add the chicken, and spread it evenly in one layer in the wok. Cook undisturbed for 1 minute, letting the chicken begin to sear. Stir-fry 30 seconds or until the chicken is almost completely opaque. Add the ginger, garlic, and the paprika mixture, and stir-fry 1 minute or until the aromatics are fragrant and the chicken is well coated in the spices.

3. Add the red and green bell peppers, reduce the heat to medium, and stir-fry 2 minutes or until the peppers begin to soften. (Do not be alarmed if the

spices stick a little to the bottom of the wok.) Add the fish sauce, chilies, zucchini, and the remaining ¼ teaspoon salt, and stir-fry 1 minute or until almost all the liquid has evaporated. Restir the cornstarch mixture, swirl it into the wok, increase the heat to high, and stir-fry 1 minute or until the chicken is just done and the vegetables are crisp-tender. Remove the wok from the heat and stir in the chili powder.

Serves 3 as a main dish with rice or 4 as part of a multicourse meal.

Irene Khin Wong

Chinese Indian Chicken Manchurian

The Cantonese chefs at Chinese Mirch restaurant in New York City showed me how to make this stir-fry, an extraordinary blend of Chinese and Indian tastes. According to owner Vik Lulla, whose family owns several Chinese restaurants in Bangalore, Indians have a special fondness for Chinese food. In Hindi mirch *means "spicy." Indian customers expect Chinese food to be fiery hot, and when it comes to stir-fries they want them to be saucy to replicate the experience of eating a curry. As a consequence, their Chicken Manchurian is very saucy, perfect for eating with lots of rice.*

At the restaurant, the chicken is first deep-fried before stir-frying, but Lulla advised me that for home cooking the chicken should just be stir-fried. He also told me that they slice the chilies to "control" the heat level. If the dish is too hot, a customer can simply remove the sliced chilies, unlike minced chilies. I've given a range of chilies for those who want the heat to be a little tamer. For only a hint of heat, remove the chili seeds. The original recipe calls for garlic mashed in a mortar and pestle; it's such a small amount that I just put the garlic through a garlic press.

1 pound skinless, boneless chicken thigh, cut into
 ¼-inch-thick bite-sized slices
2 tablespoons egg white, lightly beaten
2½ teaspoons cornstarch
2 teaspoons mashed plus 1 teaspoon minced garlic
3 teaspoons minced ginger
¾ teaspoon salt
3 tablespoons peanut or vegetable oil
½ cup chicken broth
1 tablespoon soy sauce
⅓ cup chopped onions

1 to 2 Thai chilies, cut into ¼-inch-thick slices, with
 seeds
¼ cup cilantro sprigs
1 tablespoon chopped scallion

1. In a medium bowl combine the chicken, egg white, cornstarch, the 2 teaspoons mashed garlic, 2 teaspoons of the ginger, 1 teaspoon cold water, and salt. Stir to combine. Stir in 1 tablespoon of the oil. Put the chicken uncovered in the refrigerator 30 minutes. In a small bowl combine the broth and soy sauce.

2. Heat a 14-inch flat-bottomed wok or 12-inch skillet over high heat until a bead of water vaporizes within 1 to 2 seconds of contact. Swirl in the remaining 2 tablespoons oil, add the onions, chilies, and the remaining 1 teaspoon minced garlic and 1 teaspoon ginger, then, using a metal spatula, stir-fry 30 seconds or until the onions begin to wilt. Push the onion mixture to the sides of the wok, carefully add the chicken, and spread it evenly in one layer in the wok. Cook undisturbed 1 minute, letting the chicken begin to sear. Then stir-fry 1 minute, or until the chicken is lightly browned but not cooked through.

3. Swirl the broth mixture into the wok, add the cilantro, and stir-fry 1 to 2 minutes or until the chicken is cooked through and the sauce is just thickened. Stir in the scallion.

Serves 2 to 3 as a main course with rice or 4 as part of a multicourse meal.

Chinese Vietnamese Lemongrass Chicken

This is my adaptation of a favorite dish I used to eat in a Chinese Vietnamese restaurant when I first moved to New York City. The chicken was so mellow, with a balance of sweet, spicy, garlicky, and salty flavors laced with an undertone of lemongrass. It took me a long time to replicate the sauce. I am fond of this dish because no one flavor is overpowering. Should you want more heat, use 2 teaspoons or more of the chilies.

When buying fresh lemongrass, select plump stalks with no signs of dryness. Cut off about ½ inch from the bottom and chop off the woody top section. Then peel away the tough outer layers of the stalk until you reach the tender portion, the most flavorful part, about 3 to 8 inches long, depending on the original size of the stalk. Slice the lemongrass as thin as possible before mincing it. Do not be alarmed if the chicken seems to be "dry" after marinating.

1 pound skinless, boneless chicken thigh or breast, cut into ¼-inch-thick bite-sized slices

2 teaspoons cornstarch

½ teaspoon salt

½ teaspoon freshly ground pepper

1 teaspoon plus 2 tablespoons peanut or vegetable oil

⅓ cup chicken broth

1 tablespoon fish sauce

2 stalks fresh lemongrass, minced (about ¼ cup)

1 tablespoon minced garlic

1 to 2 teaspoons chopped jalapeño chilies, with seeds

1 small yellow onion, thinly sliced (about ¾ cup)

1 teaspoon brown sugar

1. In a medium bowl combine the chicken, cornstarch, salt, and pepper. Stir to combine. Stir in 1 teaspoon of the oil. In a small bowl combine the broth and fish sauce.

2. Heat a 14-inch flat-bottomed wok or 12-inch skillet over high heat until a bead of water vaporizes within 1 to 2 seconds of contact. Swirl in 1 tablespoon of the oil, carefully add the chicken, and spread it evenly in one layer in the wok. Cook undisturbed 1 minute, letting the chicken begin to sear. Then, using a metal spatula, stir-fry 1 minute or until the chicken is lightly browned but not cooked through. Transfer the chicken to a plate.

3. Swirl the remaining 1 tablespoon oil into the wok, add the lemongrass, garlic, and chilies, and stir-fry over medium heat 10 seconds or until the aromatics are fragrant. Add the onions and stir-fry 1 minute or until the onions begin to brown. Return the chicken with any juices that have accumulated to the wok and increase the heat to high. Swirl the broth mixture into the wok, sprinkle on the brown sugar, and stir-fry 1 to 2 minutes or until the chicken is just cooked through.

Serves 2 to 3 as a main dish with rice or 4 as part of a multicourse meal.

Lessons from a Simple Stir-Fry: Hakka Cooking in Indonesia

Fah Liong

Fah Liong, a Chinese home cook who grew up in Indonesia, learned classic Hakka cooking (see The Hakka Diaspora, page 102) from her mother. Some people think Chinese cooking requires all manner of exotic ingredients, but the Hakka are known for their simple cuisine. Watch Fah Liong make her Hakka-Style Stir-Fried Shrimp and Vegetables (page 175) and she will ease any apprehensions a novice cook might have that stir-frying is too complicated or difficult to master. The recipe doesn't even require soy sauce or ginger.

Fah Liong

Liong pours a couple of tablespoons of vegetable oil into the well of a preheated wok. Next she adds a generous spoonful of chopped garlic, and while it sizzles, perfuming the air, she adds sliced carrots that have been soaked in water. She stir-fries the carrots and then adds a small bowlful of peeled shrimp. Tossing the shrimp with a few quick turns of the spatula, she then adds several handfuls of sliced Napa cabbage, stir-fries it briefly, and finally empties a small colander full of broccoli and cauliflower florets into the wok. She adds a generous splash of the carrot water before covering the wok and leaving it to bubble furiously for half a minute. Finally, she swirls in

a little of the carrot water mixed with cornstarch and gives a quick stir-fry before pronouncing it done. A delectable seafood sauce studded with garlic coats the shrimp and vegetables. Tasting it reminds me that there is nothing that compares to simple, honest food.

Ask Liong why she soaks the carrots in water and she will tell you it makes the carrots crisper and the water adds sweetness and flavor to the dish. Indeed, the soaking water has a faint orange color, but it is difficult to discern any hint of carrot flavor. Yet this is how her mother and countless generations have passed along this recipe, so typical of the subtle tricks Chinese home cooks use to extract flavor and texture in the most subtle ways. Fah Liong's stir-fry is a revelation not just for its everyday ingredients and uncomplicated preparation, but also for the deeper story it tells about the Chinese philosophy of cooking and eating.

Liong remembers her family served this recipe with plenty of rice, along with several vegetable side dishes that incorporated eggs, tofu, or even a little meat. So fundamental is rice to the Chinese way of cooking that the word for meal in Chinese, *fan*, is the same as the word for cooked rice. The term *soong fan*, or "rice-sending dishes," describes the intention of dishes as a topping for rice. In many parts of China, it is the custom to eat several bowls of plain rice with just a few spoonfuls of each of the various dishes to flavor—"send"—the rice.

As a child, my parents taught me to eat rice by

bringing the rice bowl up to my lips to transport the grains into my mouth with chopsticks as well as to better savor the rice's fragrance. By contrast, in the West, the idea of eating plain rice is unheard of; the dishes are the focal point, with rice as an afterthought. I have witnessed countless meals during which the rice was hardly touched.

I once met an American who had lived in a Taiwanese home as an exchange student. At her first dinner she declined the bowl of rice offered her; she was on a diet and preferred to eat only the dishes. While her host family was polite, she sensed dismay and, only weeks later, after becoming immersed in the culture did she recognize the rudeness of her behavior. Once she learned to eat Chinese-style, she was amazed at how a diet rich in rice and vegetables and low in protein and fat caused her to become naturally leaner.

As we finish our cooking session, Liong tells me her mother liked to stir-fry Napa cabbage and just before it was done she would crack an egg into the center of the mixture, stir-frying it until the egg melded with the cabbage (page 204). "When we were kids it was a favorite meal with rice," says Liong. Although Liong has lived in the United States since 1962, she still adheres to the old Chinese customs of eating moderately. The modest half pound of shrimp in her stir-fry is a meager amount of protein by Western standards, even when rounded out with additional vegetable dishes. With dietary preferences like Liong's, it is not difficult to satisfy the latest nutritional recommendations for eating a variety of vegetables for optimal health.

In his book *The Food of China*, the Chinese scholar E. N. Anderson explains, "The basic (Chinese) diet includes several grains and tubers. . . . The rest of the diet consists primarily of soybean products and vegetables, especially those of the mustard and cabbage family (Brassicaceae). . . . Meat is rare (except among the rich) and eaten only in small quantities. Fish (locally) and eggs provide some animal protein, but the great protein sources everywhere are grain and soybeans."

The old Cantonese expression *Yum sik chut fun bao* means: "Drink and eat until seventy percent full." Chinese food remains one of the most popular ethnic cuisines in America, yet few understand this underlying principle. Modest consumption may have resulted out of necessity, but its enormous health benefits reveal the wisdom of the old ways.

Chinese Trinidadian Stir-Fried Shrimp with Rum

Fish and Shellfish

RECIPES

ESSENTIALS FOR STIR-FRYING FISH AND SHELLFISH

Buy Fresh

Freshness is of vital importance for all ingredients, but especially for fish and shellfish. Cook fish and shellfish the day of purchase, and refrigerate until ready to use. Never use fish or shellfish that has been previously frozen, because freezing ruins the texture. The exception is frozen shrimp that have been defrosted, but fresh is always preferable.

Preparing Fish and Shellfish

Slicing Fish Fillets: Put the fish fillet skin side down on a cutting board. Remove any visible bones with your finger tips or fish tweezers. As an additional precaution you can also run your fingertips up and down the length of the fillet in search of any bones not visibly apparent. Cut a few bite-sized slices from the narrowest end. Then, halve the fish lengthwise along the deep natural crease of the fillet into 2 strips, each roughly 2 inches wide (**1**). One strip at a time, cut crosswise into ¼- to ½-inch-thick bite-sized pieces.

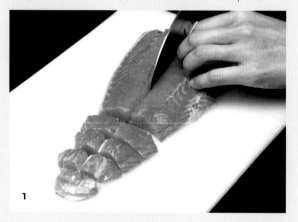

1

Note: A sharp chef's knife or cleaver must be used to cut fish. Even though you have removed visible bones, you are likely to be cutting through some bones. Chinese diners are accustomed to eating fish slices that have tiny bones. I always warn diners to watch out for bones even though the bones should be no more than the thickness of a bite-sized slice, about ¼ to ½ inch. If you are uncomfortable with the idea of eating fish with tiny bones you should not prepare stir-fried fish.

Rinsing and Slicing Scallops: When buying fresh sea scallops, it is common to find a range of sizes in the same batch. Rinse the scallops under cold water, removing the small flap of muscle and any visible bits of shell or grit. Then halve any larger scallops so that all of the scallops have a similar thickness and will stir-fry in the same amount of time.

Cleaning Squid: Gently pull the tentacles from the squid body, removing the entrails as you separate the two pieces. Cut the tentacles just above the eyes, reserving only the tentacles. Remove the internal cartilage and ink sac from the squid body and discard. Peel off the delicate purple membrane from the body. Wash the squid in several changes of cold water, removing any remaining entrails and black ink from the body, and drain in a colander. About 1½ pounds whole squid yield about 1 pound cleaned squid.

Note: Squid is frequently available already cleaned at fish markets and even some supermarkets. Even though it is "cleaned," I recommend rinsing it again.

2

3

Deveining Shrimp in the Shell: Shrimp is often stir-fried in the shell in order to retain its succulence and juiciness. Use kitchen shears to remove the legs. Then, starting at the head end, cut through the shell two-thirds of the length down the back of the shrimp (**2**). Use the tip of a knife to pull out the black vein. Rinse the shrimp under cold water while keeping the shell intact.

Peeling and Deveining Shrimp: The easiest way to remove the shell and devein shrimp quickly is to use an inexpensive shrimp deveiner. Slip the deveiner between the shell and the flesh on the head end of the shrimp. As you push the tip of the shrimp deveiner toward the tail, the shell along with the legs will automatically pull off and it will strip out the black vein at the same time (**3**). Rinse the shrimp under cold water. You can also peel the shrimp by hand. Using a paring knife, make a scant ⅛-inch-deep cut down the back of the shrimp to expose the vein. Use the tip of the knife to pull out the black vein and rinse the shrimp as described above.

Cutting Squid: The squid body is typically cut in half lengthwise and then lightly scored with a crisscross pattern. The squid is then cut into squares. The tentacles are cut into small pieces. Once stir-fried, the squares of squid curl up and the scoring makes an attractive decorative pattern.

Drying Scallops, Squid, and Shrimp Before Stir-Frying: After rinsing scallops, squid, and shrimp, dry them well with paper towels before stir-frying. This can be done several hours in advance. Arrange the scallops, squid, and shrimp in an even layer on a large plate lined with several paper towels. Put several more towels on top of the seafood and refrigerate until ready to use. This is an important step as any excess moisture on shellfish when it is added to the wok will cause additional spattering of the hot oil.

Further, it will turn a stir-fry into a braise. Discard the paper towels before stir-frying begins because the shellfish will sometimes stick to the towels.

Discarding Unsafe Clams or Mussels

Before stir-frying, discard any raw clams or mussels that have open shells. Likewise, after stir-frying, discard any unopened clams or mussels; these mollusks are unsafe for eating.

Bring Fish or Shellfish to Room Temperature

Ingredients will stir-fry more evenly if they are removed from the refrigerator and set at room temperature for 10 to 15 minutes before stir-frying. This is especially important for ice-cold shrimp and scallops that can be seared on the outside but remain raw within.

No Need to Marinate Fish or Shellfish

Fish and shellfish generally do not require marinating because of their natural tenderness. A marinade is sometimes used to enhance flavor, but if it is too acidic, it can also toughen seafood. Chef Richard Chen of Wing Lei restaurant in Las Vegas considers it important to protect the delicate flavor of seafood. "The less we do the better," he advises.

Avoid Overfilling the Wok

When stir-frying, do not crowd a wok or skillet with too much fish or shellfish. If a wok is overcrowded, the temperature drops, and ingredients begin to braise rather than stir-fry. *As a general rule, in a 14-inch wok or 12-inch skillet, do not stir-fry more than 1 pound fish; 1 pound shrimp; 12 ounces raw scallops or 1 pound blanched scallops; 1½ pounds littleneck clams (about 1½ dozen); 1 pound mussels (about 2 dozen); 8 ounces raw squid or 1 pound blanched squid.*

Stir-Frying Fish Is Slightly Different

Right after adding the fish slices to the oil in the preheated wok, spread the pieces into an even layer and do not touch them for 30 seconds. The normal stir-fry action of tossing and turning is too harsh for fragile, bite-sized pieces of fish. Fish is much more delicate than meat, poultry, or shellfish and must be stir-fried gently to prevent it from falling apart. *The term "stir-frying" is more suggestive than applicable when it comes to fish—just turning the fish slices over once or twice is typically sufficient.* Velveted fish or shellfish, if stir-fried correctly, should never be browned.

The Sizzle Means . . .

The moment fish or shellfish is added to a preheated wok there should be a sizzling sound that remains steady throughout stir-frying. If there is no audible sizzle, it indicates that the wok was not sufficiently heated (see Stir-Frying with Proper Heat and Control, page 52), or that the wok's heat has been reduced by wet ingredients or crowding the wok with too large a quantity of fish or shellfish. If this happens, your stir-fry has become a braise.

Spread the Fish or Shellfish in an Even Layer to Sear

Right after adding fish or shellfish to the oil in a preheated wok, spread the pieces in an even layer and do not touch them for 30 seconds to 1 minute (**4**). The tendency of the home cook is to begin stir-frying the fish or shellfish immediately, but this is counterproductive. By not moving the ingredients for the designated time, you are allowing them to sear. Letting shellfish cook undisturbed is particularly important when stir-frying on a residential range as these stoves do not produce the ideal amount of heat for stir-frying. If you do have a powerful range, the ingredients can be stir-fried immediately. Once the outside surface of the pieces sear, use a Chinese metal spatula or pancake turner (this is preferable to a wooden spatula because its thinner edge is more effective in getting under the fish or shellfish) and stir-fry as directed in the recipe.

Addition of Liquid Ingredients

Swirl in the liquid ingredients in a thin stream along the sides of the wok. The liquid adds flavor and also deglazes the pan, loosening and dissolving the browned bits formed from stir-frying.

Stir-Frying in a Malaysian Village

Mei Chau

Growing up in Dungun village in Malaysia during the 1960s, Mei Chau, the youngest of eleven siblings, learned to cook watching her mother and sisters. Chau remembers life was not easy. The family raised one hundred pigs and grew coconuts and durian. Having no refrigerator, they were forced to shop for food morning and night.

At the age of thirteen, Chau was put in charge of cooking for her father and brothers. Her mother, who had been a farmer since the age of eight, had opened a canteen for workers in the jungle, three hours away, which prevented her from coming home frequently. Chau's sisters had been sent away to school in Kuala Lumpur; she was the only girl still left at home. "It was assumed I would cook all the meals, and I felt the pressure to make the food delicious," says Chau. "My brothers and father were very criti-

Mei Chau

cal. They wouldn't hesitate to tell me if they thought something was lousy."

"I cooked in the morning and then went to school in the afternoon," says Chau. "I made a lot of stir-fries because it's fast cooking. The weather was hot and humid and I hated to chop the wood and to start up the fire," she recalls. A good fire is critical to the quality of stir-fry cooking, and the logistics of Chau's "kitchen" did not make her work any eas-

ier. The family didn't have a real stove. Instead, the wok was set on two cement blocks, too high for her to reach without a stool. Fortunately, because both her parents were of Chinese Hakka descent (see The Hakka Diaspora, page 102), the typical family fare was plain and simple.

Chau fondly recalls that when the family went out they enjoyed eating spicy, chili-filled Malaysian dishes. Over time the family's cooking evolved to reflect the influences of Chinese and Malaysian traditions. "We learned to love eating stir-fries with fresh sliced chilies doused with a little soy sauce and vinegar. But for my father who was born in the village of Qing Yuan in Southern China, the chilies were too spicy." By the time Chau was fifteen, she joined her sisters in Kuala Lumpur where she was still in charge of the cooking. Despite the chore she appreciated the convenience of having a modern gas-fueled stove for cooking her stir-fries.

In the 1990s, Chau immigrated to New York City, where she met her husband, Marc Kaczmarek, a native of France. In 1993, the two opened Franklin Station Café, a successful Tribeca restaurant. There, for fifteen years, until it closed in 2008, connoisseurs and casual diners alike savored Chau's cooking, a unique blend of Chinese, Malaysian, and French influences.

Malaysian-Style Stir-Fried Turmeric Shrimp

A stir-fry can reflect the influences of many different cultures. This recipe comes from Mei Chau (see opposite page) who is of Hakka descent, born in Malaysia, and whose husband is a native of France. Chau says the origins of this dish are Malaysian, characterized by the use of turmeric, curry leaves, and chilies.

Curry leaves have a wonderful fragrance, and Chau uses them here to infuse the shrimp with a fresh citrus flavor. I was completely surprised when she told me fresh dill can be used in place of the leaves—this unexpected substitution is inspired no doubt by her exposure to French cuisine. I have cooked the dish with dill sprigs, and while the flavor they impart is totally different from that of the curry leaves, the stir-fry remains scrumptious. Curry leaves are most often found in Indian markets and in stores specializing in Southeast Asian ingredients. The chilies are soaked in water to enhance their flavor. When cutting them pour out the water they have absorbed.

2 small dried red chilies, or ½ teaspoon red
  pepper flakes
1 pound large shrimp
9 fresh curry leaves cut into strips, or 1 tablespoon
  chopped fresh dill sprigs
¼ teaspoon ground turmeric
⅛ teaspoon freshly ground pepper
½ teaspoon sugar
2 tablespoons peanut or vegetable oil
1 tablespoon chopped garlic
1 tablespoon chopped shallots
½ teaspoon salt

1. In a small bowl cover the chilies in cold water for 1 hour. Drain the chilies and cut into ½-inch pieces with the seeds. Using kitchen shears, cut through the shrimp shells two-thirds of the length down the back of the shrimp. Remove the legs and devein the shrimp, leaving the shells and tails on. In a medium bowl combine the shrimp, chilies, curry leaves, turmeric, and pepper. Stir to combine and marinate at room temperature for 20 minutes. Stir in the sugar.

2. Heat a 14-inch flat-bottomed wok or 12-inch skillet over high heat until a bead of water vaporizes within 1 to 2 seconds of contact. Swirl in the oil, add the garlic and shallots, then, using a metal spatula, stir-fry 10 seconds or until the aromatics are fragrant. Push the aromatics to the sides of the wok, carefully add the shrimp, and spread them evenly in one layer in the wok. Cook undisturbed 30 seconds, letting the shrimp begin to sear. Then stir-fry 1 minute or until the shrimp just begin to turn orange. Sprinkle on the salt and stir-fry 1 to 2 minutes or until the shrimp turn completely orange. Cover and allow to stand 30 seconds off heat. Uncover and stir-fry a few seconds or until the shrimp are just cooked through.

Serves 2 as a main dish with rice or 4 as part of a multicourse meal.

Stir-Fried Chili Scallops with Baby Bok Choy

This is a simple, elegant stir-fry, perfect for entertaining. Scallops have a delicate flavor that is complemented by strong seasonings; in this recipe chili bean sauce, ginger, and garlic bring that flavor to life. I have called for small baby bok choy, which may sound redundant, but baby bok choy can range in length from 3 to 8 inches. The vegetables are stir-fried for only 2 minutes, so you must choose the very small, tender, truly "baby" or dwarf bok choy.

12 ounces medium fresh sea scallops

2 tablespoons chicken broth

1 tablespoon chili bean sauce

2 teaspoons soy sauce

½ teaspoon cornstarch

2 tablespoons peanut or vegetable oil

1 tablespoon minced ginger

2 teaspoons minced garlic

½ teaspoon salt

8 small baby bok choy, trimmed and halved lengthwise (about 4 cups)

1 large red bell pepper, cut into ½-inch-wide strips (about 2 cups)

⅓ cup chopped scallions

1. Rinse the scallops under cold water, removing the muscle and any visible bits of shell or grit, and set on paper towels. With more paper towels, pat the scallops dry. Cut the scallops horizontally in half so that all the pieces are about ½ inch thick. In a small bowl combine the broth, chili bean sauce, soy sauce, and cornstarch.

2. Heat a 14-inch flat-bottomed wok or 12-inch skillet over high heat until a bead of water vaporizes within 1 to 2 seconds of contact. Swirl in 1 tablespoon of the oil, add the ginger and garlic, then, using a metal spatula, stir-fry 10 seconds or until the aromatics are fragrant. Push the aromatics to the sides of the wok. Carefully add the scallops and spread them evenly in one layer in the wok. Cook undisturbed 1 minute, letting the scallops begin to sear. Sprinkle on ¼ teaspoon of the salt and stir-fry 30 seconds or until the scallops are opaque but not cooked through. Transfer the scallops to a plate.

3. Swirl the remaining 1 tablespoon oil into the wok, add the bok choy and bell peppers, sprinkle on the remaining ¼ teaspoon salt, and stir-fry 1 minute or until the bok choy just begins to turn bright green. Return the scallops with any juices that have accumulated to the wok. Restir the broth mixture, swirl it into the wok, and stir-fry 1 minute or until the scallops are just cooked. Stir in the scallions.

Serves 2 to 3 as a main dish with rice or 4 as part of a multicourse meal.

Stir-Fried Garlic Snow Pea Shoots with Crabmeat

This is one of the most decadent of stir-fry dishes, reserved for special occasions. Snow pea shoots are the tender tips of snow pea plants and are regarded as a great delicacy. There are two varieties sold in Asian produce markets: farm-grown and a hothouse variety. I only buy the farm-grown, as I find the hothouse variety lacks flavor and texture. The pea shoots are best from winter to early spring when they are young, tender, and sweet. When the shoots are young they can simply be washed and towel-dried before stir-frying. By late spring the shoots are often very tough and fibrous, and the woody stems must be removed. Homemade chicken broth is essential for this dish; do not diminish the quality of the finished product by using canned. Depending on the saltiness of the broth, you may need to add a little more salt to the crabmeat as it simmers.

1 cup Homemade Chicken Broth (page 284)

1 tablespoon cornstarch

1 large egg white, lightly beaten

8 ounces lump crabmeat, picked over to remove cartilage (about 1½ cups)

⅛ teaspoon ground white pepper

2 tablespoons peanut or vegetable oil

2 medium garlic cloves, smashed

8 ounces young snow pea shoots (about 6 cups packed)

¼ teaspoon salt

1. In a 1-quart saucepan bring ¾ cup of the broth to a boil over high heat. Meanwhile, in a small bowl whisk the remaining ¼ cup broth and cornstarch. When the broth comes to a boil, whisk in the cornstarch mixture. Return to a boil, reduce the heat to medium, and whisk constantly 30 seconds to 1 minute or until the broth is just slightly thickened and glossy. Whisk in the egg white and cook, whisking 30 seconds to 1 minute or until the egg white is just opaque. Stir in the crabmeat and pepper, and cook about 30 seconds to 1 minute or until the mixture returns to a gentle simmer. Cover and remove from the heat.

2. Heat a 14-inch flat-bottomed wok or 12-inch skillet over high heat until a bead of water vaporizes within 1 to 2 seconds of contact. Swirl in the oil, add the garlic, and stir-fry 10 seconds or until the garlic is fragrant. Add the snow pea shoots, sprinkle on the salt, and stir-fry 2 to 3 minutes or until the pea shoots are just wilted, bright green, and crisp-tender. Transfer the vegetables to a platter and spoon the crabmeat mixture over the center of the greens.

Serves 2 as a main dish with rice or 4 as a vegetable side dish.

Velvet Orange Scallops

The texture of the scallops after velveting (see Velvet Stir-Fry, page 100) becomes luxuriously smooth and dense. Rich and silky, this stir-fry is redolent with the flavors of fresh orange and is also laced with a little heat. I prefer medium-sized scallops, about ¾ inch thick. If any are thicker, cut them to match the thickness of the other scallops. When adding the scallops to the hot water to blanch them, you must work quickly. I find using a wok skimmer is the easiest and safest way to add them. Then have a colander ready in the sink to drain the scallops quickly.

1 pound medium fresh sea scallops

2 tablespoons egg white, lightly beaten

2 tablespoons cornstarch

2 tablespoons Shao Hsing rice wine or dry sherry

1 teaspoon salt

3 tablespoons peanut or vegetable oil

1 tablespoon chicken broth

1 tablespoon soy sauce

1 tablespoon rice vinegar

1 teaspoon sugar

Zest of 1 orange

¼ teaspoon red pepper flakes

1 tablespoon minced ginger

2 teaspoons minced garlic

1 cup thinly sliced carrots

2 scallions, finely shredded

1. Rinse the scallops under cold water, removing the muscle and any visible bits of shell or grit. Put the scallops in a colander and shake out the excess water. In a medium bowl combine the scallops, egg white, cornstarch, 1 tablespoon of the rice wine, and ¾ teaspoon of the salt. Stir until the cornstarch is totally dissolved and no clumps are visible. Stir in 1 tablespoon of the oil. Put the scallops uncovered in the refrigerator for 30 minutes. In a small bowl combine the broth, soy sauce, rice vinegar, sugar, orange zest, red pepper flakes, and the remaining 1 tablespoon rice wine.

2. In a 2-quart saucepan bring 1 quart water to a boil over high heat. Add 1 tablespoon of the oil to the boiling water. Reduce the heat to low. When the water is barely simmering, carefully add the scallops, gently stirring them so that the pieces do not clump together. Cook 15 seconds or until the scallops just turn opaque but are not cooked through. Carefully drain the scallops in a colander, shaking the colander to remove excess water.

3. Heat a 14-inch flat-bottomed wok or 12-inch skillet over high heat until a bead of water vaporizes within 1 to 2 seconds of contact. Swirl in the remaining 1 tablespoon oil, add the ginger and garlic, then, using a metal spatula, stir-fry 10 seconds or until the aromatics are fragrant. Add the carrots, sprinkle on the remaining ¼ teaspoon salt, and stir-fry 1 minute or until the carrots are crisp-tender. Add the scallops to the wok, restir the broth mixture, swirl it into the wok, and stir-fry 1 minute or until the scallops are just cooked through. Stir in the scallions.

Serves 2 to 3 as a main dish with rice or 4 as part of a multicourse meal.

Stir-Fried Mussels with Ginger and Scallions

When Chef Danny Chan prepared this recipe for me he used New Zealand greenshell mussels that were meaty and delicious. I have had equally excellent results with both wild and cultivated black mussels. It is critical to stir-fry mussels immediately after removing each mussel's beard, which looks like a tuft of hairy fibers. Mussels must be alive when cooked, and they die soon after the beard is removed. This is an example of a "raw stir-fry." There are no ingredients that require precooking before stir-frying.

1 pound mussels (about 2 dozen)

2 tablespoons Shao Hsing rice wine or dry sherry

2 teaspoons soy sauce

1 teaspoon dark soy sauce

¼ teaspoon freshly ground pepper

½ teaspoon cornstarch

2 tablespoons peanut or vegetable oil

1 tablespoon finely shredded ginger

1 tablespoon thinly sliced garlic

1 tablespoon chopped scallion, white part only, plus
    2 scallions, cut into 2-inch sections

1 teaspoon sesame oil

1. Thoroughly wash the mussels in several changes of cold water, discarding any open mussels. Grab the beard near the shell opening and give it a firm tug to remove it. Scrub the shells with a stiff brush to remove the grit and rinse well. Drain the mussels in a colander, shaking out excess water. Pat dry with paper towels. In a small bowl combine the rice wine, soy sauce, dark soy sauce, and pepper. In a separate small bowl combine the cornstarch and 1 tablespoon cold water.

2. Heat a 14-inch flat-bottomed wok or 12-inch skillet over high heat until a bead of water vaporizes within 1 to 2 seconds of contact. Swirl in the peanut oil, add the ginger, garlic, and the 1 tablespoon chopped scallions, and stir-fry 10 seconds or until the aromatics are fragrant. Add the mussels and swirl the rice wine mixture into the wok. Cover and cook on high heat 1 minute. Uncover, restir the cornstarch mixture, and swirl it into the wok. Add the remaining cut scallions and stir-fry 1 to 2 minutes or until the mussels have just opened. Stir in the sesame oil. Discard any unopened mussels.

Serves 2 as a main course with rice or 4 as part of a multicourse meal.

Stir-Fried Crystal Shrimp

The seasonings are subtle in this dish—the stir-fry is to be appreciated for the sweet, succulent flavor and crisp texture of the shrimp. The key to achieving this is to first wash the shrimp in salt. Chinese home cooks use many variations for cleaning shrimp with salt and water (see page 166). Velveting chicken, scallops, or fish (see Velvet Stir-Fry, page 100) ensures a satiny, smooth texture, but when the technique is applied to shrimp it bestows a crisp, crystal-like texture the Chinese revere. Always buy the highest-quality shrimp.

1 pound large shrimp, peeled and deveined

2¼ teaspoons salt

2 tablespoons egg white, lightly beaten

1 tablespoon plus ½ teaspoon cornstarch

2 tablespoons peanut or vegetable oil

⅓ cup chicken broth

1 tablespoon Shao Hsing rice wine or dry sherry

⅛ teaspoon ground white pepper

3 slices ginger, smashed

3 scallions, halved lengthwise and cut into
   2-inch sections

½ cup frozen peas, defrosted

1. In a large colander rinse the shrimp. Sprinkle 1 teaspoon of the salt over the shrimp and with a wooden spoon stir the shrimp in a vigorous circular motion for about 1 minute. Rinse the shrimp under cold water, then shake out the excess water. Sprinkle 1 more teaspoon of salt over the shrimp and repeat the washing process, stirring again for 1 minute. After the shrimp has been thoroughly rinsed, set on several sheets of paper towels. With more paper towels, pat the shrimp dry. In a medium bowl combine the shrimp, egg white, and 1 tablespoon of the cornstarch. Stir until the cornstarch is totally dissolved and no clumps are visible. Put the shrimp mixture uncovered in the refrigerator for 1 hour.

2. In a 3-quart saucepan bring 1½ quarts water to a boil over high heat. Add 1 tablespoon of the oil to the boiling water. Reduce the heat to low. When the water is barely simmering, carefully add the shrimp, gently stirring them so that the pieces do not clump together. Cook 1 minute or until the shrimp just turn orange but are not cooked through. Carefully drain the shrimp in a colander, shaking the colander to remove any excess water. In a small bowl combine the broth, rice wine, the remaining ½ teaspoon cornstarch, and pepper.

3. Heat a 14-inch flat-bottomed wok or 12-inch skillet over high heat until a bead of water vaporizes within 1 to 2 seconds of contact. Swirl in the remaining 1 tablespoon oil, add the ginger and scallions, then, using a metal spatula, stir-fry 10 seconds or until the aromatics are fragrant. Add the shrimp to the wok, add the peas, and sprinkle on the remaining ¼ teaspoon salt. Restir the broth mixture, swirl it into the wok, and stir-fry 1 to 2 minutes or until the shrimp are just cooked and the sauce just clings to the shrimp.

Serves 2 as a main dish with rice or 4 as part of a multicourse meal.

Stir-Fried Salmon with Wine Sauce

I had never stir-fried salmon until my friend Chef Danny Chan prepared this exceptional dish for me. He lightly marinates the fillet, first cut into slices, in a mixture of garlic, peanut oil, a touch of rice wine, sesame oil, and pepper. Then he adds a little egg white to give it a "semi" velveting, stopping there and forgoing blanching in hot oil or water. Chef Chan then briefly cooks the salmon in a small amount of broth and after that stir-fries it very gently. In a wok the salmon slices will lightly brown with this method. You can stir-fry the salmon in a skillet, but the fish will not brown.

Stir-frying fish is tricky: it cannot be stir-fried with the same vigor as you would vegetables, for example, because it's easy for the fish to fall apart, but salmon, with its firm and meaty flesh, is ideal for stir-frying. When slicing the raw salmon, Chef Chan suggests lightly feeling the surface of the fish to remove any loose bones; you should still warn guests to watch out for bones as they eat. When possible I recommend purchasing wild salmon; it is more expensive than farm-raised, but the flavor and texture are far superior. Chef Chan likes to serve this stir-fry on a bed of blanched Shanghai bok choy.

1 pound salmon fillet, with skin

2½ teaspoons cornstarch

2 teaspoons plus 2 tablespoons peanut
    or vegetable oil

2 teaspoons minced garlic

3 teaspoons Shao Hsing rice wine or dry sherry

1¼ teaspoons sesame oil

¼ teaspoon freshly ground pepper

2 tablespoons egg white, lightly beaten

½ teaspoon salt

2 tablespoons plus ¼ cup chicken broth

2 tablespoons chopped scallions

1 tablespoon finely shredded ginger

½ cup drained and rinsed canned straw
    mushrooms

¼ cup thinly sliced carrots

8 snow peas, strings removed

1. Remove any visible bones from the fish. Halve the fish lengthwise along the deep natural crease of the fillet into 2 strips, each roughly 2 inches wide. Cut one strip at a time crosswise into scant ½-inch-thick bite-sized slices. In a medium bowl gently combine the fish, cornstarch, 2 teaspoons of the peanut oil, garlic, 1 teaspoon of the rice wine, ¼ teaspoon of the sesame oil, and pepper. Stir until the cornstarch is totally dissolved and no clumps are visible. Stir in the egg white and add ¼ teaspoon of the salt. In a small bowl combine 2 tablespoons of the broth with the remaining 2 teaspoons rice wine.

2. Heat a 14-inch flat-bottomed wok or 12-inch skillet over high heat until a bead of water vaporizes within 1 to 2 seconds of contact. Swirl in the remaining 2 tablespoons peanut oil, add the scallions and ginger, then, using a metal spatula, stir-fry 10 seconds or until the aromatics are fragrant. Push the aromatics to the sides of the wok, carefully add the salmon and spread it evenly in one layer in the wok. Cook undisturbed for 30 seconds. Swirl in the broth mixture, sprinkle the mushrooms and carrots on top of the fish, and cook undisturbed 1 minute. Gently loosen the fish with the spatula but do not begin to stir-fry. Swirl in the remaining ¼ cup broth, sprinkle on the remaining ¼ teaspoon salt, and continue to cook undisturbed 2 minutes, continuing to gently loosen the fish with the spatula. If the pan is dry, swirl 2 tablespoons water into the wok. Gently turn the fish over once. The salmon will be lightly browned. Add the snow peas, cover the wok, and cook 45 sec-

onds or until the fish is just cooked through. Do not overcook. Uncover, drizzle on the remaining 1 teaspoon sesame oil, and gently stir-fry a few seconds just to combine the ingredients.

Serves 2 to 3 as a main dish with rice or 4 as part of a multicourse meal.

Is Stir-Frying a Healthy Way to Cook?

Stir-frying involves cooking food quickly over high heat in a small amount of oil. Vegetables are typically the main ingredient of a stir-fry, with meat protein used as a condiment or flavoring agent. I asked Dr. Marion Nestle, Professor of Nutrition, Food Studies, and Public Health at New York University, and the author of *What to Eat*, about the nutritional implications of this age-old cooking technique.

How are the nutrient content and flavor of vegetables affected by the stir-fry method?

The high heat brings out the flavor and preserves the bright colors of vegetables. And it is just enough to soften them, making them easier to digest. When done well, stir-frying is so fast that it does not destroy too much of the more delicate vitamins. So you don't lose much vitamin C or folic acid, for example. And the fat aids the absorption of fat-soluble nutrients like vitamin A, vitamin E, and carotenoids in vegetables.

What are the nutritional implications of eating meals that emphasize vegetables and are lower in meat protein?

People who eat plenty of vegetables tend to be healthier than people who don't. They have lower rates of chronic diseases such as heart disease and certain cancers. All cooking oils used in stir-frying are low in the saturated fatty acids that raise the risk of coronary heart disease. It's best if the oils are not hydrogenated, of course, so they are free of trans fatty acids, which also raise heart disease risk. Eating small amounts of meat in a meal is a healthy way to eat. Meat provides vitamin B_{12} and higher amounts of B vitamins and minerals like zinc and iron than are found in vegetables.

What are the benefits of using less fat in cooking?

These days, everyone worries about calories. Fat has twice the calories per unit weight of either protein or carbohydrate. The little amount of oil used for stir-frying is enough to help the body absorb fat-soluble nutrients and carotenoids found in vegetables.

Some fats are adversely affected by being heated to a high temperature. Is peanut oil, the traditional oil for stir-frying, safe for cooking on high heat?

When stir-frying on high heat, it's key to use oils with a high smoking point (like peanut oil), which prevents the oil from breaking down. As with all oils, when one starts looking and smelling bad, it's time to get rid of it.

Stir-frying emphasizes the use of seasonal and local vegetables. Are vegetables from a farmers' market a healthier choice for cooking?

I like buying vegetables at farmers' markets. They are fresher and taste better. I like supporting farmers in my community.

Is it true that cooking in cast-iron or carbon-steel cookware adds iron to your food?

Yes, but only in unfinished cast-iron or carbon-steel woks—the kind that rust.

Cooks of Two Cultures: The Sizzle of Singapore

Julie Tay

"In America," says Julie Tay, a Chinese cooking teacher and musician based in New York's Chinatown, "I prepare a meal leisurely, perhaps pouring myself a glass of wine or turning on the television." But in Singapore, where Tay grew up, "The culture of cooking is entirely different. The kitchen is stifling hot because of the tropical climate, so you get in and out of the kitchen as quickly as possible, making stir-fries all the more practical. When men cook, they're usually naked to the waist," explains Tay. "In America, the rhythm of life is so different. Preparing a meal can be a social occasion, but in Singapore cooking is considered work. No one has time for interruptions or chit-chat. The process is much faster."

In San Francisco, where I was raised, even if there was no tropical heat, the kitchen was still a place of serious business. My parents cooked in exactly the way Tay describes (except my father was never naked to the waist). My mom, a force of nature, was in the kitchen within moments of her arrival from work, washing vegetables, marinating meat, putting a pot of rice on the fire to cook, switching from task to task with grace and efficiency. The atmosphere of her no-nonsense kitchen discouraged me and my brother from hanging out there. In fact, we knew in no uncertain terms not to wander in.

Julie Tay

Like Tay, I will occasionally turn on the television or listen to the radio as I prepare my evening meal, and there are times when I enjoy a glass of wine. I find cooking dinner to be relaxing, and I enjoy the distractions of chatting with my husband, Michael, or with guests if we're entertaining. In my parents' home, guests never once even saw our kitchen. They sat at the dining room table as my parents presented dish after dish, whisking stir-fries to the table in record time, so they arrived still breathing wok heat.

When I approached Julie Tay to talk about the differences in cooking in New York from her native Singapore, I was anticipating a response about the quality of ingredients or the lack of certain specialty food items in America. It never occurred to me that my question would prompt a behavioral discussion.

Asian home cooks share a pragmatic approach to culinary chores that defines a devotion to the meal. My mother considered cooking to be a chore but she also relished the products of her kitchen. Each spring she marveled at the first taste of stir-fried snow pea shoots; in mid-November she eagerly anticipated the arrival of Dungeness crabs. She praised my father on his skill at finely shredding scallions and cutting ginger paper-thin. My mother, like Tay's mother, I learn, was a perfectionist about slicing ginger. I confess to Tay that my own ginger slices have never been thin enough to impress my parents. Our parents share the same critical nature, it seems, but more important, the love of eating well.

Classic Dry-Fried Pepper and Salt Shrimp

There are many versions of this beloved dry stir-fry (see Dry Stir-Frying and Moist Stir-Frying, page 121). The absence of liquid in the stir-fry allows you to experience a concentrated shrimp flavor accented by garlic, ginger, chilies, and Sichuan peppercorns. For this reason, it's imperative to use the freshest ingredients. In recent years my fishmonger has been carrying fresh shrimp, and in this recipe you can really taste the difference. Defrosted frozen shrimp will work; just make sure it's the best quality possible.

2 tablespoons plus ½ teaspoon salt

1 pound large shrimp, peeled and deveined

¼ teaspoon sugar

¼ teaspoon roasted and ground Sichuan peppercorns (see page 6)

2 tablespoons peanut or vegetable oil

1 tablespoon minced garlic

1 tablespoon minced ginger

1 teaspoon minced jalapeño chili, with seeds

1. In a large bowl combine 1 tablespoon of the salt with 1 quart cold water. Add the shrimp and swish the shrimp in the water with your hand for about 30 seconds. Drain. Add 1 more tablespoon salt to the bowl with 1 quart of cold water and repeat. Rinse the shrimp under cold water and set on several sheets of paper towels. With more paper towels, pat the shrimp dry. In a small bowl combine the remaining ½ teaspoon salt, sugar, and ground Sichuan peppercorns.

2. Heat a 14-inch flat-bottomed wok or 12-inch skillet over high heat until a bead of water vaporizes within 1 to 2 seconds of contact. Swirl in 1 tablespoon of the oil, add the garlic, ginger, and chili, then, using a metal spatula, stir-fry 10 seconds or until the aromatics are fragrant. Push the garlic mixture to the sides of the wok, carefully add the shrimp, and spread them evenly in one layer in the wok. Cook undisturbed 1 minute, letting the shrimp begin to sear. Swirl in the remaining 1 tablespoon oil and stir-fry 1 minute or until the shrimp just begin to turn orange. Sprinkle on the salt mixture and stir-fry 1 to 2 minutes or until the shrimp are just cooked.

Serves 2 as a main dish with rice or 4 as part of a multicourse meal.

Stir-Fried Clams with Spicy Bean Sauce

When George Chew (see Stir-Frying in Brooklyn's Great Outdoors, page 281) stir-fries this dish, he uses soft belly clams. Since the clams are not widely available and are difficult to clean, he told me I could adapt the recipe using littleneck clams. The sauce, with its salty, hot, and sweet notes from the clams, is delicious over rice.

Littleneck clams can vary dramatically in size; ask your fishmonger to choose clams that are uniform in size to ensure even cooking. I prefer the smaller ones, no more than 2 inches at their widest point. Littleneck clams are easy to clean, needing a wash in several changes of cold water as well as a scrubbing with a brush to remove the grit. Old-fashioned Chinese cooks, however, swear that placing a carbon-steel cleaver in a bowl of clams soaking in water is the best way to clean them. The iron is said to draw out the grit. Wet clams added to hot oil will cause a lot of spattering. Because of that, in addition to draining the clams in a colander, I suggest patting them dry with paper towels.

1½ dozen littleneck clams (about 1½ pounds)

⅓ cup chicken broth or clam juice

1 tablespoon bean sauce

1 teaspoon soy sauce

2 tablespoons peanut or vegetable oil

1 tablespoon chopped shallots

2 teaspoons minced garlic

2 teaspoons minced ginger

¼ teaspoon minced Thai chili, with seeds,
    or ¼ teaspoon red pepper flakes

¼ cup chopped scallions

1. Thoroughly wash the clams in several changes of cold water, discarding any open clams. Scrub the shells with a stiff brush to remove grit and rinse well. Drain the clams in a colander, shaking out the excess water. Pat dry with paper towels. In a small bowl combine the broth, bean sauce, and soy sauce.

2. Heat a 14-inch flat-bottomed wok or 12-inch skillet over high heat until a bead of water vaporizes within 1 to 2 seconds of contact. Swirl in the oil, add the shallots, garlic, and ginger, and stir-fry 15 seconds or until the aromatics are fragrant. Add the clams and stir-fry 1 minute. Sprinkle on the chili and stir-fry 30 seconds or until well combined. Swirl the broth mixture into the wok, cover, and cook 4 minutes, stirring every minute. Uncover and stir-fry 1 minute or until the shells are fully open. Transfer any opened clams to a platter and continue stir-frying uncovered over high heat 1 to 2 minutes or until all the shells have opened and the broth mixture is reduced to a saucy consistency. Discard any unopened clams. Add the scallions and pour the sauce over the clams.

Serves 2 as a main dish with rice or 4 as part of a multicourse meal.

Stir-Fried Squid with Black Bean Sauce

When Chef Danny Chan taught me this recipe he explained that squid, which can easily become tough when cooked, cannot be marinated before stir-frying because a marinade can give it a chewy texture. Most home cooks stir-fry raw squid, but chefs blanch it first to shorten the stir-frying time. The concern is that if squid is stir-fried even a minute or two too long it becomes overcooked and loses its tenderness. The other benefit of blanching is that you can stir-fry a pound of blanched squid in a 14-inch wok (with raw squid only a half pound can be stir-fried). Once the squid is blanched, be sure to pat it dry with paper towels. If the squid is wet, the stir-fry will become a braise.

1 pound fresh cleaned squid

2 tablespoons chicken broth

2 teaspoons oyster sauce

2 teaspoons soy sauce

1 teaspoon dark soy sauce

1 teaspoon sesame oil

½ teaspoon cornstarch

2 tablespoons peanut or vegetable oil

2 tablespoons fermented black beans, rinsed and mashed

1 tablespoon chopped scallion, white part only

1 tablespoon thinly sliced garlic

¾ cup thinly sliced onions

2 teaspoons finely shredded ginger

½ cup julienned red bell peppers

¼ teaspoon salt

⅛ teaspoon freshly ground pepper

1 tablespoon Shao Hsing rice wine or dry sherry

12 snow peas, strings removed

1. Cut each squid body in half lengthwise. Using a very sharp knife, lightly score the inside of the bodies in a crisscross pattern. Cut the squid into 1½-inch squares and the tentacles into 2-inch pieces.

2. In a 2-quart saucepan bring 1 quart water to a boil covered over high heat. Add the squid and blanch 10 seconds or until the squid turns opaque and curls. Drain well in a colander, shaking out all the excess water. Set the squid on paper towels and blot dry to remove excess moisture. In a small bowl combine 1 tablespoon of the broth, oyster sauce, soy sauce, and dark soy sauce. In another small bowl combine the sesame oil, cornstarch, and the remaining 1 tablespoon broth.

3. Heat a 14-inch flat-bottomed wok or 12-inch skillet over high heat until a bead of water vaporizes within 1 to 2 seconds of contact. Swirl in the peanut oil, add the fermented black beans, scallion, and garlic and stir-fry 10 seconds or until the aromatics are fragrant. Add the onions and ginger and stir-fry 1 minute or until the onions just wilt. Add the bell peppers, sprinkle on the salt and pepper, and stir-fry 30 seconds or until the bell pepper begins to soften. Add the rice wine and stir-fry 20 seconds or until just combined. Add the squid and snow peas to the wok, swirl in the soy sauce mixture, and stir-fry 1 minute or until the snow peas are bright green. Restir the cornstarch mixture, swirl it into the wok, and stir-fry 30 seconds or until the squid is just cooked.

Serves 2 as a main dish with rice or 4 as part of a multicourse meal.

Singapore-Style Stir-Fried Lobster

This recipe comes from Julie Tay (see Cooks of Two Cultures, page 165), a native of Singapore; it is the classic Chinese way of eating lobster: cut into pieces and stir-fried in the shell. The lobster is meaty and succulent, with a decadent spicy sauce and a hint of sweetness. This is clearly a luxurious dish, one for special occasions, and definitely an "advanced" stir-fry recipe. If you have solid knife skills and are familiar with boiling a lobster, then you know how to handle the most complicated parts of this recipe.

Traditionally the lobster would be chopped raw through the shell, but Tay has adapted the recipe for American kitchens: the lobster is partially cooked by parboiling it. When it has cooled, the claws are separated from the body, and the shell is cracked with a mallet to make it easier for eating. I recommend holding the lobster claws with a clean kitchen towel as this is the messiest part of the preparation—there will be some spattering on your cutting board. I use kitchen shears to cut through the translucent part of the lobster tail (not the hard shell). Then I carefully cut the tail crosswise with a chef's knife or cleaver using a rocking motion. The body is the softest part and the easiest to cut through. Once the lobster is in pieces, the actual stir-frying is quick, and soon you'll be enjoying one of the most delicious ways to eat lobster.

One 2-pound live lobster

2 tablespoons ketchup

2 teaspoons soy sauce

2 teaspoons rice vinegar

½ teaspoon sugar

½ teaspoon salt

2 tablespoons peanut or vegetable oil

2 tablespoons minced garlic

2 tablespoons minced ginger

2 tablespoons chopped shallots

½ to 1 teaspoon minced Thai chili, with seeds

½ cup chicken broth

1 large egg white, lightly beaten

1 teaspoon Shao Hsing rice wine or dry sherry

1. In an 8-quart pot bring 6 quarts water to a boil over high heat. Use a sturdy pair of tongs to plunge the lobster headfirst into the boiling water, cover tightly, and cook 3 minutes from the time the lobster enters the water until the water returns to a rolling boil. Carefully transfer the lobster with tongs to a large bowl of ice and cold water to stop the cooking. Drain the lobster in a colander.

2. When cool enough to handle, put the lobster on a large cutting board. Remove the legs and the 2 main claws by twisting them from the body. Wrap one claw at a time in a clean kitchen towel, and, using a mallet or hammer, gently crack the shell of the claw and break the claw in half at the joint. Arch the back of the lobster until it cracks and separate the tail from the lobster body. Halve the tail through the translucent part of the shell lengthwise with kitchen shears. Carefully cut the tail crosswise into 3 or 4 pieces, using kitchen shears and a cleaver or a chef's knife. Remove the body from the hard shell. Cut the body in half lengthwise with kitchen shears, and remove and discard the sand sacs from inside the head. Cut the body in half again crosswise. Transfer the lobster pieces to a bowl. Drain any liquid from the bowl.

3. In a small bowl combine the ketchup, soy sauce, rice vinegar, sugar, and ¼ teaspoon of the salt.

4. Heat a 14-inch flat-bottomed wok over high heat until a bead of water vaporizes within 1 to 2 seconds

of contact. Swirl in the oil, add the garlic, ginger, and shallots, then, using a metal spatula, stir-fry 2 minutes or until the mixture is golden brown. Carefully add the ketchup mixture, which will start to spatter, and stir-fry 10 seconds or until the mixture is fragrant. Add the cut-up lobster, chili, and broth, sprinkle on the remaining ¼ teaspoon salt, and stir-fry 10 seconds or until just combined. Add the egg white and stir-fry 1 minute or until the egg white is well combined with the rest of the ingredients. Cover and cook 2 minutes. Swirl 2 tablespoons cold water into the wok and stir-fry 30 seconds. Cover and cook 2 minutes, stirring occasionally. Swirl the rice wine into the wok and stir-fry 10 seconds or until the lobster meat is opaque and just cooked through.

Serves 2 as a main dish with rice or 4 as part of a multicourse meal.

Malaysian-Style Stir-Fried Squid and Pineapple

Mei Chau (see Stir-Frying in a Malaysian Village, page 152) learned to love squid growing up in a fishing village in Malaysia, where her mother's stir-fried squid was simply cooked in the Hakka style. After years of living in Malaysia, Chau gradually adapted her tastes to the more highly seasoned and fiery Malaysian cuisine and started to stir-fry squid with hot sauce and tropical fruit. Chau favors a hot sauce with a distinct sweet and spicy taste with just the right amount of heat and prefers Lingham's Hot Sauce. When Lingham's is unavailable, as a last resort she uses 1 to 1½ teaspoons Tabasco and adds more sugar and tomato to the dish.

It is best to use a small quantity of raw squid for stir-frying. More than 8 ounces of raw squid crowds a 14-inch wok, which releases moisture creating a braise rather than a stir-fry. The squid must be thoroughly blotted dry with paper towels to prevent the stir-fry from becoming too wet.

8 ounces fresh cleaned squid

2 tablespoons peanut or vegetable oil

1 tablespoon minced garlic

1 tablespoon chopped shallots

1½ cups sliced fresh pineapple, cut into ½-inch-thick bite-sized pieces

½ medium ripe tomato, cut into thin wedges

1 tablespoon Asian-style hot sauce

1 teaspoon sugar

½ teaspoon salt

1 scallion, chopped

1. Cut each squid body in half lengthwise. Using a very sharp knife, lightly score the inside of the bod-ies in a crisscross pattern. Cut the squid into 1½-inch squares and the tentacles into 2-inch pieces. Blot dry the squid with paper towels to remove any excess moisture.

2. Heat a 14-inch flat-bottomed wok or 12-inch skillet over high heat until a bead of water vaporizes within 1 to 2 seconds of contact. Swirl in the oil, add the garlic and shallots, and stir-fry 10 seconds or until the aromatics are fragrant. Add the squid and stir-fry 2 minutes or until the squid turns opaque, curls, and is just cooked. Add the pineapple and stir-fry 10 seconds or until just combined. Add the tomato and hot sauce, sprinkle on the sugar and salt, and stir-fry 30 seconds or until the flavors have blended. Sprinkle on the scallion.

Serves 2 as a main course with rice or 4 as part of a multicourse meal.

Hakka-Style Stir-Fried Shrimp and Vegetables

Fah Liong's (see Lessons from a Simple Stir-Fry, page 144) Hakka family originally came from northern China and migrated south to Guangdong province. In the 1880s her grandfather emigrated from southern China to Sumatra, Indonesia, bringing with him his Hakka cooking traditions. Liong recalls the family only cooked traditional Hakka foods; the culinary traditions of Indonesia never influenced their cooking.

When I visited Liong in her home in Redwood City, California, she prepared this stir-fry, which she learned to make over forty years ago. She varies the vegetables depending on the season, but whenever she uses carrots she soaks them in cold water and then uses the soaking water in the stir-fry. If you don't have time to soak the carrots, just use water or vegetable broth. In addition to the broccoli florets, you can also add the broccoli stems if they are peeled and cut into ¼-inch-thick slices. Since broccoli and cauliflower cook in the same amount of time, you can also vary it by using all broccoli or all cauliflower.

This stir-fry reflects the economy of Chinese cooking. By Western standards, a half pound of shrimp is not enough to serve two to three guests as a main dish even when accompanied by vegetables and rice, but this is typical of how little protein the Chinese traditionally eat in a meal.

1 cup thinly sliced carrots
½ teaspoon cornstarch
2 tablespoons peanut or vegetable oil
1 tablespoon plus 1 teaspoon chopped garlic
½ pound medium shrimp, peeled, deveined, and patted dry

2 cups Napa cabbage, cut crosswise into 1-inch-wide pieces
1½ cups small bite-sized broccoli florets
1½ cups small bite-sized cauliflower florets
¾ teaspoon salt
¼ teaspoon ground white pepper

1. Soak the carrots in about 1 cup cold water 1 hour. In a small bowl combine 1 tablespoon of the carrot soaking water with the cornstarch. In another small bowl measure ⅓ cup of the carrot water. Drain the carrots, shaking out any excess water.

2. Heat a 14-inch flat-bottomed wok or 12-inch skillet over high heat until a bead of water vaporizes within 1 to 2 seconds of contact. Swirl in the oil, add all the garlic, and stir-fry 20 seconds or until fragrant. Add the drained carrots and stir-fry 1 minute or until the garlic begins to brown. Add the shrimp and stir-fry 30 seconds or until the shrimp just begin to turn orange. Add the cabbage and stir-fry 30 seconds or until the cabbage just begins to wilt. Add the broccoli and cauliflower and stir-fry 30 seconds or until the broccoli begins to turn bright green. Sprinkle on the salt and pepper, swirl in the reserved ⅓ cup carrot water, and stir-fry a few seconds or until just combined. Cover and cook 30 seconds. Uncover, restir the cornstarch mixture, swirl it into the wok, and stir-fry 30 seconds or until the shrimp are just cooked.

Serves 2 to 3 as a main dish with rice or 4 as part of a multicourse meal.

Fujianese-Style Stir-Fried Fish with Peppers

I learned the recipe for this amazing stir-fried fish from Kian Lam Kho, who writes a popular blog on Chinese home cooking (redcook.net). Interestingly, the dish, which is typical of Kian's family's Fujianese-style cooking, reminded me of a famous Shanghainese-style stir-fried fish in wine sauce.

When Kian demonstrated this recipe in his New York City kitchen, he took a whole carp and impressively filleted it, then cut each fillet into thin slices. Since carp is not widely available, he recommends cod, scrod, or any other firm-fleshed white fish, with the skin. Kian told me the key to success is velveting (see Velvet Stir-Fry, page 100) the fish to ensure it has a silky texture before stir-frying it with the peppers. Typically, ingredients are marinated in an egg white-cornstarch mixture, but Kian's method uses only egg white and salt. It is also important to remember that fish needs to be stir-fried gently to prevent it from falling apart and that velveted fish is stir-fried only until just cooked; the slices should never be browned. Don't forget to alert guests to watch out for small bones.

12 ounces carp, cod, or scrod fillet, skin on

2 tablespoons egg white, lightly beaten

1 teaspoon salt

3 tablespoons chicken broth

2 tablespoons Shao Hsing rice wine or dry sherry

2 teaspoons cornstarch

½ teaspoon sugar

2 cups peanut or vegetable oil

1 tablespoon minced garlic

1 tablespoon finely shredded ginger

1 cup julienned yellow or red bell peppers

1 cup finely shredded scallions

1. Remove any visible bones from the fish. Halve the fish lengthwise, along the deep natural crease of the fillet, into 2 strips, each roughly 2 inches wide. Cut one strip at a time crosswise into ¼-inch-thick bite-sized slices. In a medium bowl gently combine the fish, egg white, and ½ teaspoon of the salt. Stir to combine. In a small bowl combine the broth, rice wine, cornstarch, sugar, and the remaining ½ teaspoon salt.

2. Heat the oil in a 14-inch flat-bottomed wok over high heat until the oil registers 280°F on a deep-frying thermometer. Using a slotted metal spoon, carefully add the fish to the hot oil, gently stirring so that the pieces do not clump together. Cook 30 seconds or until the fish is barely opaque and is not cooked through. Remove the wok from the heat. Remove the fish with the slotted spoon to a plate. Carefully remove the oil from the wok and reserve. Wash the wok and dry it thoroughly.

3. Heat the wok over high heat until a bead of water vaporizes within 1 to 2 seconds of contact. Swirl in 2 tablespoons of the reserved oil. Add the garlic and ginger, then, using a metal spatula, stir-fry 10 seconds or until the aromatics are fragrant. Add the bell peppers and stir-fry 30 seconds or until the peppers begin to soften. Return the fish to the wok and add the scallions. Restir the broth mixture and swirl it into the wok. Gently stir-fry the fish 30 seconds to 1 minute or until the fish is just cooked through and the ingredients are combined.

Serves 2 as a main dish with rice or 4 as part of a multicourse meal.

Kian Lam Kho

Taiwanese-Style Stir-Fried Scallops and Shrimp with Yellow Chives

Justin Guo, who grew up in Taiwan, fondly remembers stir-fried eel was a favorite street food. He learned to make this version of that dish with shrimp and scallops from his mother. Yellow chives are grown in the dark and have a mild, delicate garlic flavor. Just rinse them in cold water and remove any light brown tips or stems.

8 ounces medium fresh sea scallops

8 ounces medium shrimp, peeled and deveined

2 tablespoons Japanese sake or dry sherry

1 tablespoon finely shredded ginger

¾ teaspoon salt

¼ teaspoon ground white pepper

2 tablespoons peanut or vegetable oil

3 medium garlic cloves, smashed

2 teaspoons chili bean sauce

4 ounces yellow chives, cut into 2-inch sections
   (about 2 cups)

1. Rinse the scallops, removing the muscle and any visible bits of shell or grit and shake out water. Cut the scallops horizontally in half so that all the pieces are about ½ inch thick. Rinse the shrimp and shake out water. In a bowl combine the scallops, shrimp, 1 tablespoon of the sake, ginger, ½ teaspoon of the salt, and pepper. Put the seafood uncovered in the refrigerator for 45 minutes.

2. Heat a 14-inch flat-bottomed wok or 12-inch skillet over high heat until a bead of water vaporizes within 1 to 2 seconds of contact. Swirl in 1 tablespoon of the oil, add 1 of the smashed garlic cloves, then, using a metal spatula, stir-fry 10 seconds or until fragrant. Push the garlic to the side of the wok, add the scallop and shrimp mixture, and spread it evenly in one layer in the wok. Cook undisturbed 1 minute, letting the scallops and shrimp begin to sear. Stir-fry 30 seconds until the scallops are opaque and the shrimp have just turned orange but are not cooked through. Transfer the scallops and shrimp to a plate.

3. Swirl the remaining 1 tablespoon oil into the wok. Add the remaining 2 garlic cloves and stir-fry 10 seconds or until fragrant. Return the seafood with any juices that have accumulated to the wok, add the bean sauce, and stir-fry 1 minute until well combined. Add the chives and the remaining 1 tablespoon sake, sprinkle on the remaining ¼ teaspoon salt, and stir-fry 45 seconds or until well combined. Cover, reduce the heat to medium, and cook for 10 seconds. Uncover, increase the heat to high, and stir-fry 1 minute or until the shrimp and scallops are just cooked through.

Serves 2 as a main dish with rice or 4 as part of a multicourse meal.

Justin Guo

Chinese American Shrimp with Lobster Sauce

George Chew's (see Stir-Frying in Brooklyn's Great Outdoors, page 281) shrimp with lobster sauce is an extravagantly rich and delectable eating experience. Key to the success of this dish is making a stock with the shrimp shells. George makes his own clam broth and I was surprised to discover that even with bottled clam juice, homemade shrimp stock gives that seafood essence that elevates the dish. Of course, George's shrimp with lobster sauce has spoiled me forever. Every dish I've sampled in a restaurant since has been a disappointment, memorable mainly for its gloppy, tasteless sauce.

1 pound large shrimp
One 8-ounce bottle clam juice
1¼ teaspoons cornstarch
2 teaspoons soy sauce
¼ teaspoon freshly ground pepper
2 tablespoons peanut or vegetable oil
1 teaspoon minced garlic
1 teaspoon minced ginger
¼ cup ground pork (about 2 ounces)
⅛ teaspoon minced Thai chili, with seeds
1 tablespoon fermented black beans, rinsed
1 large egg, lightly beaten
2 scallions, chopped

1. Peel and devein the shrimp, reserving the shells. Rinse the shrimp under water and set on paper towels.

2. In a 1-quart saucepan combine the clam juice and the reserved shrimp shells and bring to a boil over high heat. Using a spoon, press the shells into the liquid to extract as much flavor as possible. Cover, reduce the heat to low, and simmer 2 minutes or until the shells are bright orange. Transfer the mixture to a colander set over a bowl and strain to yield about 1 cup. Set the liquid aside to cool and discard the shells. When the shrimp stock has cooled, measure 2 tablespoons in a small bowl and combine with the cornstarch. To the remaining shrimp stock add 1 teaspoon of the soy sauce and ⅛ teaspoon of the pepper.

3. Heat a 14-inch flat-bottomed wok or 12-inch skillet over high heat until a bead of water vaporizes within 1 to 2 seconds of contact. Swirl in 1 tablespoon of the oil, carefully add the shrimp, and spread them evenly in one layer in the wok. Cook undisturbed 1 minute, letting the shrimp begin to sear. Sprinkle on the remaining ⅛ teaspoon pepper and 1 teaspoon soy sauce, then, using a metal spatula, stir-fry 30 seconds or until the shrimp just begins to turn orange but are not cooked through. Transfer the shrimp to a plate.

4. Swirl the remaining 1 tablespoon oil into the wok, add the garlic, ginger, and pork, and stir-fry 1 minute, breaking up the pork with the spatula. Add the minced chili and stir-fry 30 seconds or until the pork begins to change color. Add the fermented black beans, swirl the reserved shrimp stock mixture into the wok, return the shrimp with any juices that have accumulated to the wok. When the stock comes to a full boil, restir the cornstarch mixture, swirl it into the wok, and stir-fry 30 seconds or until the sauce is slightly thickened. Add the beaten egg and scallions, and stir-fry 15 seconds or until the egg is barely set and the shrimp are just cooked.

Serves 2 to 3 as a main dish with rice or 4 as part of a multicourse meal.

Chinese Trinidadian Stir-Fried Shrimp with Rum

When I was in Trinidad, Winnie Lee Lum (see A Culinary Remembrance, page 103) showed me how to make this superb dish, which beautifully demonstrates the convergence of Chinese and Trinidadian cooking traditions. Of course, the taste was extraordinary because Lee Lum only cooks with fresh local shrimp that her husband, Tony, purchases for her. Before cooking, she rinses the shrimp in lime juice, a Trinidadian cooking practice said to remove the "fishy" taste. She prefers the Chinese custom of cooking the shrimp in the shell to protect the shrimp's succulence and flavor (see Essentials for Stir-Frying Fish and Shellfish, page 148). Rather than rice wine, Lee Lum insists on using dark Jamaican-style rum; according to her, white rum is too harsh for cooking. This is one of the easiest dishes to stir-fry, and it is guaranteed to satisfy. (See photo, page 146.)

1 pound large shrimp

Juice of ½ lime

3 tablespoons ketchup

3 tablespoons dark Jamaican rum

2 teaspoons soy sauce

¼ teaspoon ground white pepper

2 tablespoons peanut or vegetable oil

1 tablespoon minced garlic

1 tablespoon minced ginger

½ teaspoon salt

1 medium ripe tomato, cut into thin wedges

1 large green bell pepper, cut into thin strips

1 small onion, cut into thin wedges

1 tablespoon finely chopped cilantro

1. Using kitchen shears, cut through the shrimp shells two-thirds of the length down the back of the shrimp. Remove the legs and devein the shrimp, leaving the shells and tails on. In a medium bowl toss the shrimp with the lime juice for a few seconds. Rinse the shrimp, drain, and set on a plate lined with paper towels. With more paper towels pat the shrimp dry. In a small bowl combine the ketchup, rum, soy sauce, and ground white pepper.

2. Heat a 14-inch flat-bottomed wok or 12-inch skillet over high heat until a bead of water vaporizes within 1 to 2 seconds of contact. Swirl in the oil, add the garlic and ginger, then, using a metal spatula, stir-fry 10 seconds or until the aromatics are fragrant. Push the aromatics to the sides of the wok, carefully add the shrimp and spread them evenly in one layer in the wok. Cook undisturbed 1 minute, letting the shrimp begin to sear. Sprinkle on the salt and stir-fry 30 seconds or until the shrimp begin to turn orange. Add the tomatoes, bell peppers, and onions and stir-fry 1 minute or until the shrimp have turned almost totally orange. Swirl the ketchup mixture into the wok and stir-fry 1 minute or until the shrimp are just cooked through and the sauce coats the shrimp. Stir in the cilantro.

Serves 2 to 3 as a main dish with rice or 4 as part of a multicourse meal.

Partners in Stir-Frying

Wai Ching Wong and Ken Lo

Some cooks work best as a team, especially when stir-frying. Ken Lo, a *chi gung* master and Chinese cooking instructor, stir-fried happily for over ten years with his mother-in-law, Wai Ching Wong. "I don't cook well with my wife—our ideas differ," explains Lo, "but I get along really well in the kitchen with my mother-in-law. She's a perfectionist. She isn't quick, but everything she cuts is absolutely uniform. When I come home from teaching every night, she has everything beautifully prepared for me. All I have to do is *chau* (stir-fry)."

I arrive at Lo's home to find him alone in the kitchen, busily cutting ingredients. Mrs. Wong has sustained a shoulder injury and will not be able to assist. As he prepares to slice ginger, Lo holds up his cutting board. "Look at all these hack marks she made. She has such tremendous strength, she dents my knives." When I finally meet Mrs. Wong, who joins us for lunch, she is not the powerfully built, Julia Child–sized woman I imagined her to be after hearing Lo describe her as being "rough in the kitchen." Instead she is petite, spry, and a little girlish, especially for one who is ninety years old. I

Wai Ching Wong

am even more charmed when I learn Mrs. Wong is an avid Taiwanese tango dancer.

For lunch we share Lo's steamed tilapia, *ma po* tofu, stir-fried lotus root (page 193), and steamed rice. Every dish is delicious: the tilapia delicate and succulent, served with fine shreds of ginger and scallion; the lotus root offers a contrast of textures, combining unique savory flavors from the Chinese bacon and the seasoning of rice wine and sesame oil. Mrs. Wong thoroughly enjoys the food, eating heartily although she cannot resist telling Lo that the lotus root could have been cut thinner, and the green beans, not a traditional ingredient in a lotus root stir-fry, are not to her taste. Lo is more amused than offended by the criticism and says to me almost proudly, "No detail escapes her. Everything she cooks, she cooks really well."

I wish I could have seen Lo and Mrs. Wong do their culinary dance, but a few months after my visit Mrs. Wong passed away. Every now and then, I make a lotus root stir-fry, and when I do I think of Mrs. Wong making an extra effort to cut the lotus root thinly and precisely. I hope my slicing would pass muster with Mrs. Wong's sharp eye and charming exactitude.

Stir-Fried Vegetarian Five-Spice Tofu

Vegetable and Tofu

RECIPES

ESSENTIALS FOR STIR-FRYING VEGETABLES AND TOFU

Stir-Frying with the Seasons

The technique of stir-frying vegetables intensifies their natural flavor, texture, and color, so it makes sense to cook with vegetables that are in their prime. Buying vegetables in season is the best value for your pocketbook and for quality. If you have the luxury of shopping at a farmers' market, there is nothing that compares to the flavor and texture of vegetables that have just been harvested. If you are unsure of the seasonality of a favorite vegetable, check with the growers at your local farmers' market (most markets only allow produce to be brought in from within a few hundred miles). Some supermarkets are now making an effort to post signs over the produce that indicate if it is locally grown. Even better, if you have a vegetable garden, consider adding Asian vegetables to your selection. A source for vegetable seeds is included in Sources (see page 287). If you have access to an Asian market, the choice of Asian produce there is generally superior to what's available in an American supermarket.

Sadly, it is difficult to tell what is in season by what's sold in a supermarket these days. Factory farming and international trade have made it possible for just about any vegetable to be available year-round. Generally, such vegetables are inferior because they have been picked before they fully mature and have sat in a cold storage warehouse for days if not weeks before reaching your supermarket. Many supermarkets offer packaged precut stir-fry vegetables. I am never tempted by these convenience items as they are overpriced, the freshness is sometimes questionable, and the pieces are so large that they are better suited for chunky stews or crudités than they are for stir-frying.

Use Fresh

Use vegetables within a few days of purchasing them. Do not buy vegetables too far in advance and let them deteriorate in your refrigerator.

Buying and Storing Tofu

The best tofu for stir-frying is firm, extra-firm, and pressed (five-spice) tofu. Avoid silken tofu, which will completely break apart if stir-fried, resembling scrambled eggs. If you have the good fortune to buy tofu in a store specializing in tofu in Chinatown, it is sold in individual squares. However, in supermarkets or health food stores the most common form of firm and extra-firm tofu is a large rectangular block in a sealed plastic container. I generally buy the organic tofu since the price is not significantly higher. Check the expiration date on the package. Store the tofu in the refrigerator. Once the container is opened, change the water daily. Tofu should have a clean, nonsour smell.

Five-spice tofu is sold in individual squares and is not available in plastic containers. Unlike firm and extra-firm tofu it is not stored in water. You can substitute baked tofu found in the refrigerator section of health food stores but I find it to be inferior because the texture is grittier and not as smooth as the Chinese version. All tofu is extremely perishable and should be used within 2 to 3 days.

The Importance of Drying Vegetables Before Stir-Frying

When stir-frying vegetables, it is critical that they be dry to the touch. The temperature of the wok will drop the moment vegetables still wet from rinsing are added. That excess moisture will steam vegetables, transforming a stir-fry into a soggy braise. Wet vegetables also cause unnecessary spattering when added to hot oil. To dry vegetables, pat them dry with a kitchen towel or wash them a few hours ahead of time and allow them to air-dry in a colander. For leafy vegetables, one of my favorite methods is to whirl them dry in a salad spinner.

Categorize, Then Stir-Fry

When stir-frying, group vegetables by texture into the following categories:

Hard: Chinese broccoli stems, broccoli, carrots, cauliflower, lotus root, potatoes, chayote, parsnips

Medium-hard: asparagus, bell peppers, long beans, green beans, fuzzy melon, zucchini, button mushrooms, shiitake mushrooms, snow peas, sugar snap peas, eggplant, water chestnuts, mature bok choy, cut corn, fava beans

Soft/leafy: Chinese broccoli leaves, spinach, water spinach, snow pea shoots, baby bok choy, bean sprouts, Napa cabbage, green cabbage, *yau choi*, lettuce, watercress, tomatoes

The Need for a Uniform Cut

Cut vegetables as uniformly as possible into bite-sized pieces so they will cook in the same amount of time. This is especially critical for hard and medium-hard vegetables. If vegetables are cut differently and vary in size and shape, by the time bigger pieces are ready, the smaller ones are likely to be overcooked or burned.

Tips for Stir-Frying Hard Vegetables

There are several methods to handle stir-frying hard vegetables:

- Blanch the vegetables in boiling water 1 to 2 minutes. Shake out all the excess water from the vegetables in a colander or pat dry before proceeding to stir-fry. If desired, blanched vegetables can be "shocked" in cold water to stop the cooking. By blanching vegetables, you reduce the amount of oil necessary to stir-fry them, creating a lighter taste; you also shorten the stir-fry time. It is not advisable to blanch soft/leafy vegetables or some medium-hard vegetables. Unlike hard vegetables, these vegetables can absorb too much water, which in turn makes a stir-fry a soggy braise.

- Cut the vegetables in thin pieces so that they will cook faster, i.e., ¼-inch-thick carrot slices stir-fry in less time than 1-inch-thick chunks.

- After stir-frying vegetables 1 to 2 minutes, swirl a small amount of liquid (usually water, rice wine, or broth) into the wok, cover, and cook 1 to 2 minutes, then uncover and continue stir-frying until just crisp-tender.

Stir-Frying Vegetables That Are Both Hard and Soft

A few vegetables, such as Chinese broccoli, qualify as both hard and soft. In such cases, separate the hard stems from the leafy greens, cut the stems into uniform ¼- to ½-inch-thick bite-sized pieces, and stir-fry them for a minute or two before adding the broccoli leaves.

No Need to Spread Vegetables in an Even Layer

Vegetables, unlike protein, can be stir-fried immediately, without first having to be spread in an even layer in the wok.

The Best Spatula for Stir-Frying Vegetables and Tofu

A Chinese metal spatula, a pancake turner, or a wooden spatula are all equally good for stir-frying vegetables. However, use a metal spatula for tofu because its thinner edge is more effective in getting under tofu.

Avoid Overfilling the Wok

When stir-frying, do not crowd the wok or skillet with too many vegetables. A crowded wok means vegetables are difficult to move. Vegetables caught on the bottom are likely to overcook or burn, along with the aromatics, while those in the middle and top remain raw. If you're cooking for a large group, stir-fry vegetables one recipe at a time; do not try and double the amount in a wok. *As a general rule, in a 14-inch wok or 12-inch skillet, do not stir-fry more than 4 cups hard or medium-hard vegetables.* Soft/leafy vegetables vary in bulk depending on the vegetable, e.g., 12 ounces of spinach = 16 cups, but 12 ounces of Napa cabbage = 6 cups; *check individual recipes to see the maximum amount of leafy vegetables called for.*

Use a Wok for Stir-Frying Leafy Vegetables

Stir-frying leafy vegetables (which start off with great volume before they cook down) in a 14-inch wok is far superior to stir-frying them in a skillet. For example, in a skillet 16 cups of spinach are difficult to move, let alone stir-fry, without the spinach falling out of the pan. If you don't want to use a wok, a 6-quart Dutch oven is an alternative, but the high sides make it awkward to stir-fry in.

Dry Firm Tofu Before Stir-Frying

After rinsing firm or extra-firm tofu, cut it into julienne, cubes, or bite-sized slices and then place it on paper towels before stir-frying. This can be done several hours in advance. Put several more paper towels on top of the tofu and refrigerate until ready to use. This is an important step as firm tofu is very moist and will cause spattering. Five-spice tofu does not have this moisture, because it has been pressed and therefore does not require towel drying. If however, you are using baked tofu as a substitute, it must be dried with paper towels because it is a moist product.

The Sizzle Means . . .

The moment vegetables and tofu are added to a wok there should be a sizzling sound that remains steady throughout stir-frying. If there is no audible sizzle, it indicates that the wok was not sufficiently heated (see Stir-Frying with Proper Heat and Control, page 52), or that the wok's heat has been reduced by the addition of wet vegetables, wet tofu, or overcrowding. If this happens, your stir-fry has become a braise.

Sprinkle in the Dry Seasonings

Sprinkle in dry seasonings, like salt and pepper, so they are well distributed and do not clump in one spot. This is more critical when stir-frying leafy vegetables.

How to Gauge Doneness

Use the cooking time of any recipe as a guideline only; a variety of factors such as the power of the stove and the age of vegetables will affect times. As a general rule, stir-fry hard and medium-hard vegetables until crisp-tender; stir-fry soft/leafy vegetables until just wilted, or until the vegetables are done to your liking.

How to Estimate Cooking Times for Different Vegetables

Stir-fry vegetables from the same category together since their cooking times are similar. If stir-frying vegetables with different textures, stir-fry hard vegetables for a few minutes first, then add medium-hard, and finally soft/leafy vegetables. Cooking times will also be influenced by the freshness and maturity of the vegetables.

Bok choy: Cut off about ¼ inch of the base of the bok choy head. Then separate the bok choy into stalks.

Cut each stalk of bok choy into 2-inch pieces.

Lotus root: Trim the lotus root ends. Peel and rinse the lotus root. Shave a thin slice off and put the cut side down on the cutting board.

Cut the lotus root lengthwise in half. Cut each half into ¼-inch-thick slices.

Chinese broccoli: Cut the stalks into 2-inch pieces, keeping the stalk ends separate from the leaves.

Water chestnuts: Peel the entire surface of the water chestnut as you would an apple; be careful to remove just the peel.

The Conundrum of Chop Suey

There is some debate about the provenance of chop suey. Those who believe its origins are Chinese generally cite E. N. Anderson's *Food of China* where he states, "Last of all, chop suey is not—as many would-be connoisseurs believe—an American invention." Anderson's source is Li Shu-fan, who referred to chop suey as a Toisan dish from southern China in his 1964 autobiography *Hong Kong Surgeon*. I do not know anything about Li's background, and I'm not sure why his statement holds such culinary authority.

Most of the great twentieth-century Chinese cooking experts in America seemed to make a special effort to disassociate themselves from chop suey. Florence Lin, Irene Kuo, Virginia Lee, and Buwei Yang Chao included neither recipes nor references to chop suey in their cookbooks. Doreen Yen Hung Feng mentions it in her introduction to *The Joy of Chinese Cooking* (1950) only to note that it "is known to us Chinese only as an agreeable foreign dish." Grace Zía Chu did publish a chop suey recipe in her 1962 cookbook, *The Pleasures of Chinese Cooking*. The book's first recipe chapter is entitled "Popular Dishes in Chinese-American Restaurants" and includes a section called "This Business of Chop Suey and Chow Mein." Chu writes:

"Is chop suey a Chinese dish? The best answer seems to be: More or less. Webster's dictionary makes a valiant attempt at defining chop suey as 'a mélange served in Chinese restaurants, consisting typically of bean sprouts, onions, mushrooms, etc., and sliced meats fried and flavored with sesame oil.' In its usual wisdom, the dictionary neatly side-steps the issue of whether chop suey is a genuine product of China.

"But it is generally conceded by people who worry about such things that chop suey was indeed invented by the Chinese—the Chinese who had migrated to America."

In Craig Claiborne's *New York Times* review of the cookbook he writes, "There is a fascinating collection of recipes in the book, although why Mrs. Chu saw fit to include a recipe for that all-American bore called chop suey is anybody's guess."

In 1963, the famous San Francisco Chinese restaurateur Johnny Kan and his coauthor Charles L. Leong made a special point of stating in the introduction to their cookbook *Eight Immortal Flavors,* "In the first place, Chop Suey is no more authentic in Chinese cuisine than Irish stew." The 1953 menu from Kan's renowned restaurant includes a quote from legendary *San Francisco Chronicle* newspaper columnist Herb Caen:

"But for the authentic delicacies of the Chinese menu—and they are many and delightful—it has been necessary to know a Chinese family, or one of the tiny basement restaurants that cater almost exclusively to the Oriental trade.

"This, fortunately, is no longer the case, now that Johnny Kan has elected to preside over a first-rate Chinese restaurant dedicated to all that is genuine and worthwhile in Chinese cooking. On his menu you will find Peking Duck, Melon Cup Soup, Squab Stuffed with Bird's Nest, Gold Coin Chicken, Pressed Mandarin Duck—dishes that heretofore have been denied to all but the cognoscenti.

"But a word of warning. Don't ask for chop suey. The highest compliment to Kan's conception of Chinese food is the absence of this most ersatz of Oriental dishes from his menu."

Similarly, the Imperial Palace, one of San Francisco's most elegant Chinese restaurants from the 1960s and '70s, makes a special point on its menu: "Ancient eggs, shark's fin soup, bitter melon . . . anything but Chop Suey."

What appeals to me about chop suey is how it revolutionized the American perception of Chinese food, but in my opinion, it lacks the qualities of a dynamic stir-fry. The respected Chinese cooking authority Kenneth Lo describes it best in his cookbook *Chinese Food:* "Chop-suey is the antithesis of real Chinese culinary art, which requires that flavours are kept distinct, and not jumbled, however savoury the result; and chop-suey is really no more than a savoury mess! At its worst, the bean-sprouts in chop-suey are stale and limp, or in some cases, for lack of enough bean-sprouts, shredded cabbage is added, along with shredded meat which may also be stale and indeterminate, and there is far too much tomato sauce. The result is a dish not only quite alien to any Chinese tradition, but to any concept of good food."

Stir-Fried Baby Bok Choy with Sichuan Pepper and Salt

Baby bok choy can vary from about 3 to 8 inches in length. Shanghai bok choy is sold in both Asian produce sections and in Western markets, where it can also be labeled "baby bok choy." For Shanghai bok choy, I like to trim the bottoms and separate the bok choy stalks before rinsing them under cold water. This makes it easier to remove all the grit. After rinsing, I put the bok choy in a salad spinner to remove excess water, then I cut the stalks into roughly 2-inch pieces. If you have access to an Asian produce market keep your eye out for the dwarf bok choy, about 3 inches in length and the most tender. When using the dwarf variety, I trim about ¼ inch from the bottoms and then halve the heads lengthwise.

2 tablespoons chicken broth

2 tablespoons Shao Hsing rice wine or dry sherry

¼ teaspoon cornstarch

2 tablespoons peanut or vegetable oil

3 ginger slices, smashed

1 cup thinly sliced carrots

12 ounces baby bok choy (about 6 cups packed)

½ teaspoon salt

¼ teaspoon roasted and ground Sichuan peppercorns (see page 6)

1. In a small bowl combine the broth, rice wine, and cornstarch.

2. Heat a 14-inch flat-bottomed wok or 12-inch skillet over high heat until a bead of water vaporizes within 1 to 2 seconds of contact. Swirl in 1 tablespoon of the oil, add the ginger slices, and stir-fry 10 seconds or until the ginger is fragrant. Add the carrots and stir-fry 30 seconds or until the carrots are just coated with the oil. Swirl in the remaining 1 tablespoon oil, add the bok choy, sprinkle on the salt and ground Sichuan peppercorns, and stir-fry 1 minute or until the leaves are just limp and the bok choy is bright green. Restir the broth mixture and swirl it into the wok. Cover and cook 30 seconds. Uncover and stir-fry 30 seconds to 1 minute or until the bok choy is just crisp-tender.

Serves 4 as a vegetable side dish.

Hong Kong–Style Chinese Broccoli

Chinese broccoli is available year-round in Asian markets, but it is best in the winter months. When selecting broccoli, choose stalks that only have buds and dark green leaves. White flowers and yellowing leaves indicate that the broccoli is older and past its prime. This is one of my favorite vegetable combinations. The bittersweet flavor of the broccoli complements the smoky-sweet flavor of the Chinese bacon. The bacon is sold in roughly 1-inch-thick slabs and is available in Chinese butcher shops and some Asian markets (see photo, page 39). You'll need only a small portion of the bacon for this recipe. Wrap the extra bacon in freezer paper and it will keep in the freezer for one to two months.

9 medium stalks Chinese broccoli (about 12 ounces)
2 ounces Chinese bacon
2 tablespoons Shao Hsing rice wine or dry sherry
2 teaspoons soy sauce
1 tablespoon peanut or vegetable oil
3 slices ginger, smashed
1 teaspoon sugar
¼ teaspoon salt

1. Trim ¼ inch from the bottom of each broccoli stalk. Cut the stalks in half lengthwise if more than ½ inch in diameter. Cut the stalks and leaves into 2-inch-long pieces, keeping the stalks separate from the leaves.

2. Remove the hard rind and thick layer of fat attached to the Chinese bacon and discard. Cut the bacon crosswise into scant ¼-inch-thick slices to make about ½ cup. In a small bowl combine the rice wine and soy sauce.

3. Heat a 14-inch flat-bottomed wok or 12-inch skillet over high heat until a bead of water vaporizes within 1 to 2 seconds of contact. Swirl in the oil, add the ginger slices, and stir-fry 10 seconds or until the ginger is fragrant. Add the bacon and stir-fry 45 seconds or until it begins to release its fat. Add only the broccoli stalks and stir-fry 1 to 1½ minutes until the stalks are bright green. Add the leaves and stir-fry for 1 minute until the leaves are just limp. Swirl the rice wine mixture into the wok. Sprinkle on the sugar and salt and stir-fry 1 minute or until the broccoli is just crisp-tender.

Serves 4 as a vegetable side dish.

Stir-Fried Lotus Root with Bacon and Vegetables

This is the delectable recipe Ken Lo (see Partners in Stir-Frying, page 181) prepared for me the day I went to visit him. In deference to the memory of his mother-in-law, Wai Ching Wong, I have omitted the green beans he included that day. The dish is a classic example of the Cantonese siu chau, or "simple stir-fry" (see The Simple Stir-Fry, page 201). Lotus root comes in three connected pieces: the large piece is typically used for stir-fries because it is said to have a crisper texture; the two smaller pieces are reserved for soups. Use extra care when halving the lotus root. Once it has been peeled, it can be slippery and difficult to hold. I like to shave a thin slice off so that it can sit securely on a cutting board cut side down before I halve it lengthwise.

¼ cup cloud ears
1 large lotus root section (about 8 ounces)
2 ounces Chinese bacon
2 tablespoons chicken broth
1 tablespoon Shao Hsing rice wine or dry sherry
1 teaspoon soy sauce
1 teaspoon sesame oil
1 tablespoon peanut or vegetable oil
4 slices ginger, smashed
8 ounces snow peas, strings removed
½ cup thinly sliced carrots
½ teaspoon salt
¼ teaspoon ground white pepper
½ cup finely shredded scallions

1. Put the cloud ears in a small bowl with enough cold water to cover for 30 minutes. When softened, drain and discard the water. Remove the hard spots from the cloud ears, cut into bite-sized pieces, and set aside.

2. Trim the lotus root ends. Using a vegetable peeler, peel the lotus root, removing the rootlike strands, and rinse under cold water. Slice the lotus root lengthwise in half. Cut each half into ¼-inch-thick slices to make about 2 cups. Rinse the lotus root again in case there is any mud lodged in it. Drain the slices in a colander and shake out any excess water.

3. Remove the hard rind and thick layer of fat attached to the Chinese bacon and discard. Cut the bacon crosswise into scant ¼-inch-thick slices to make about ½ cup. In a small bowl combine the broth, rice wine, soy sauce, and sesame oil.

4. Heat a 14-inch flat-bottomed wok or 12-inch skillet over high heat until a bead of water vaporizes within 1 to 2 seconds of contact. Swirl in the peanut oil, add the ginger slices, and stir-fry 10 seconds or until the ginger is fragrant. Add the bacon and stir-fry 45 seconds or until it begins to release its fat. Add the lotus root and stir-fry 1 minute or until well combined. Add the snow peas, carrots, and cloud ears and stir-fry 1 minute or until well combined. Swirl the rice wine mixture into the wok, sprinkle on the salt and pepper, and stir-fry 1 to 2 minutes or until the lotus root and snow peas are crisp-tender. Stir in the shredded scallions.

Serves 4 as a vegetable side dish.

The Chinese New Year and the Stir-Fry

Chinese New Year is celebrated for two weeks anytime from mid-January to mid-February (depending on the lunar calendar). Each year is named after one of the twelve Chinese zodiac animals: rat, ox, tiger, hare, dragon, snake, horse, goat, monkey, rooster, dog, and pig. The holiday is steeped in tradition and superstitions, and families decorate the home with peonies, lilies, or cherry blossoms in the hope that the buds will open on New Year's Day, portending growing fortunes. It is a time of positive thinking and any type of argument or negative behavior is regarded as bad luck. The classic table centerpiece is composed of pomelos, oranges, and tangerines, preferably with stems and fresh green leaves intact, and decorated with *lai see*, the red packet of lucky money. Throughout the celebration family and friends greet each other with *gung hay fat choy* (in Cantonese) or *gong xi fa cai* (in Mandarin), wishing each other Happy New Year. The literal translation is "Congratulations and Prosperity."

The festivities begin with the New Year's Eve meal, the most sumptuous of the year, symbolizing thanksgiving and family unity. The feast is designed around meaning-laden foods to ensure auspicious blessings for the coming year based on the Chinese belief that "you are what you eat." Some foods are symbolic of good fortune while other foods are homonyms in Chinese for words that mean "good luck" or "prosperity." Typical dishes for a New Year's Eve meal might include salt-baked chicken, because a chicken symbolizes happiness and wealth in addition to signifying a proper beginning and end to the year; steamed sea bass with scallions and ginger, because the word

for fish in Cantonese *yu* is a homonym for "abundance" and portends having a surplus in the coming year; and Stir-Fried Shiitake Mushrooms with Dried Scallops (page 215), which represents prosperity, because mushrooms grow quickly. There are numerous recipes in this collection appropriate for a New Year's Eve celebration. If you choose to serve a stir-fry, be sure to feature one or more of the following ingredients:

Ingredient	Symbolism/Homonym
shrimp	happiness and laughter
eggs	fertility
mushrooms	growing fortunes
lettuce	prosperity and wealth
chicken	a proper beginning and end
scallions	intelligence
clams and scallops	prosperity
noodles	longevity
lobster	auspicious symbol of the dragon
fish	abundance and surplus
cilantro	compassion
pork	bounty and family unity
five-spice tofu	happiness
oysters	good business
hard liquor	longevity

Stir-Fried Lettuce with Garlic Chili

Stir-fried lettuce is an auspicious dish to serve for Chinese New Year, birthdays, and graduations. The Cantonese word for lettuce, saang choi, *is a homonym for "growing money." In China, lettuce is a popular vegetable to eat in the summer months, enjoyed for its yin, or cooling, attributes. Romaine lettuce is well suited for stir-frying because the quick, intense cooking accentuates its natural sweetness.*

2 tablespoons Shao Hsing rice wine or dry sherry
1 tablespoon chicken broth
2 teaspoons soy sauce
2 tablespoons peanut or vegetable oil
3 medium garlic cloves, smashed
1 teaspoon minced jalapeño chili, with seeds
1 medium head of romaine, cut crosswise into
    1-inch-wide pieces (about 1 pound)
½ teaspoon salt
⅛ teaspoon ground white pepper

1. In a small bowl combine the rice wine, broth, and soy sauce.

2. Heat a 14-inch flat-bottomed wok or 12-inch skillet over high heat until a bead of water vaporizes within 1 to 2 seconds of contact. Swirl in the oil, add the garlic and chili, and stir-fry 10 seconds or until the garlic is fragrant. Add the lettuce, sprinkle on the salt and pepper, and stir-fry 1 minute or until the lettuce begins to wilt. Swirl the rice wine mixture into the wok, cover, and cook 15 seconds. Uncover and stir-fry 30 seconds to 1 minute or until the lettuce is crisp-tender and bright green.

Serves 4 as a vegetable side dish.

Stir-Fried *Yau Choi* with Oyster Sauce

When George Chew (see Stir-Frying in Brooklyn's Great Outdoors, page 281) stir-fries yau choi *(also known as* choi sum*) he's able to cook twice the amount called for in this recipe because of the power of his Wolf range. For cooks using stoves with average power, no more than 12 ounces should be cooked. Check the width of the stalks about 1 inch from the bottom: if they are ½ inch or more in diameter, cut the stalks in half lengthwise. If you don't halve the thicker stalks, once the delicate leaves are cooked the stalks will still be raw. George trims the bottom of the* yau choi *stalks before washing and then dries the vegetables in a salad spinner.*

I've tried stir-frying yau choi *in a skillet, but the wok is preferable because its deeper bowl shape makes it easier to stir-fry bulky vegetables. This combination of oyster sauce and fish sauce is also delicious with other greens such as Chinese broccoli and bok choy. If the vegetable seems dry in the wok, George swirls in 1 to 2 tablespoons of white wine or sake.*

12 ounces *yau choi* (about 9 stalks)
2 teaspoons oyster sauce
1 teaspoon fish sauce
2 tablespoons peanut or vegetable oil
2 teaspoons minced garlic
⅛ teaspoon ground white pepper

1. Trim ¼ inch from the stem end of each *yau choi* stalk. Cut the stalks in half lengthwise if ½-inch or more in diameter. In a small bowl combine the oyster sauce and fish sauce.

2. Heat a 14-inch flat-bottomed wok over high heat until a bead of water vaporizes within 1 to 2 seconds of contact. Swirl in the oil, add the garlic, and stir-fry 10 seconds or until the garlic is fragrant. Add the *yau choi* and stir-fry 30 seconds or until the pieces are lightly coated in the oil. Sprinkle on the pepper and stir-fry 1 minute or until the leaves are just limp and the *yau choi* is bright green. Add the oyster sauce mixture to the wok and stir-fry 30 seconds to 1 minute or until the *yau choi* is just crisp-tender.

Serves 4 as a vegetable side dish.

Stir-Fried Napa Cabbage with Prosciutto

Napa cabbage's mild flavor is enriched here by the addition of ham and a little chicken broth. Typically Chinese cooks in America use Smithfield country ham, which is similar in taste to a famous ham from Yunnan, China. However, country ham requires a lot of work, because it must first be soaked in water to remove excess salt before cooking. My mother prefers using domestic prosciutto. The flavor is more delicate and there is no need to soak it. Just make sure when you add the prosciutto to incorporate it well with the cabbage so that it doesn't clump in one spot.

1 small head Napa cabbage (about 1 pound)
3 tablespoons chicken broth
2 tablespoons Shao Hsing rice wine or dry sherry
½ teaspoon cornstarch
2 tablespoons peanut or vegetable oil
2 teaspoons minced ginger
½ teaspoon salt
¼ teaspoon sugar
1 ounce prosciutto, julienned (about ⅓ cup)

1. Quarter the cabbage lengthwise, cutting out and discarding the hard core from each quarter. Then cut each quarter crosswise at 1-inch intervals to make about 8 cups. In a small bowl combine the broth, rice wine, and cornstarch.

2. Heat a 14-inch flat-bottomed wok or 12-inch skillet over high heat until a bead of water vaporizes within 1 to 2 seconds of contact. Swirl in the oil, add the ginger, and stir-fry 10 seconds or until the ginger is fragrant. Add the cabbage, sprinkle on the salt and sugar, and stir-fry 1 minute or until the leaves begin to wilt. Restir the broth mixture and swirl it into the wok. Stir-fry 15 seconds or until just combined. Cover and cook on high heat 30 seconds. Uncover and stir-fry 1 to 2 minutes or until the cabbage is crisp-tender. Stir in the prosciutto, making sure it is evenly distributed.

Serves 4 as a vegetable side dish.

Stir-Fried Bean Sprouts with Chili Bean Sauce

Bean sprouts are extremely delicate and perishable. I like to purchase them in Asian markets or specialty tofu shops that sell them in open bins so I can check to make sure they are plump, with "horns" that are yellow, not brown. If possible, avoid buying the bean sprouts that are sold in sealed plastic bags; the plastic seems to suffocate them, making them deteriorate faster. I cook bean sprouts the day of purchase and keep them refrigerated until cooking time. I pick through the sprouts and remove any brown or limp pieces. Stir-frying is the best method for preparing bean sprouts: the quick toss in a hot wok accentuates their crunchy texture.

1 tablespoon Shao Hsing rice wine or dry sherry

2 teaspoons chili bean sauce

1 teaspoon soy sauce

2 tablespoons peanut or vegetable oil

2 teaspoons minced garlic

6 cups bean sprouts, rinsed and patted dry, (about 12 ounces)

½ cup julienned carrots

½ cup finely shredded scallions

¾ teaspoon salt

1. In a small bowl combine the rice wine, chili bean sauce, and soy sauce.

2. Heat a 14-inch flat-bottomed wok or 12-inch skillet over high heat until a bead of water vaporizes within 1 to 2 seconds of contact. Swirl in the oil, add the garlic, and stir-fry 10 seconds or until the garlic is fragrant. Add the bean sprouts and carrots and stir-fry 1 minute or until the sprouts are just limp. Add the scallions and sprinkle on the salt. Restir the sauce, swirl it into the wok, and stir-fry 30 seconds to 1 minute or until the sprouts are just crisp-tender.

Serves 4 as a vegetable side dish.

The Simple Stir-Fry

While the exact translation of *siu chau* is "small stir-fry," its true meaning is "simple" or "home-style" stir-fry. Never found in a banquet meal or a formal cooking institution, a *siu chau* requires ingredients and seasonings to be added one by one to the hot wok, and then they are stir-fried over a hot flame. There are no fancy advance preparations such as velveting, oil-blanching ingredients, or cooking different components separately before combining them in the wok. The Chinese Cuisine Training Institute in Hong Kong does not consider *siu chau* to be a cooking method, but, rather, a type of dish, like dim sum or barbecued foods.

Chef Chow Chung of Chow Chung Restaurant in Hong Kong explains that the Cantonese *siu chau* varies slightly from village to village and is the specialty of home cooks. Many Cantonese claim this elemental dish as their own, although, in fact, it is made throughout China and Southeast Asia, where small inexpensive eateries, most notably outdoor food stalls or hawker stands, specialize in *siu chau* dishes. "These cooks are stir-frying like home cooks without fancy stoves," says Chef Yong Soon of Toronto, Canada. Without the luxury of a real kitchen, most are typically using only a single wok set over a crude metal drum fueled with coal, or a wok stove. The *siu chau* is thus the easiest and most practical stir-fry for cooks to execute. Many people regard a *siu chau* as "fast food" because the stir-fry time is so short. The Cantonese take such pride in their execution of the dish that *siu chau* often appears as its own category on Cantonese restaurant menus.

The mastery comes from the freshness of the ingredients and the cook's exact timing and control of the heat. Unsurprisingly, Cantonese connoisseurs judge a *siu chau* by its *wok hay*—the breath of a wok—and its *heung hui*, or fragrance. This classic stir-fry is heralded for its range of textures, tastes, aromas, and the intensity of wok heat seared into the food.

One popular example of a *siu chau* is stir-fried lotus root (page 193), or *leen ngao siu chau*, in which aromatic slices of ginger are stir-fried in a wok with a little oil until fragrant. Thinly sliced Chinese bacon is then added and cooked quickly until the fat is just rendered. Next, delicate half-moon slices of lotus root are stir-fried briefly, before snow peas, sliced carrots, and cloud ears are added and stir-fried another minute. Then a mixture of broth, rice wine, soy sauce, and sesame oil is splashed into the wok with salt and pepper and fine shreds of scallions added last. The contrasting textures of the crisp lotus root, carrots, and snow peas, all with different levels of sweetness, combine with the earthy hints of bacon to make this a revered stir-fry classic.

Stir-Fried Garlic Spinach

This is a classic example of a clear stir-fry, or ching chau *(see Stir-Fry Purist's Dish, page 217). I recommend using only a wok to stir-fry spinach. Twelve ounces of spinach (16 cups) is too much to stir-fry in a skillet without spilling. A wok, on the other hand, with its deep bowl, makes stir-frying such an amount much easier.*

This dish is especially good when made with young spinach, when the stems are still pink, and the leaves are tender. Lettuce, more exotic greens like amaranth, and snow pea shoots can also be stir-fried in this style. When stir-frying such a large amount of greens as this, it's important to sprinkle on the salt and sugar to distribute them throughout; you don't want them to land on just one part of the greens.

2 tablespoons peanut or vegetable oil
3 medium garlic cloves, smashed
1 bunch spinach, ends trimmed (12 ounces,
    about 16 cups)
½ teaspoon salt
⅛ teaspoon sugar

Heat a 14-inch flat-bottomed wok over high heat until a bead of water vaporizes within 1 to 2 seconds of contact. Swirl in the oil, add the garlic, and stir-fry 10 seconds or until the garlic is fragrant. Add the spinach and stir-fry 30 seconds or until the spinach just begins to wilt. Sprinkle on the salt and sugar and stir-fry 1 minute or until the spinach is just wilted but still bright green.

Serves 4 as a vegetable side dish.

Stir-Fried Tofu with Pickled Ginger

When I'm in the mood for a light vegetarian dish I stir-fry tofu. Combined with pickled and fresh ginger, seasoned with rice wine and soy sauce, the tofu becomes infused with rich, pungent flavors. Before chopping the pickled ginger, pat it dry with paper towels to remove excess moisture so that it doesn't spatter when stir-fried. Do not be concerned if the tofu breaks up a little as you stir-fry it. In summer, this is a yin dish to cool the body of excess heat, best served warm or at room temperature.

One 14-ounce package firm tofu, rinsed
2 tablespoons Shao Hsing rice wine or dry sherry
1 tablespoon soy sauce
1½ teaspoons plus 1 tablespoon peanut
   or vegetable oil
2 teaspoons minced ginger
½ cup ¼-inch diced carrots
2 tablespoons chopped pickled ginger
⅓ cup chopped scallions
¼ teaspoon salt
⅛ teaspoon ground white pepper

1. Cut the tofu into roughly 1-inch cubes. Pat the tofu dry with paper towels. In a small bowl combine the rice wine and soy sauce.

2. Heat a 14-inch flat-bottomed wok or 12-inch skillet over high heat until a bead of water vaporizes within 1 to 2 seconds of contact. Swirl in 1½ teaspoons of the oil, add the tofu, and spread it evenly in the wok. Cook undisturbed 1 minute, letting the tofu begin to brown. Then, using a metal spatula, stir-fry 1 minute or until the tofu is a little brown but is not cooked through. Transfer the tofu to a plate.

3. Swirl in the remaining 1 tablespoon oil, add the fresh ginger and carrots, and stir-fry 30 seconds or until well combined. Add the pickled ginger, scallions, and tofu and stir-fry 30 seconds or until well combined. Swirl the sauce mixture into the wok, sprinkle on the salt and pepper, and stir-fry 1 to 2 minutes or until the carrots are crisp-tender.

Serves 2 as a main course with rice or 4 as part of a multicourse meal.

Hakka-Style Stir-Fried Cabbage and Egg

Growing up in Indonesia, Fah Liong (see Lessons from a Simple Stir-Fry, page 144) fondly remembers her mother serving this simple Hakka-style vegetable stir-fry with rice for family dinners. Do not overcook the cabbage; it should still have a little crunch. If you're just learning to stir-fry, I suggest cracking the egg in a bowl ahead of time, which saves having to waste seconds reaching for the egg and cracking it over a hot wok, making the stir-fry action more fluid.

1 small head Napa cabbage (about 1 pound)
2 tablespoons peanut or vegetable oil
2 tablespoons chopped garlic
¾ teaspoon salt
⅛ teaspoon ground white pepper
1 large egg

1. Quarter the cabbage lengthwise, cutting out and discarding the hard core from each quarter. Then cut crosswise into ½-inch-wide pieces to make about 8 cups.

2. Heat a 14-inch flat-bottomed wok or 12-inch skillet over high heat until a bead of water vaporizes within 1 to 2 seconds of contact. Swirl in the oil, add the garlic, and stir-fry 20 seconds or until the garlic is fragrant and just begins to brown. Add the cabbage and stir-fry 1 to 2 minutes or until the leaves just begin to wilt. Cover and cook on high heat 30 seconds or until the leaves have just wilted. Uncover, sprinkle on the salt and pepper, and stir-fry 30 seconds or until well combined. Crack the egg into the center of the vegetables and stir-fry about 30 seconds or until the egg is just cooked and flecked throughout the mixture and the cabbage is crisp-tender. Do not overcook.

Serves 4 as a vegetable side dish.

Stir-Fried Vegetarian Five-Spice Tofu

This dish is a classic siu chau, *or simple stir-fry (see The Simple Stir-Fry, page 201), characterized by its many ingredients and seasonings added to the wok without any precooking. Having to cut all the vegetables may strike you as rather labor intensive, but it's no more work than making a salad. The fresh water chestnuts add sweetness and a distinct, fresh crisp texture. (For instructions on peeling them see page 187.) If you cannot find fresh ones, do not use the canned variety, which are an inferior substitute. Instead, try peeled jicama, or a peeled, unripe Asian or Bosc pear, all of which have a similar crunchy texture and sweetness.*

Five-spice tofu is sold in Asian markets in small squares. You can also substitute with 1 square, about 4 ounces, of firm tofu. Unlike five-spice tofu you must pat it dry with paper towels after cutting into julienne pieces. (See photo, page 182.)

1 tablespoon soy sauce

1 tablespoon Shao Hsing rice wine or dry sherry

2 teaspoons sesame oil

2 tablespoons peanut or vegetable oil

1 cup julienned five-spice or firm tofu (1 square)

1 tablespoon minced garlic

1 cup julienned carrots

1 cup julienned red bell peppers

1 cup julienned yellow bell peppers

1 cup thinly sliced fresh shiitake mushrooms

½ teaspoon salt

¼ teaspoon ground white pepper

¼ teaspoon sugar

4 fresh water chestnuts, peeled and thinly sliced (about ½ cup)

⅓ cup thinly sliced scallions

¼ cup chopped pickled ginger

¼ cup cilantro sprigs

1. In a small bowl combine the soy sauce, rice wine, and sesame oil.

2. Heat a 14-inch flat-bottomed wok or 12-inch skillet over high heat until a bead of water vaporizes within 1 to 2 seconds of contact. Swirl in 1 tablespoon of the peanut oil, carefully add the tofu, reduce the heat to medium, then, using a metal spatula, stir-fry 1 minute, or until it begins to brown. Add the garlic and stir-fry 10 seconds or until the garlic is fragrant.

3. Swirl in the remaining 1 tablespoon peanut oil, add the carrots, red and yellow bell peppers, and mushrooms, increase the heat to high, and stir-fry 1 minute or until the vegetables begin to wilt. Sprinkle on the salt, pepper, and sugar. Swirl the soy sauce mixture into the wok, add the water chestnuts, scallions, and pickled ginger, and stir-fry 1 to 2 minutes or until the vegetables are crisp-tender. Stir in the cilantro sprigs.

Serves 2 as a main course with rice or 4 as a vegetable side dish.

Yin Yang Beans

Firmer vegetables like asparagus, carrots, and green beans sometimes are blanched to partially cook them before stir-frying. It is very important that blanched vegetables be well drained. Any water on the vegetables will turn a stir-fry into a braise. I devised this recipe when I was in the mood for Dry-Fried Sichuan Beans (page 233) but didn't have the Sichuan preserved vegetable. This has a similar complement of salty, tangy, and spicy flavors and is more convenient to make.

¾ teaspoon salt

1 pound green beans, ends trimmed (about 6 cups)

1 tablespoon soy sauce

1 tablespoon Shao Hsing rice wine or dry sherry

1 tablespoon peanut or vegetable oil

1 tablespoon minced garlic

1 tablespoon minced ginger

¼ teaspoon red pepper flakes

2 tablespoons ground pork (about 1 ounce)

1 tablespoon minced pickled ginger

¼ cup chopped scallions

1. In a 3-quart saucepan bring 1½ quarts water and ½ teaspoon of the salt to a boil over high heat. Add the beans and cook 1 minute or until they are bright green and the water almost returns to a boil. Drain the beans in a colander, shaking well to remove all excess water. In a small bowl combine the soy sauce and rice wine.

2. Heat a 14-inch flat-bottomed wok or 12-inch skillet over high heat until a bead of water vaporizes within 1 to 2 seconds of contact. Swirl in the oil, add the garlic, fresh ginger, and red pepper flakes and stir-fry 10 seconds or until the aromatics are fragrant. Add the pork, and using a metal spatula, break up the pork, and stir-fry 30 seconds to 1 minute or until the pork is no longer pink. Add the beans, pickled ginger, and scallions and sprinkle on the remaining ¼ teaspoon salt. Swirl the soy sauce mixture into the wok and stir-fry 1 minute or until the pork is cooked through and the beans are crisp-tender.

Serves 4 as a vegetable side dish.

Stir-Fried Sugar Snap Peas with Shiitake Mushrooms

Young sugar snaps are perfect for stir-frying because the quick cooking accentuates their natural sweetness and crisp delicacy. They are best in the late spring when they first come into season and the pods are about 3 inches in length. Later into the summer they become tough and more fibrous. You can substitute sliced button or cremini mushrooms for the shiitakes.

¼ cup plus 1 tablespoon chicken broth

1 tablespoon Shao Hsing rice wine or dry sherry

2 teaspoons soy sauce

3 tablespoons peanut or vegetable oil

1 tablespoon minced ginger

8 medium fresh shiitake mushrooms, stems removed and caps quartered (about 4 ounces)

8 ounces sugar snap peas, strings removed (about 2½ cups)

½ teaspoon salt

1. In a small bowl combine ¼ cup of the broth, rice wine, and soy sauce.

2. Heat a 14-inch flat-bottomed wok or 12-inch skillet over high heat until a bead of water vaporizes within 1 to 2 seconds of contact. Swirl in 2 tablespoons of the oil, add the ginger, and stir-fry 10 seconds or until the ginger is fragrant. Add the mushrooms and stir-fry 30 seconds or until they have absorbed all the oil. Swirl the broth mixture into the wok, cover, and cook 30 seconds to 1 minute or until about only 1 tablespoon of broth remains. Swirl in the remaining 1 tablespoon oil, add the sugar snaps, sprinkle on the salt, and stir-fry 1 minute or until the sugar snaps are bright green. Swirl the remaining 1 tablespoon broth into the wok and stir-fry 30 seconds to 1 minute or until the sugar snaps are just crisp-tender.

Serves 4 as a vegetable side dish.

Stir-Fried Aromatic Potatoes

There are some cooks who insist that potatoes should be soaked in cold water or be rinsed to remove excess starch before cooking. If you soak or rinse the potatoes, be sure to dry them thoroughly with paper towels. The potatoes should be stir-fried until they are crisp-tender and still have a slight al dente crunch. If overcooked, they will be mushy and likely to fall apart. I hand-cut the potatoes, but you can also use a mandoline so that you get nice long strands a little bigger than bean sprouts. I prefer using a wok for this stir-fry; the potatoes tend to stick in a skillet and you will need more oil.

2 large new potatoes, peeled (about 1 pound)
2 tablespoons peanut or vegetable oil
1 tablespoon minced garlic
1 tablespoon finely shredded ginger
½ cup finely shredded scallions
1 teaspoon rice vinegar
¾ teaspoon salt
⅛ teaspoon ground white pepper

1. Cut the peeled potatoes into matchsticks, about a scant ¼ inch thick and 2 inches long, to make about 3½ cups.

2. Heat a 14-inch flat-bottomed wok over high heat until a bead of water vaporizes within 1 to 2 seconds of contact. Swirl in the oil, add the garlic and ginger, then, using a metal spatula, stir-fry 10 seconds or until the aromatics are fragrant. Add the potatoes and stir-fry 2 minutes or until the potatoes are light golden and just beginning to wilt. Reduce the heat to medium and continue to stir-fry 2 to 3 minutes or until the potatoes are crisp-tender but not raw. Do not overcook. Add the scallions and vinegar, sprinkle on the salt and pepper, and stir-fry 1 minute or until the scallions are just wilted.

Serves 4 as a vegetable side dish.

Stir-Fried Water Spinach with Fermented Bean Curd

Water spinach is a wonderful vegetable to enjoy during the late spring and throughout the summer. It bears no resemblance to regular spinach. Two-thirds of a stalk of water spinach is a hollow reedlike stem. I prefer water spinach with stems no wider than ¼ inch; bigger stems are tougher and more fibrous. Water spinach is extremely perishable so I try to use it within the first day of purchase; otherwise the leaves will begin to wilt quickly. If you have to hold it for a day or two in the refrigerator, trim about ¼ inch from the base of the stems and wrap the stems in wet paper towels. Cover in plastic and place in the vegetable crisper bin.

I recommend stir-frying water spinach only in a wok. Twelve ounces of water spinach is the equivalent of about 16 cups—an impossible amount to move in a skillet without the ingredients falling out. As soon as you add the water spinach to the wok, begin to stir-fry by digging the spatula into the spinach, lifting the bottom pieces to the top. If your wok is stabilized on a wok ring or you have someone to hold the wok handle securely for you, I suggest stir-frying the spinach with two spatulas so that you're tossing the vegetable as you would a salad. Within 2 minutes of stir-frying, the 16 cups cooks down to about 3 cups.

12 ounces water spinach

2 cubes wet bean curd with chili (about 1 tablespoon)

1 tablespoon Shao Hsing rice wine or dry sherry

2 tablespoons peanut or vegetable oil

1 tablespoon roughly chopped garlic

¼ teaspoon salt

⅛ teaspoon sugar

1. Break off about 2 inches from the bottom of each water spinach stem and discard. Remove any wilted leaves. Break each stem by hand into 4-inch pieces, rinse in several changes of cold water, and drain thoroughly in a colander or salad spinner until dry to the touch. You should have about 16 loosely packed cups. In a small dish stir the wet bean curd and rice wine until almost smooth.

2. Heat a 14-inch flat-bottomed wok over high heat until a bead of water vaporizes within 1 to 2 seconds of contact. Swirl in the oil, add the garlic, and stir-fry 10 seconds or until the garlic is fragrant. Add the water spinach and stir-fry 1 minute or until the spinach just begins to wilt. Add the bean curd mixture, sprinkle on the salt and sugar, and stir-fry 1 minute or until the spinach is just wilted but still bright green.

Serves 4 as a vegetable side dish.

Spicy Long Beans with Sausage and Mushrooms

Long beans are sold only in Asian markets. There are two varieties: one is dark green and the other pale green. The darker colored long bean is preferable for stir-frying because it has a crunchier texture. This dish is all about texture and flavor; the salty, sweet, and peppery accents complement the contrasting textures. It is delicious served piping hot, warm, or even at room temperature.

8 medium dried shiitake mushrooms

1 bunch Chinese long beans (about 12 ounces)

2 ounces Sichuan preserved vegetable (about ¼ cup)

1 tablespoon soy sauce

1 tablespoon Shao Hsing rice wine or dry sherry

1 teaspoon sesame oil

2 tablespoons peanut or vegetable oil

¼ cup ground pork (about 2 ounces)

1 Chinese sausage, diced into ¼-inch pieces

⅓ cup thinly sliced scallions

¼ cup cilantro sprigs

½ teaspoon salt

½ teaspoon sugar

¼ teaspoon ground white pepper

1. In a medium shallow bowl soak the mushrooms in ¾ cup cold water for 30 minutes or until softened. Drain and squeeze dry, reserving 2 tablespoons of the soaking liquid. Cut off the stems and mince the mushrooms.

2. Trim ¼ inch from the ends of the long beans. Cut the long beans into ¼-inch-long pieces to make about 3 cups.

3. Rinse the preserved vegetable in cold water until the red chili paste coating is removed and pat dry. Finely chop to make about ¼ cup. In a small bowl combine the soy sauce, rice wine, and sesame oil.

4. Heat a 14-inch flat-bottomed wok or 12-inch skillet over high heat until a bead of water vaporizes within 1 to 2 seconds of contact. Swirl in 1 tablespoon of the peanut oil, add the pork and sausage. Using a metal spatula, break up the pork, and stir-fry 1 minute or until the pork is no longer pink. Add the mushrooms and stir-fry 1 minute. Swirl in the remaining 1 tablespoon peanut oil, add the beans, and stir-fry 1 minute. Swirl in the 2 tablespoons reserved mushroom liquid. Cover and cook 30 seconds. Uncover and add the preserved vegetable, scallions, and cilantro. Swirl the soy sauce mixture into the wok. Sprinkle on the salt, sugar, and pepper, and stir-fry 1 to 2 minutes or until the pork and sausage are cooked and the vegetables are crisp-tender.

Serves 4 as a vegetable side dish.

Stir-Fried Cauliflower with Rice Wine

The easiest way to handle cauliflower is to first remove the tough outer leaves, then hollow out the inner core. Once the core has been removed, the head can be separated into individual florets. Large florets should be cut in half or quartered so that all the pieces will cook in the same amount of time. Without blanching, florets can sometimes remain raw in the middle even after stir-frying.

1 teaspoon salt
12 ounces cauliflower, cut into bite-sized florets
   (about 4 cups)
1 tablespoon Shao Hsing rice wine or dry sherry
1 tablespoon rice vinegar
1 tablespoon peanut or vegetable oil
3 slices ginger, smashed

1. In a 2-quart saucepan bring 1 quart water to a boil over high heat. Add ½ teaspoon of the salt and the cauliflower and cook, stirring, 1 minute or until the cauliflower has changed color and the water has almost returned to a boil. Drain the cauliflower in a colander, shaking well to remove excess water. In a small bowl combine the rice wine and vinegar.

2. Heat a 14-inch flat-bottomed wok or 12-inch skillet over high heat until a bead of water vaporizes within 1 to 2 seconds of contact. Swirl in the oil, add the ginger slices, and stir-fry 10 seconds or until the ginger is fragrant. Add the blanched cauliflower, swirl in the rice wine mixture, sprinkle on the remaining ½ teaspoon salt, and stir-fry 1 to 2 minutes or until the cauliflower begins to brown a little and is crisp-tender.

Serves 4 as a vegetable side dish.

Stir-Fried Shiitake Mushrooms with Dried Scallops

This is an intensely flavorful vegetable dish and a specialty of George Chew (see Stir-Frying in Brooklyn's Great Outdoors, page 281). Chinese dried scallops are a delicacy reserved for special occasions, and they are especially delicious in combination with fresh shiitake mushrooms. The scallops are expensive, but well worth it for their rich flavor. Do not ruin this dish by using canned chicken broth—homemade broth is a must.

4 dried scallops (about 1 ounce)
1 pound fresh shiitake mushrooms
½ cup Homemade Chicken Broth (page 284)
2 teaspoons oyster sauce
1 teaspoon soy sauce
3 tablespoons peanut or vegetable oil
3 tablespoons minced shallots
¼ teaspoon ground white pepper

1. In a small bowl soak the dried scallops in ⅓ cup cold water, occasionally turning the scallops over, about 1 hour or until softened. Drain, reserving the liquid. There should be about ¼ cup. Remove the small hard muscle from the side of the scallops. Finely shred the scallops by hand to make about a scant ½ cup.

2. Trim the tough mushroom stems. Cut the mushrooms in half to measure about 8 cups. In a small bowl combine the broth, oyster sauce, soy sauce, and the reserved scallop liquid.

3. Heat a 14-inch flat-bottomed wok or 12-inch skillet over high heat until a bead of water vaporizes within 1 to 2 seconds of contact. Swirl in the oil, add the shallots, and stir-fry 1 minute or until the shallots begin to brown. Add the mushrooms, sprinkle on the pepper, and stir-fry 1 minute or until the mushrooms have absorbed all the oil. Swirl in the broth mixture, add the scallops, and stir-fry 10 seconds to combine. Cover, reduce the heat to low, and simmer 5 minutes or until the mushrooms are firm but tender and have absorbed all but a few tablespoons of the liquid.

Serves 4 as a vegetable side dish.

Stir-Fried Ginger Broccoli

This is a great vegetable side dish that goes equally well with a Chinese menu or with roast chicken. Broccoli is a "hard" vegetable that benefits from a quick blanching before stir-frying. Without the blanching, broccoli requires longer stir-frying, which in turn means using more oil. Just make sure all the florets are the same size, even if you have to halve or quarter larger florets. Sometimes I mix in the broccoli stems, sliced ¼ inch thick.

¾ teaspoon salt
12 ounces small broccoli florets (about 6 cups)
1 tablespoon soy sauce
2 teaspoons ginger juice (see page 43)
2 tablespoons peanut or vegetable oil
3 slices ginger, smashed
¼ teaspoon sugar

1. In a 3-quart saucepan bring 1½ quarts of water to a boil over high heat. Add ½ teaspoon of the salt and the broccoli and cook, stirring the broccoli, 1 minute or until the broccoli is bright green and the water has almost returned to a boil. Drain the broccoli in a colander, shaking well to remove excess water. In a small bowl combine the soy sauce and ginger juice.

2. Heat a 14-inch flat-bottomed wok or 12-inch skillet over high heat until a bead of water vaporizes within 1 to 2 seconds of contact. Swirl in the oil, add the ginger slices, and stir-fry 10 seconds or until the ginger is fragrant. Add the broccoli, swirl the ginger juice mixture into the wok, sprinkle on the sugar and the remaining ¼ teaspoon salt, and stir-fry 1 minute or until the broccoli is just crisp-tender.

Serves 4 as a vegetable side dish.

Stir-Fry Purist's Dish: Clear Stir-Fry

Ching chau, or "clear stir-fry," generally refers to the stir-frying of a solitary ingredient so that its individual character is maintained. The Chinese Cuisine Training Institute in Hong Kong describes *ching chau* as a pure stir-fry because "no additional ingredients are added." According to Chinese food authority Fuchsia Dunlop, a *ching chau* is "a 'clear stir-fry' or 'distinct stir-fry,' taking the sense of *ching* as 'clear, unmixed, distinct.'"

Although the *ching chau* method can be rendered to seafood, meats, and poultry, it is in its full glory when applied to vegetables. The *ching chau* technique is valued for the use of minimal seasonings, which allows the concentrated essence of a vegetable, prepared when it is in season, to achieve its peak flavor. With focus strictly on the vegetable, its quality must be superior. The vegetable is basically stir-fried in oil and then seasoned simply with salt. Occasionally, the oil in a *ching chau* is flavored with an aromatic, such as ginger, followed by the addition of bok choy or garlic and spinach (page 202). The vegetable is then lightly seasoned with salt and possibly a dash of sugar. In rare instances a *ching chau* can consist of two vegetables, such as bean sprouts and yellow chives being stir-fried together.

If fried rice is the first stir-fry dish (see Fried Rice: The Stir-Fry for Rookies, page 257) a young cook learns to make, a vegetable prepared in the *ching chau* style represents the next level of stir-fry proficiency. Vegetables, while easy to stir-fry, are more complicated because the timing requires precise attention. Every vegetable has its own cooking time and, if stir-fried a minute too long, its color, texture, and vibrancy of flavor diminish. When stir-fried, vegetables, unlike rice which absorbs excess oil, will also spatter, especially if not properly dried after washing or rinsing.

A *ching chau* typically involves no addition of liquid beyond a possible sprinkling of water or broth. One variation is the use of rice wine when stir-frying Chinese broccoli or snow pea shoots. The wine is swirled in after a minute or two of stir-frying to contribute aroma and to heighten the flavor. No starch thickening is ever permitted. And if a condiment such as soy sauce, oyster sauce, or fermented bean curd is added, the dish is no longer classified as *ching chau*. It is the pure essence and spirit of the vegetable that is the hallmark of vegetables stir-fried in the *ching chau* style.

Summer Pepper Corn

From July through September the farmers' markets in New York City have the best corn and bell peppers. I associate this stir-fry with the taste of summer, when peppers and corn are at their peak and a minimal amount of seasonings is all that is needed to enhance the natural flavors of the vegetables. When I'm being lazy I use the red pepper flakes to add a little heat, but this is even better with about a teaspoon of freshly minced jalapeño. To make it hotter still, add the seeds.

1 tablespoon peanut or vegetable oil

2 slices ginger, smashed

2 medium garlic cloves, smashed

1 teaspoon minced jalapeño chili, without the
    seeds, or ¼ teaspoon red pepper flakes

2 medium red bell peppers, cut into ½-inch dice
    (about 2½ cups)

2 medium ears corn, kernels scraped off (about
    1½ cups)

½ teaspoon salt

¼ teaspoon sugar

Heat a 14-inch flat-bottomed wok or 12-inch skillet over high heat until a bead of water vaporizes within 1 to 2 seconds of contact. Swirl in the oil, add the ginger, garlic, and chili, and stir-fry 10 seconds or until the aromatics are fragrant. Add the bell peppers and corn, sprinkle on the salt and sugar, and stir-fry 2 to 3 minutes or until the bell peppers and corn are crisp-tender.

Serves 4 as a vegetable side dish.

Stir-Fried Garlic Shanghai Bok Choy

Shanghai bok choy has spoonlike stems, an overall pale jade green color, and a delicate, sweet flavor. The smallest heads are 4 to 5 inches long and the slightly more mature ones 7 to 8 inches. If it is not available, regular bok choy can be substituted, but it will be much tougher and more fibrous and will require longer cooking.

12 ounces Shanghai bok choy
¼ cup chicken broth or vegetable broth
1 tablespoon Shao Hsing rice wine or dry sherry
2 teaspoons soy sauce
¼ teaspoon cornstarch
1 tablespoon peanut or vegetable oil
3 medium garlic cloves, smashed
¼ teaspoon salt
¼ teaspoon sugar

1. Trim ¼ inch from the bottom of each head. Separate the bok choy into stalks. Cut the stalks and leaves into 2-inch-long pieces. You should have about 8 cups. In a small bowl combine the broth, rice wine, soy sauce, and cornstarch.

2. Heat a 14-inch flat-bottomed wok or 12-inch skillet over high heat until a bead of water vaporizes within 1 to 2 seconds of contact. Swirl in the oil, add the garlic, and stir-fry 10 seconds or until the garlic is fragrant. Add the bok choy, sprinkle on the salt and sugar, and stir-fry 1 minute or until the leaves begin to wilt and just turn bright green. Restir the broth mixture and swirl it into the wok. Stir-fry 1 minute or until the bok choy is just crisp-tender.

Serves 4 as a vegetable side dish.

Wok-Seared Vegetables

This recipe is a template for how to stir-fry vegetables with hard, medium-hard, and soft textures. "Hard" carrots are cut into ¼-inch-thick julienne pieces so that they cook quickly. Blanching the "medium-hard" asparagus enables it to be stir-fried together with the shiitake mushrooms and "soft" cherry tomatoes. This is a dish I like to make in the spring when asparagus comes into season. I prefer using grape tomatoes because they have more flavor than regular tomatoes that time of the year. You can substitute button mushrooms for the shiitakes.

12 ounces medium asparagus, trimmed and cut
    into 2-inch pieces (about 2 cups)

3 tablespoons Shao Hsing rice wine or dry sherry

1 tablespoon soy sauce

1 tablespoon rice vinegar

2 tablespoons peanut or vegetable oil

1 shallot, thinly sliced (about ¼ cup)

1 tablespoon minced ginger

1 tablespoon minced garlic

1 cup julienned carrots

8 medium fresh shiitake mushrooms, stems
    removed and caps quartered (about 4 ounces)

1 cup grape or cherry tomatoes, halved

¾ teaspoon sugar

¾ teaspoon salt

1. In a 2-quart saucepan bring 3 cups water to a boil over high heat. Add the asparagus and cook, stirring, 1 minute or until the asparagus is bright green and the water has almost returned to a boil. Drain the asparagus in a colander, shaking well to remove excess water. In a small bowl combine the rice wine, soy sauce, and rice vinegar.

2. Heat a 14-inch flat-bottomed wok or 12-inch skillet over high heat until a bead of water vaporizes within 1 to 2 seconds of contact. Swirl in the oil, add the shallot, ginger, and garlic, and stir-fry 10 seconds or until the aromatics are fragrant. Add the asparagus, carrots, and shiitake mushrooms and stir-fry 1 minute or until the mushrooms begin to wilt. Add the tomatoes, sprinkle on the sugar and salt, swirl the rice wine mixture into the wok, and stir-fry 1 minute or until the vegetables are crisp-tender.

Serves 4 as a vegetable side dish.

Stir-Fried Cilantro with Bean Sprouts and Shrimp

I was immediately intrigued when my friend Chef Yong Soon told me his mother, Potsam Loo, a Hakka home cook from Malaysia, makes a delicious stir-fry deeply infused with the delicate aroma and taste of cilantro. If the cilantro has roots, remove them before cutting the entire bunch, including the stems, into 2-inch pieces. I then put the cilantro in the colander portion of a salad spinner and wash it under cold water before spinning it several times to remove all the excess water. There will be about 5 cups of cilantro after it's been spun. If you desire a subtler cilantro flavor, reduce the amount by half and increase the bean sprouts to 4 cups.

Loo's family's village, Hui Zhou in China, makes a version of this recipe that calls for about ⅓ cup dried shrimp. According to Chef Soon, the villagers like their food pungent and the dried shrimp has a stronger flavor. If using dried shrimp, soak it in about ⅔ cup cold water for 30 minutes or so to soften. Drain and pat dry before adding it as you would the fresh to the stir-fry. You will want to reduce the salt if using dried shrimp.

2 tablespoons peanut or vegetable oil

2 tablespoons chopped garlic

1 teaspoon minced ginger

4 ounces small shrimp, peeled and deveined

3 cups bean sprouts, rinsed and patted dry (about 6 ounces)

½ cup julienned carrots

1 bunch cilantro, cut into 2-inch pieces (about 4 ounces)

¾ teaspoon salt

¼ teaspoon sugar

Heat a 14-inch flat-bottomed wok or 12-inch skillet over high heat until a bead of water vaporizes within 1 to 2 seconds of contact. Swirl in the oil, add the garlic and ginger, and stir-fry 15 seconds or until the garlic begins to brown. Add the shrimp and stir-fry 30 seconds to 1 minute or until the shrimp begin to turn orange but are not cooked through. Add the bean sprouts and stir-fry 5 seconds. Add the carrots and stir-fry 30 seconds or until the bean sprouts just begin to wilt. Sprinkle the cilantro over the entire mixture without stirring it in. Cover and cook on high heat for 20 seconds. Uncover and stir-fry 10 seconds until combined. Sprinkle on the salt and sugar and stir-fry 30 seconds to 1 minute or until the shrimp are just cooked and the cilantro is just wilted.

Serves 4 as a vegetable side dish.

Potsam Loo

Stir-Fried Bok Choy with Pancetta

This recipe is from my friend Pang-Mei Chang's late Aunt Maejeane. She was a great home cook and loved to entertain during the years she worked in Paris. Unable to find the traditional Chinese Yunnan ham, she used pancetta and stir-fried it either with bok choy or Napa cabbage. When the wok is covered after stir-frying, the pancetta flavor penetrates the vegetables. Bok choy that is sold in American supermarkets can be extremely mature and, therefore, very fibrous and tough. I look for bok choy that is no more than 11 inches long, with fresh green leaves.

1 pound bok choy

¼ cup chicken broth

1 tablespoon Shao Hsing rice wine or dry sherry

1 teaspoon soy sauce

¼ teaspoon cornstarch

2½ teaspoons peanut or vegetable oil

1 ounce pancetta, cut into ¼-inch dice (about ¼ cup)

1 tablespoon finely shredded ginger

2 teaspoons minced garlic

½ teaspoon salt

¼ teaspoon sugar

1. Trim ¼ inch from the bottom of each head. Separate the bok choy into stalks. Cut the stalks and leaves into 1-inch pieces to make about 8 cups. In a small bowl combine the broth, rice wine, soy sauce, and cornstarch.

2. Heat a 14-inch flat-bottomed wok or 12-inch skillet over high heat until a bead of water vaporizes within 1 to 2 seconds of contact. Swirl in ½ teaspoon of the oil, add the pancetta, reduce the heat to low, and stir-fry 1 minute or until the pancetta begins to brown and releases its fat. Swirl in the remaining 2 teaspoons oil, add the ginger and garlic, increase the heat to high, and stir-fry 10 seconds or until the ginger and garlic are fragrant. Add the bok choy, sprinkle on the salt and sugar, and stir-fry 1 minute or until the leaves are just beginning to wilt. Restir the broth mixture and swirl it into the wok. Cover and cook 1 minute. Uncover and stir-fry a few seconds. Cover and cook 1 minute or until the bok choy stems are just crisp-tender and the sauce lightly coats the bok choy.

Serves 4 as a vegetable side dish.

Shanghainese-Style Stir-Fried Fava Beans

I had never heard of stir-frying mashed beans until Florence Lin (see Stir-Frying in Old China, page 235) taught me this recipe. Lin says this dish is regarded by the Chinese as one that is good for the old or the young as it's easy to digest. The beans have the consistency of mashed potatoes. It is an unusual stir-fry because the mixture is one big mass that clings to the spatula.

Fresh fava beans in the pod come into season in the spring. They are time-consuming to prepare, but they are well worth the effort. Fava beans or broad beans are well liked in China, and the combination of fava beans and pickled vegetables is especially favored in Shanghai, where it is also a popular soup. Most Asian markets carry frozen shelled fava beans, but they are not nearly as delicious as the fresh. Occasionally you can find frozen fava beans that have the tough outer skin removed; if the beans have not been skinned, you'll need to do that by hand. A one-pound bag of frozen fava beans with skin yields about 2 cups of peeled beans.

When Florence Lin first came to the United States she substituted sauerkraut (not the canned variety) if Chinese pickled cabbage wasn't available. Both are technically shredded cabbage that has been salted, but the Chinese canned pickled cabbage is made with mustard greens, so the flavor is much more pungent. Lin's favorite brand of pickled cabbage is Ma Ling. Whichever cabbage you use must be blotted dry with paper towels.

In the 1980s, while visiting China, Lin was served stir-fried mashed fava beans that had been molded and chilled. She says she and her friends still recall with fondness how impressed they were at the presentation and how delicious the puree was served as an appetizer along with fine rice wine.

2½ pounds fresh fava beans

2 tablespoons peanut or vegetable oil

2 tablespoons well-drained pickled cabbage, or sauerkraut, chopped

3 tablespoons chicken broth

¼ teaspoon sugar

¼ teaspoon salt

1. Split open the fava pods and remove the beans. In a 2-quart saucepan bring 3 cups water to a boil over high heat. Add the beans to the boiling water and cook 2 minutes. Pour the beans into a colander and rinse under cold water until cool enough to handle. With your fingernail, pierce the skin of each bean near one end and squeeze the bean to pop it free of the skin. You will have about 2 cups.

2. Put the skinned beans in a food processor and process 15 to 30 seconds or until almost smooth. Transfer to a bowl.

3. Heat a 14-inch flat-bottomed wok or 12-inch skillet over high heat until a bead of water vaporizes within 1 to 2 seconds of contact. Swirl in the oil, add the pickled cabbage, and stir-fry 10 seconds or until the cabbage is fragrant. Add the mashed fava beans, and stir-fry 1 minute or until all the oil has been absorbed. Reduce the heat to medium-high, swirl in the broth, sprinkle on the sugar and salt, and stir-fry 1 minute or until all the liquid has just evaporated.

Serves 4 as a vegetable side dish.

Stir-Fried Garlic Eggplant with Pork

My friend Peipei Chang (see The Alchemy of Stir-Frying, page 62) taught me this recipe, which is typical of her native Shanghai, where soy sauce and sugar are favorite ingredients. According to Chang, the key to the success of this dish is adding the smashed garlic cloves toward the end of cooking and letting the raw garlic perfume the eggplant off the heat. For a spicier variation, she adds a teaspoon of minced fresh jalapeño chilies with seeds along with the smashed garlic. I often serve this at room temperature. According to Chinese medicine, eggplant cools the body of internal heat. Omit the pork and this makes a fine vegetarian dish.

¼ cup ground pork (about 2 ounces)

2 teaspoons plus ¼ cup minced scallions

1 teaspoon plus 3 tablespoons soy sauce

½ teaspoon minced ginger

1 teaspoon plus ¼ cup peanut or vegetable oil

1 tablespoon chopped garlic, plus 2 medium garlic cloves, smashed

3 medium Asian eggplants (about 1 pound), halved lengthwise and cut into ½-inch-thick slices (about 6 cups)

¼ cup Shao Hsing rice wine or dry sherry

½ teaspoon sugar

1. In a small bowl combine the pork and 1 teaspoon cold water. Stir in 2 teaspoons of the scallions, 1 teaspoon of the soy sauce, and ginger. Add 1 teaspoon cold water and stir until the pork absorbs all of the water. In another small bowl combine the remaining 3 tablespoons soy sauce and ¼ cup cold water.

2. Heat a 14-inch flat-bottomed wok or 12-inch skillet over high heat until a bead of water vaporizes within 1 to 2 seconds of contact. Swirl in 1 teaspoon of the oil, add the pork mixture, and, using a metal spatula, break up the pork. Stir-fry 30 seconds or until the pork is opaque but still slightly rare. Transfer the pork to a plate.

3. Swirl in the remaining ¼ cup oil and heat the oil a few seconds or until hot but not smoking. Carefully add the 1 tablespoon chopped garlic and stir-fry 10 seconds or until the garlic is fragrant. Add the eggplant and stir-fry 2 minutes or until the eggplant flesh has changed color and has absorbed all the oil. Swirl the rice wine into the wok, immediately cover the wok, reduce the heat to medium, and cook 30 seconds. Uncover and sprinkle on the sugar. Swirl the soy sauce mixture into the wok, increase the heat to high, and stir-fry 1 minute. Return the pork to the wok. Cover and cook 2 minutes or until almost all the liquid has been absorbed by the eggplant and the eggplant is just tender when pierced with a knife. Uncover and stir-fry 15 seconds. Stir in the remaining 2 smashed garlic cloves. Cover, remove the wok from the heat, and set aside for 1 minute or until the pork is just cooked through. Sprinkle on the remaining ¼ cup scallions.

Serves 4 as a vegetable side dish.

Chinese American Stir-Fried Cabbage with Bacon

Tane Ong Chan remembers her mom making this dish in Albuquerque, New Mexico, when she was growing up in the 1940s. This is a very simple stir-fry typical of what Chinese Americans living outside of Chinese communities in America were forced to cook. Unable to find Napa cabbage or Chinese bacon, Chan's mom substituted regular cabbage and American-style bacon. Years later, when ginger and dry sherry became available, her mom added those ingredients to enhance the flavor. If the bacon is very lean and does not release much fat, the cabbage will be too dry to stir-fry and may begin to stick to the pan. Just add 1 to 2 tablespoons of peanut or vegetable oil and continue stir-frying. The amount of salt added will depend on the saltiness of the bacon. Cut the cabbage as you would for coleslaw.

4 slices bacon, cut into ½-inch-wide pieces (about
   3 ounces)
2 teaspoons minced garlic
1 pound green cabbage, cored and cut crosswise
   into ¼-inch-wide shreds (about 8 cups)
¼ cup chicken broth or water
2 teaspoons soy sauce
¼ teaspoon salt
⅛ teaspoon freshly ground pepper

Spread the bacon pieces in an even layer in a cold 14-inch flat-bottomed wok or 12-inch skillet. Cook over medium heat undisturbed 1 minute or until the bacon begins to release its fat. Then, using a metal spatula, stir-fry on medium heat 2 minutes or until the bacon begins to brown and more fat has been released. Add the garlic and stir-fry 10 seconds or until the garlic is fragrant. Add the cabbage and stir-fry 2 minutes or until the cabbage just begins to wilt. If mixture is dry add 1 to 2 more tablespoons oil. Swirl in the broth, cover the wok, and cook 30 seconds. Uncover, add the soy sauce, sprinkle on the salt and pepper, and stir-fry 1 minute or until the cabbage is crisp-tender.

Serves 4 as a vegetable side dish.

Tane Ong Chan

Stir-Frying Watermelon Rind

When teaching me the recipe for Stir-Fried Fuzzy Melon and Ginger Pork (see page 232), Beverly Low, a home cook in San Francisco, explained how her relatives from China make the same recipe using peeled watermelon rind as a substitute for the fuzzy melon. Low speculates that the family stir-fries watermelon rind as a way to avoid wasting food. Indeed, once stir-fried, the rind tastes remarkably like fuzzy melon. I subsequently tried stir-frying fuzzy melon and watermelon rind together and was astounded at how similar they tasted. The combination was delicious, the watermelon rind creating a beautiful color contrast with its hint of pink from the watermelon flesh.

Low's mention of cooking with watermelon rind was not the first I had heard of it: Tane Ong Chan, owner of The Wok Shop in San Francisco, grew up in New Mexico in the 1940s, when Chinese vegetables were not available. Her mother longed for Chinese winter melon. Chan remembers the day her mother sat staring at some leftover watermelon rind before deciding that she would substitute the rind for the missing winter melon to make soup. Delighted at how well the watermelon rind mimicked the winter melon, Mrs. Chan made it that way for years.

Florence Lin, the legendary Chinese cooking authority who grew up in Ningbo, near Shanghai, remembers in the summertime stir-fried watermelon rind was a common home-cooked dish. "No one would go to the market looking for watermelon rind for cooking," she explains. "But once the melon was purchased it was natural to save the rind for stir-frying. Food in China was precious and we wasted nothing. After the green watermelon skin was removed and the rind was cut into slices, we would lightly salt the rind and let it sit for 30 minutes before pouring off the water that was released. We did this to give the rind more bite once it was cooked. My family loved the combination of diced tomatoes and sliced watermelon rind stir-fried in a little oil. We didn't even use garlic or ginger. The only seasoning was a dash of sugar to bring out the tomato flavor and sometimes a little broth. Both ingredients cook quickly, so it only required 2 or 3 minutes to make a delectable vegetarian stir-fry."

At first the idea of cooking watermelon rind struck me as extremely odd, until I was reminded that in Eastern Europe and in America's South there is a long tradition of eating pickled watermelon rind. Curiously, in my research I even came across a recipe for tomato and watermelon rind salad—the American salad version of Lin's stir-fry. Watermelon rind is, in fact, quite healthful. One hundred percent of the watermelon is edible and it contains citrulline, an amino acid that the body converts to arginine, another amino acid that scientific studies have suggested may be beneficial to the heart and the immune system. According to Chinese medicine, watermelon reduces the internal heat in the body caused by summer weather. Whether you follow Western or Chinese medicine, stir-fried watermelon rind is delicious.

How to Prepare Watermelon Rind for Stir-Frying

Select watermelon rind that does not have any visible fibers, an indication that the rind is old and woody. Avoid seedless watermelon as the rind is too thin. Cut the watermelon into 1-inch-thick slices. With a knife, trim away and discard the tough green skin of the watermelon, leaving only the white fleshy portion of the rind intact. Separate the rind from the red flesh with the knife. Reserve the fruit for eating. Do not be concerned if there is a hint of pink fruit that remains on the rind. If you start with about 1½ pounds of watermelon rind, you will have about 1 pound of the white flesh once the green skin is removed. Cut the white flesh into 2-inch-wide strips, and then cut each strip into ¼-inch-thick slices to make about 4 cups. Follow the recipe for Stir-Fried Fuzzy Melon and Ginger Pork (page 232), substituting the watermelon rind for the fuzzy melon.

Stir-Fried Fuzzy Melon and Ginger Pork

In my family we used fuzzy melon only for soups or braises. It never occurred to me to stir-fry it until Beverly Low, a home cook in San Francisco, taught me this recipe. Fuzzy melon is more like zucchini than melon; it is in season year-round but is best in the summer. The skin has short, fine prickly hairs, which account for the name; use a vegetable peeler to remove the skin. I like fuzzy melon a little al dente, but if you like your vegetables softer increase the stir-fry time by 1 to 2 minutes. Low also makes this with dried shrimp in place of the ground pork. She briefly soaks a small handful of the dried shrimp in cold water, drains them, and then stir-fries them as she would the pork.

¼ cup ground pork (about 2 ounces)

1 tablespoon plus ¼ cup minced scallions

2 teaspoons soy sauce

¼ teaspoon cornstarch

3 tablespoons chicken broth

1 teaspoon plus 2 tablespoons peanut
    or vegetable oil

3 slices ginger, smashed

1 medium fuzzy melon (about 1 pound), peeled,
    halved lengthwise, and cut into ¼-inch-thick
    slices (about 4 cups)

½ teaspoon salt

⅛ teaspoon freshly ground pepper

1 teaspoon sesame oil

1. In a small bowl combine the pork and 1 teaspoon cold water. Stir in 1 tablespoon of the scallions, 1 teaspoon of the soy sauce, and cornstarch. In another small bowl combine the broth and the remaining 1 teaspoon soy sauce.

2. Heat a 14-inch flat-bottomed wok or 12-inch skillet over high heat until a bead of water vaporizes within 1 to 2 seconds of contact. Swirl in 1 teaspoon of the peanut oil, add the pork mixture, then, using a metal spatula, break up the pork, and stir-fry 30 seconds or until the pork is opaque but still slightly rare. Transfer the pork to a plate.

3. Swirl in the remaining 2 tablespoons peanut oil, add the ginger slices, and stir-fry 10 seconds or until the ginger is fragrant. Add the fuzzy melon, sprinkle on the salt and pepper, and stir-fry 1 minute or until the melon slices begin to wilt. Swirl the broth mixture into the wok and stir-fry 1 minute. Return the pork to the wok and stir-fry 1 minute or until almost all the liquid has evaporated, the fuzzy melon is just tender when pierced with a knife, and the pork is cooked through. Remove from the heat. Stir in the sesame oil. Sprinkle on the remaining ¼ cup scallions.

Serves 4 as a vegetable side dish.

Dry-Fried Sichuan Beans

This is a classic example of the technique of "dry stir-frying" (see Dry Stir-Frying and Moist Stir-Frying, page 121). To intensify the flavor and to impart a more caramelized taste, the beans are first stir-fried slowly for a longer period of time. I only make this dish in a wok. The longer stir-frying requires more oil in a skillet and makes the pan more difficult to wash. Make sure the beans are bone-dry before stir-frying. If the beans are older be sure to remove the strings. The saltiness of the Sichuan preserved vegetable can vary wildly, so the amount of salt may need to be adjusted. The vegetable must be rinsed before chopping. When stir-frying the beans on low heat, if they seem too dry you can add an additional tablespoon or two of oil.

1 tablespoon plus 1 teaspoon peanut
    or vegetable oil
12 ounces green beans, ends trimmed and cut into
    2-inch pieces (about 4 cups)
¼ teaspoon salt
1 tablespoon minced ginger
¼ cup ground pork (about 2 ounces)
3 tablespoons finely chopped Sichuan preserved
    vegetable
¼ teaspoon sugar
2 tablespoons soy sauce

1. Heat a 14-inch flat-bottomed wok over high heat until a bead of water vaporizes within 1 to 2 seconds of contact. Swirl in 1 tablespoon of the oil, add the beans, and sprinkle on the salt. Adjust the heat between low and medium-low so that the beans are barely sizzling, and cook undisturbed 1 minute, then stir-fry a few seconds. Repeat this process 4 or 5 more times until the beans are blistered and browned, for a total cooking time of 5 or 6 minutes. Transfer the beans to a plate.

2. Swirl in the remaining 1 teaspoon oil, add the ginger, and stir-fry over high heat 10 seconds or until the ginger is fragrant. Add the pork, then, using a metal spatula, break up the pork, and stir-fry 1 minute or until the pork is no longer pink. Return the beans to the wok, add the Sichuan vegetable, and sprinkle on the sugar. Swirl the soy sauce into the wok and stir-fry 30 seconds to 1 minute or until the pork is cooked through.

Serves 4 as a vegetable side dish.

Stir-Fried Edamame with Pickled Cucumber

Florence Lin (see Stir-Frying in Old China, opposite page), the legendary Chinese cooking authority, taught me this recipe, a delicious Shanghainese way to stir-fry edamame with pickled cucumber—pickled vegetables being a favorite ingredient in the cooking of Shanghai. Pickled, or preserved, cucumber is available in 6.35-ounce jars in Chinese markets. The product comes from Taiwan and has either whole, chunks, or slices of cucumber that have been preserved in a mixture of soy sauce, water, salt, and sugar.

Lin says you can substitute Western-style pickles for the preserved cucumber just as long as they have not been pickled with vinegar. Guss' Pickles (www.gusspickle.com) in New York sells half sour, also known as "new," pickles that have been preserved in a saltwater brine; I've used them successfully as a substitute for the Chinese preserved cucumber. If I have time, after chopping the new pickles I toss them in 2 teaspoons soy sauce and ¼ teaspoon sugar, which imparts a taste even more like the Chinese product. There are, interestingly, a few commercial pickles available that have not been pickled with vinegar.

In China, soybeans are considered one of the five sacred grains. Shelled soybeans, or edamame, are available frozen in Asian markets. After defrosting, make sure the edamame are patted dry with paper towels before stir-frying to prevent spattering. This dish can be served hot, at room temperature, or even chilled.

2 tablespoons peanut or vegetable oil

2 tablespoons minced ginger

2 cups shelled frozen edamame, defrosted

6 to 8 mini pickled cucumbers or 2 new pickles,
   drained and chopped (about ⅓ cup)

2 tablespoons chicken or vegetable broth

¼ teaspoon salt

Heat a 14-inch flat-bottomed wok or 12-inch skillet over high heat until a bead of water vaporizes within 1 to 2 seconds of contact. Swirl in the oil, add the ginger, and stir-fry 10 seconds or until the ginger is fragrant. Add the edamame and stir-fry 2 minutes or until the soybeans show a hint of browning. Add the pickled cucumber, reduce the heat to medium-high, and stir-fry 1 minute or until the soybeans are lightly brown. Swirl the broth into the wok, sprinkle on the salt, and stir-fry 1 minute or until the liquid evaporates and the soybeans are crisp-tender. If you prefer more tender soybeans, continue stir-frying another few minutes and add a tablespoon or two more of broth.

Serves 4 as a vegetable side dish.

Stir-Frying in Old China

Florence Lin

In 1935, at the age of fifteen, Florence Lin accompanied her ill mother from their home in Ningbo to the house her father had built in the Chinese countryside. They traveled by sampan on a small river for the one-hour trip and lived for a year with Lin's grandmother and auntie who cared for her mother.

Their simple country life—without electricity or running water—taught Lin much about the value of food and the practice of cooking. Lin spent much of the time with her aunt, observing how she managed the kitchen help and the preparation of their meals. "Every day we walked three to four minutes to the local river where we washed our rice and vegetables. Our cooking and drinking water came from the rainwater we collected in a huge earthenware pot in our house's courtyard. The stock of precious dried rice stalks that we used to fuel the traditional hearth stove had to last the year because we had no firewood," explains Lin.

Such shortages led to staple "one-pot meals" made by cooking rice in an enormous wok on top of which sat a steam rack where several dishes could cook from the rice's intense steam, the most fuel-efficient way to cook multiple dishes at one time. The family stir-fried only every fortnight to conserve fuel, except for when guests came or an elder among them celebrated a birthday. "In those days, reaching fifty was considered quite old," says Lin. "And there were too many children for us to have birthday parties. We considered ourselves lucky if someone remembered our birthday and poached us an egg in sugar water. Sugar was a great luxury. Birthday celebrations were reserved only for adults."

The most significant days of remembrance for Lin's family were anniversaries of an ancestor's birth or death. For those occasions they would make a special trip into town to buy fresh fish, meat, or seasonal ingredients to make stir-fries along with red-cooked dishes (a Shanghainese specialty in which meats are braised in soy sauce, rice wine, and rock sugar). Although stir-frying is a fast and efficient way to cook, the oil necessary for these dishes was an extravagance. "The dishes, accompanied with rice wine, were given to the ancestors as offerings. Of course," confesses Lin, "paying our respects to the ancestors was also a great excuse for everyone to feast and to enjoy our favorite stir-fry dishes."

Florence Lin

Chop Suey

The Stir-Fry Forgery That Opened America's Door to Chinese Cooking

Edward Hopper and his wife, Jo, were fond of dining in inexpensive chop suey parlors. When they began courting in 1923, they frequented the Far East restaurant located on the second floor of 8 Columbus Circle in New York City. Restaurants like the one depicted were often found on an upper floor of a building in contrast to fine eating establishments that were located on street level. (Chop Suey, 1929, Edward Hopper, oil on canvas, Collection of Barney A. Ebsworth.)

The "stir-fry" dish most closely associated with Chinese cooking in America is the infamous chop suey, a purely Chinese American invention that has no connection to the great canon of Chinese cuisine. Ironically, this dish—much maligned by Chinese—was the portal through which Chinese immigrants and Americans first began to access each other's culture. In fact, the phenomenon of chop suey helped to facilitate the integration of the Chinese into mainstream American life.

When I was a little girl growing up in San Francisco, I remember being asked if my family ate chop suey. I had no idea what the dish was, but just the sound of the words made me cringe. When I finally spied it on a cafeteria buffet I was mortified. The unappetizing goopy concoction looked nothing like the Chinese food I knew. Many Chinese share the feelings of indignation, embarrassment, and discomfort that chop suey aroused in me. Only as an adult and a food professional did I gain a sense of the greater importance of how chop suey served as a catalyst for transforming the Chinese American experience.

The first Chinese male laborers came to America in the mid-nineteenth century during the California Gold Rush, principally from the county of Toisan (or Taishan) in the province of Guangdong in southern China. Toisan had suffered famines, floods, typhoons, earthquakes, epidemics, and a financial crisis so severe that these men arrived seeking a better life in a place they called *gam saan*, or Gold Mountain. In the beginning the Chinese worked on the railroads and in mines and at manufacturing and agricultural jobs despite the unprecedented prejudice they suffered. From the mid-1800s until the beginning of the 1900s, anti-Chinese riots erupted throughout the West. The Chinese were attacked, lynched, and expelled from white communities. Labor unions considered the Chinese willingness to work for low wages a threat to the "American" workforce and banded together to prevent their entry into the general labor pool. The only jobs remaining open to these Chinese immigrants, who were mainly of peasant stock, were in laundries and restaurants. Their food—that of self-taught cooks forced into restaurant work—reflected rural, unrefined working-class Cantonese fare.

The prejudice against the Chinese culminated in the passage of the Chinese Exclusion Act of 1882 that ended further Chinese immigration. It remains the only law in American history that barred entry into the United States based on race and ethnicity. Although the Chinese Exclusion Act was repealed in 1943, the restrictions were not significantly changed until passage of the Immigration Act of 1965, which brought new waves of Chinese to America, and with them, different regional styles of cooking radically different from the Cantonese cuisine that dominated Chinese restaurants in America.

From the time of their arrival in San Francisco and New York, the Chinese were forced to live in segregated ghettos. Eventually, their impoverished communities grew to have their own barbershops, apothecaries, boardinghouses, and a few eating establishments known as chow chows. By the 1870s, white American tourists, known as gawkers, slummers, and bohemians, began venturing into Chinatowns, curious to experience the exotic. These visitors were often accompanied by tour guides who escorted them to opium dens, curio shops, Chinese operas, gambling parlors, and brothels. Most of the visitors viewed the Chinese as barbaric rat and dog eaters who ate with sticks, shoveling rice and pungent alien foods into their mouths. The more adventurous of them were tempted by the cheap and filling food they found in chow chows, where a few American dishes such as ham and eggs, baked beans, and steak and onions were also served. The most popular dish by far, however, was chop suey. A *New York Times* article dated November 15, 1903, reported, "Sunlight and the chop suey consumer are as far apart as the poles. It is the men and women who like to eat after everybody else is abed that pour shekels into the coffers of the man who knows how to make chop suey." Tourism became a financial opportunity for the Chinese.

There are two popular legends as to how chop suey was introduced to America. The first describes an event in which a bunch of hungry, drunken white laborers who, late one night, stumble across a Chinese restaurant in San Francisco's Chinatown, where the cook is about to shut down for the night. They beg him to feed them, even though he tells them that he is out of every item on the menu. The cook, forced to make do with leftovers, concocts a dish. When pressed to give a name for his tasty dish he supposedly says, "chop suey." In Cantonese *jup suei* (*zha sui* in Mandarin) means leftover bits and pieces. One can speculate the Americans hearing *chau jup suei*—stir-fried leftovers—thought they heard the cook say "chop suey."

The second story involves a Chinese diplomat, Li Hung Chang, who came to the United States on an official visit in 1896. There are many versions of his story, but one of the most popular claims Li's cooks prepared a banquet at the Waldorf-Astoria. Americans, fascinated by Li, disseminated the tale that his favorite dish was chop suey.

Regardless of its origin, the bland dish that appealed to American tastes combined familiar ingredients with a few unthreatening foreign ones such as bean sprouts and bamboo shoots. In truth it represented the veritable antithesis of Chinese sensibilities. In China a true stir-fry requires the cook to have well-developed knife skills to cut ingredients into delicate slices or shreds. Chop suey, on the other hand, is filled with large slices of onion, celery, and water chestnuts, combined with equally thick-cut pieces of chicken, pork, or beef. In Chinese cooking, vegetables are traditionally stir-fried with aromatics, such as ginger. For Americans, who were repulsed by strong flavors like dried shrimp or fermented black beans, the ginger was deliberately omitted. Chinese cooks traditionally marinate chicken, pork, or beef in a mixture of rice wine, soy sauce, and cornstarch before stir-frying. In chop suey, the chunks of meat were not even seasoned. A Chinese stir-fry is cooked quickly over high heat, ensuring that vegetables retain their crispness and flavor. In chop suey, stock is poured in after the meat and vegetables are stir-fried, and the mixture is boiled until the ingredients are overcooked by Chinese standards. While traditional stir-fries can have a light sauce, it should never overwhelm a dish. In deference to the American fondness for gravy, a cornstarch slurry was added to chop suey at the end of the cooking time to make a goopy sauce. A dousing with soy sauce was the final touch, an effort to add Chinese flavor to the dish.

Imagine the surprise of the Chinese who, barely able to eke out a living, were suddenly flooded with American customers willing to pay good money for a dish that required the cheapest ingredients and no special cooking skills. The crude dish actually fulfilled the Americans' image of exotic Chinese food, and a craze for Chinese food ensued. In 1932, M. Sing Au wrote in his cookbook *Chinese Cookery* that chop suey "has always been surrounded with an air of mystery in the mind of the average westerner."

Throughout the early 1900s hundreds of chop suey joints or parlors opened. The *New York Times* reported in 1903, "But in New York, as in San Francisco and other cities which have large Chinese colonies, a large number of persons have learned to like chop suey. Once or twice a week, or even oftener, they have a 'hankering' for it." While the Chinese were still not welcomed in general society or the workforce, Americans managed to suspend their prejudice when eating chop suey. In 1885 New York City was reported to have had six Chinese restaurants. By 1905 there were over 100 chop suey parlors.

Enterprising Chinese merchants in San Francisco and New York capitalized on the chop suey "addiction," recognizing it as a lure to tourism and thereby to economic survival. After the San Francisco earthquake of 1906, which destroyed the original Chinatown, merchants seized on the opportunity to create a new community, free of gambling and prostitution. Chinatowns in both cities were cleaned up, and buildings were decorated with colorful pagodas, lanterns, bamboo, and other Chinese motifs to make the community more inviting to tourists.

As the popularity of chop suey grew, La Choy created cooking brochures, like this one dated 1929, to satisfy homemakers eager to cook Chinese food.

In the meanwhile, more Americans were introduced to chop suey by newspapers, magazines, brochures, and cookbooks that published chop suey recipes to satisfy homemakers eager to replicate their favorite Chinese restaurant dishes. Today, a review of chop suey (also written as *chop soi*, *chop sui*, and *chop sooy*) recipes from old cookbooks reveals some very unappealing, inedible food. It is remarkable that Americans cooking these recipes could possibly have fallen under the spell of chop suey. By 1924, La Choy company began offering canned bean sprouts and canned chop suey vegetables, making the dish easier to prepare, and even blander with the absence of fresh vegetables. Chop suey could only have become more unappetizing made with canned food, yet the infatuation with chop suey only grew.

The first Asian cookbook in English, the *Chinese-Japanese Cook Book*, published in America by Rand,

McNally & Company in 1914, has a preface that begins, "Chinese cooking in recent years has become very popular in America. . . . The restaurants are no longer merely the resort of curious idlers, intent upon studying types peculiar to Chinatown, for the Chinese restaurants have pushed their way out of Chinatown and are now found in all parts of the large cities of America. . . . There is no reason why these same dishes should not be cooked and served in any American home. When it is known how simple and clean are the ingredients used to make up these Oriental dishes, the Westerner will cease to feel that natural repugnance which assails one when about to taste a strange dish of a new and strange land." The cookbook has a small section devoted to chop suey recipes, a total of five in all, ranging from Extra White Chop Suey to Chop Suey (Plain). The recipes, though crudely written, nonetheless reflect the public's growing interest in cooking Chinese food.

Girnau's Chinese Chop Suey Chow Mein Cookbook, published in 1931 by Fredric H. Girnau Publishing Co., includes a recipe for Chinese chop suey. The instructions state to "bring cooking oil in skillet to boiling point," but does not say how much oil. After frying bite-sized pork, adding celery, onions, and soup stock, the mixture should be covered and boiled for 7 minutes. Then cornstarch, molasses, and soy sauce are added. During this time the most widely distributed soy sauce in America was what is now known as "dark" soy sauce, which is thicker and sweeter in taste than "regular" soy sauce. The resulting dish had to have been greasy and goopy, with a cloying heavy sweetness and saltiness from the molasses and dark soy sauce. In a recipe for Chinese-style brown gravy, the cookbook recommends combining soy sauce, molasses, cornstarch, and soup stock to make what is called a "highly palatable gravy," to be used with "egg foo young or chop suey."

Despite the continued racial prejudice, the Chinese began moving out of their Chinatowns in the 1900s and venturing into cities and towns across America, where they opened family-operated chop suey cafés that served a mixture of American fare and other hybrid Chinese dishes such as chow mein, egg rolls, fried rice, and sweet-and-sour pork. By 1920, there were chop suey restaurants in nearly every American city and town. These pioneering Chinese restauranteurs recognized that their food was more sought after than they themselves were and that, as the scholar and anthropologist David Y. H. Wu described, their "restaurants in the United States, and in Hawaii in particular, [were] seen to play the role of cultural ambassadors." Entering a Chinese restaurant exposed Americans to Chinese culture through its furniture, art, music, dinnerware, and even in the traditional clothing worn by the staff. Chop suey, chow mein, and hybrid Chinese American foods lay the foundation for the Chinese people and, ultimately, their true cuisine to be absorbed into mainstream America. Today, there are reported to be more than 40,000 Chinese restaurants in America. Here are a few remembrances from some of the pioneers.

Chu's Chop Suey House
Omaha, Nebraska

Terry Huey's family was instrumental in introducing Chinese food to the American heartland. His grandfather Chong Hoi Huey was born in Guangdong province in China in 1884. Unable to find work when he arrived in San Francisco in 1909, he was advised by an uncle living in Sioux City, Iowa, to relocate to Omaha, Nebraska. In 1921 Huey invested two thousand dollars along with seventy other investors to create a Chinese restaurant. In 1926 King Fong Cafe opened its doors as the first and foremost authentic Chinese restaurant in the greater Omaha area, serving Chinese food and traditional American fare. Ornately decorated with Chinese lanterns, teakwood tables, and Chinese vases and paintings, it remains a relic of old-world Chinese dining and is still run by members of the Huey family.

In 1964, Chong Hoi Huey's son, Thick Chu Huey, opened the only other Chinese eatery in Omaha, Chu's Chop Suey House. Terry Huey remembers his father explaining to him why he deliberately added the words "Steak House" to the restaurant's name in the local phone book and restaurant guides to assure customers unfamiliar with or afraid of Chinese food that it also had American entrées. The truck drivers and farmers who made up the majority of their clientele wanted American food on the menu, especially Omaha steaks. His father had to learn how to cook American-style pork chops, New York strip steak, prime rib, and even grits to satisfy customers. Those same customers came to love all the Chinese American menu staples: chop suey, chow mein, egg rolls, fried rice, crab Rangoon, and egg foo young.

The food Huey's mom prepared at home was completely different from the Chinese food offered at the restaurant. Helping out in the restaurant, Terry Huey worked in the kitchen, often stir-frying chop suey, a dish that he liked and assumed was Chinese. He remembers making up hundreds of orders of chicken chop suey: stir-frying slices of unmarinated chicken with celery, onions, bean sprouts, green peppers, bamboo shoots, and water chestnuts in an enormous wok, seasoning it with MSG, sesame oil, salt, and pepper, and making a gravy sauce with a cornstarch slurry. "We didn't even add soy sauce. Customers would douse the chop suey with soy sauce and butter and eat it with dinner rolls," he recalls.

Without a Chinese community, Huey's father had to ship in all Asian ingredients from Chicago. Frustrated with the quality of bean sprouts so necessary for chop suey and egg foo young, Huey's father purchased two devices from New York and San Francisco for growing bean sprouts, which he placed in the darkest part of the restaurant's basement. One-hundred-pound bags of sprout seeds were routinely delivered.

At the height of Chu's Chop Suey House's popularity in the mid-1970s, the kitchen regularly had fifteen woks being used simultaneously. That was also the time they served their first Chinese customer. By 2000, business had slowed to the point that only two woks were needed. "My parents should've given up the restaurant much earlier, but they kept it going because we had so many loyal customers who had been coming for over thirty years. Even though it was isolating and often lonely living in Omaha without other Asians, the restaurant allowed us to become part of the community, and in the end that was the part that was hardest to give up," recalls Huey. When the doors closed in 2004, the restaurant still served chop suey.

Chung Mei Kitchen
Pharr, Texas

Peter Lee's family has been managing Chinese restaurants in south Texas since the early 1930s, when his grandfather Ga Jim Lee partnered with some friends to open Houston Café, the first Chinese restaurant in Brownsville. The café served American food along with a few Chinese American dishes such as chop suey and chow mein. Lee himself grew up in Pharr, Texas, a community of 6,000 people comprised mainly of Mexican Americans that is located just north of Mexico. He worked in his family's restaurant, Chung Mei Kitchen, in Pharr. According to Lee, it was the only Chinese restaurant in Texas south of South San Antonio until the 1970s.

Peter's father, Du Ong Lee, graduated from the University of Texas at Austin in 1939 with a degree in finance. "My father saw his friends get jobs, but no one would hire him because he was Chinese," Peter Lee explains. For a while his father worked as a manager at Tai Shan, a fancy Chinese restaurant in San Antonio, and then eventually, he took a chance and started his own restaurant in 1950. "It took courage and fortitude to open Chung Mei Kitchen, and my dad worked fifteen-hour days, seven days a week, for over thirty years," says Lee. The menu offered various kinds of chop suey, spareribs, egg foo young, sweet-and-sour pork, fried rice, and shrimp with lobster sauce—all served with white bread that was baked on the premises. "Back in those days if you made it any more exotic they would look at you. My father always warned that if we served strictly Chinese food we'd lose the business. So we offered a mixture of Chinese and American foods. Half of the menu had American favorites like chicken-fried steak, roast beef, and baked sugar-cured ham. At first the restaurant had Chinese cooks, but it was difficult to keep them happy in a community without other Chinese, so my father switched to Mexican cooks trained by my mom. The waitresses were Mexican American, or Americans, never Chinese."

The food Peter Lee's mother cooked at home was entirely different from the Chinese food served in the restaurant. She made Cantonese-style dishes like steamed pork cake and Chinese poached chicken with finely minced ginger and scallion sauce. In the restaurant, the Chinese food wasn't even cooked with ginger. "The first time we had a Chinese customer was in the 1960s," says Lee. "When the restaurant closed in 1985, chop suey was still a mainstay on the menu.

Today, more than forty Chinese restaurants exist in a 150-mile radius of the old Chung Mei Kitchen."

Chinese Delicacies

Columbia, Missouri

In 1969, when Ellen Chou arrived in Columbia, Missouri, from Taipei, Taiwan, she was both baffled and mortified to see what Americans enjoyed as good Chinese food. Chou was raised on home-cooked dishes prepared by her mother. "Chop suey was born in America and we had never heard of it back home," says Chou.

In 1980, Ellen and her husband, Chang-Sheng Chou, both with master's degrees in journalism from the prestigious Missouri School of Journalism, came to the realization that the only way they could support their family was to open a Chinese restaurant. Without any training, the husband and wife became self-taught cooks at their restaurant, lovingly named Chinese Delicacies. In addition to cooking, Chang-Sheng worked as manager, bartender, dishwasher, and sometimes the janitor, while Ellen handled the cooking. Even their three children had to pitch in.

Although the Chous served a few Chinese American dishes like chow mein and sweet-and-sour pork, their aim at Chinese Delicacies was to serve authentic Chinese food. American tastes for Chinese food had evolved by the 1970s, and Columbia had recently gained a northern-style Chinese eatery after years of only Cantonese-style Chinese American food. The Chous offered Sichuan dishes like crispy duck, ma po tofu, fish fragrant eggplant, and stir-fried squid. The response was mixed at first.

Daughter Hsiao-Ching, who grew up thinking of chop suey as "fake" Chinese food, remembers her father as too principled to include it on his menu. Finally, after a number of years, the Chous relented and chop suey appeared, albeit with their own master sauce rather than the typical institutional chop suey sauce that came in five-gallon containers. "We realized it was not our purpose to educate customers about the Chinese way of cooking but to make everybody happy," explains Ellen.

"I think of chop suey as an Americanized dish that a segment of our customers deemed as de rigueur as sweet-and-sour pork in a goopy sauce, cream cheese wontons, and free fortune cookies," says Hsiao-Ching. "In that vein, the dish represents a lost battle in my family's effort to raise the level of Chinese cuisine in our little town."

In 2008, I finally tasted chop suey. The occasion was a lecture on chop suey sponsored by the Culinary Historians of New York, and I was one of the few Chinese attendees. The event was held at Double Harmony Restaurant in New York's Chinatown. Dinner was included in the $45 ticket price.

I arrived a little late and there were guests at several tables already noisily eating. I scanned the buffet: it included two kinds of chop suey, roast pork fried rice, shrimp egg foo young, chicken chow mein, egg rolls, and white rice, all of it looking alarmingly unappetizing. The waiter working the buffet table eyed me as if to say, "*What are you doing here?*" I asked him the difference between the two chop sueys. Suppressing a little smirk, he explained in Cantonese that the first dish was "old-world" chop suey (a stir-fry of Napa cabbage, bean sprouts, carrots, chicken, and dried shiitake mushrooms drenched in a gloppy sauce with fried noodles on top), while the other was "modern" chop suey (a stir-fry of snow peas, sliced canned mushrooms, canned water chestnuts, carrots, celery, and American broccoli in a less gloppy sauce). I could not believe the restaurant had actually invented a narrative for this awful food. I sat down with my near-empty plate to a table of enthusiastic eaters.

After the lecture as I left the restaurant, hungry and ready to find the kind of Chinese food I grew up on, I felt thankful that with Chinatown's evolution there are restaurants that cater to sophisticated Chinese tastes, no longer obliged to serve mediocre Chinese American fare for economic survival. Still, I could not help thinking that to the amazement of the Chinese, the original formula for chop suey still works. More than one hundred years after its invention, overpriced, poorly prepared Chinese American food continues to be happily eaten.

Chicken Lo Mein with Ginger Mushrooms

Rice and Noodle

RECIPES

ESSENTIALS FOR STIR-FRYING RICE AND NOODLES

Rice

When stir-frying rice (in other words, when making fried rice), there are several cardinal rules for ensuring excellence:

Rinse Raw Rice: The raw rice (whether long-grain, jasmine, brown rice, or even glutinous rice) must be rinsed several times in cold water before cooking. While American nutritionists claim this washes away nutrients, Chinese cooks always rinse prior to cooking in order to remove excess starch that can make rice gummy.

Use Cold Cooked Rice Only: When making fried rice, only use cold leftover rice; just-cooked rice is too hot and moist to use and results in gummy fried rice. Cold rice has a texture that is ideal for stir-frying. Do not allow the freshly cooked rice to cool more than a couple of hours at room temperature, particularly if the kitchen is hot. In fact, it is best to refrigerate rice in a covered container within 2 hours to prevent it from spoiling: remember, rice ferments easily, which is why vinegar and wine can be made from it. Once refrigerated, the cooked rice is best used within 3 days.

I cook rice the day before I need it unless I have leftover rice on hand. If making fried rice is a last-minute decision, I cook the rice, spread it on a jelly roll pan, and refrigerate it so the rice can cool down as quickly as possible.

Fluff Cooked Rice: After cooking rice (Classic Rice, page 283), immediately fluff the rice with a fork. Even though the rice will be refrigerated, this loosens the grains and will make them easier to stir-fry later. Without fluffing, the rice will become a compact block that will be difficult to separate when stir-frying.

Fresh Noodles

Toss Cooked Noodles in a Little Oil: When stir-frying noodles, the best pasta to use are the thick, fresh egg noodles found in the refrigerator section of most Chinese markets. After boiling the noodles according to package directions, drain them in a colander, then rinse under cold water. Vigorously shake out as much water as possible. If the noodles are too wet, it will cause extra spattering from the hot oil when they are added to the wok, in addition to turning a stir-fry into a braise. After the noodles have been well drained, toss them in a small amount of sesame or vegetable oil. This keeps the noodles separate, making it easier to stir-fry them.

Broad Rice Noodles: Also known as chow fun noodles, these are found in some Chinese bakeries and stores that sell fresh tofu, or at the checkout counters of some Chinese markets. These noodles are soft and flexible until refrigerated. They are best when used the day of purchase, without refrigeration. If they have been refrigerated, steam them for 10 minutes to resoften them, then allow them to cool before cutting. To cut the noodles, leave the fresh noodles as a slab and cut it crosswise into ½-inch-wide strips (**1**). Using your hands, separate and loosen the strips.

1

Dry Noodles

Cellophane and rice sticks (dried rice noodles) must be soaked in warm water for 20 minutes until they are soft and pliable before they can be stir-fried. After soaking, drain them in a colander. Vigorously shake out as much water as possible. If the noodles are too wet, it will cause extra spattering from the hot oil when they are added to the wok, in addition to turning a stir-fry into a braise.

Use a Wok for Stir-Frying Rice or Noodles

Stir-frying rice or noodles in a 14-inch wok is far superior to cooking either in a skillet. Most rice or noodle recipes are one-pot meals that have at least 6 to 8 cups of ingredients. In a skillet that amount of food is difficult to move, let alone stir-fry without ingredients falling out of the pan. A wok is also preferable because if your pan is well seasoned rice and noodles will not stick and very little oil is necessary.

Use a Chinese Metal Spatula or Pancake Turner

To break up the block of rice as you stir-fry, a metal spatula is preferable to a wooden spatula because its thinner edge is more effective in getting under the rice. Once the block of rice begins to break apart, it will become easier to separate it into individual grains.

Two Methods for Combining Noodles with Ingredients

When stir-frying noodles, it can be difficult to integrate the other ingredients and seasonings because the noodles become one mass. It takes practice, but here are two ways to make it easier:

- Use a pair of wooden (plastic will melt) chopsticks in one hand and a metal spatula in the other and toss the noodles as you would a salad to loosen the mass. *If the wok is not stabilized on a wok ring or if you are using a skillet, make sure someone is securely holding the wok or skillet so the pan does not flip off the burner while you do this.*

- Noodles are a symbol of longevity in Chinese culture. Traditionally, noodles are never cut before eating, because cut noodles are a symbol of bad luck. However, I have met many Chinese cooks who insist on cutting noodles into 6- to 8-inch lengths to make it easier to combine them with other ingredients.

Avoid Overfilling the Wok

When stir-frying rice or noodles, do not crowd the wok with too many ingredients. A rice or noodle stir-fry tends to be a meal in itself. If the wok is overcrowded, ingredients are difficult to move and, in the case of rice, will spill out. In addition, food on the bottom of the wok is likely to overcook or burn, along with the aromatics, while ingredients in the middle and top remain raw. As a general rule, *in a 14-inch wok do not stir-fry more than a total of 8 cups of any combination of rice or noodles, vegetables, and protein.*

The Sizzle Means . . .

The moment rice and noodles are added to the wok there should be a sizzling sound that remains steady throughout cooking. If there is no audible sizzle, it indicates the wok was not sufficiently heated (see Stir-Frying with Proper Heat and Control, page 52). Rice and noodle recipes generally have 6 to 8 cups of ingredients, and if the wok is insufficiently heated some ingredients are likely to remain raw or undercooked.

Sprinkle in the Dry Seasonings

Sprinkle in dry seasonings, like salt and pepper, so they are well distributed and do not clump in one spot. Rice and noodle recipes generally have 6 to 8 cups of ingredients, making it more challenging to disperse seasonings.

EGG PANCAKE FOR RICE AND NOODLES

Egg pancakes are often added to fried rice or noodle dishes. To make a pancake, add the beaten eggs to a preheated wok that has the bottom of the pan lightly coated with oil, tilting the pan so that the egg covers the surface as thinly as possible. Cook the pancake 30 seconds to 1 minute or until the bottom is just beginning to brown and the pancake is set. Use a metal spatula to flip the pancake and cook 5 seconds or until set.

Transfer the pancake to a cutting board. Cool before cutting the pancake in half. Stack the two halves and cut into bite-sized pieces.

Chicken Lo Mein with Ginger Mushrooms

This recipe is extremely simple to make and has a nice peppery flavor from the red pepper flakes, white pepper, and ginger. There is a variety of fresh noodles in the refrigerator section of most Chinese food markets. The best noodles for lo mein are about ¼ inch thick and are sold in 1-pound packages. If fresh shiitake mushrooms are not available, use button mushrooms. I will sometimes substitute bean sprouts for the Napa cabbage. (See photo, page 244.)

12 ounces fresh Chinese thick, round egg noodles

2 teaspoons sesame oil

12 ounces skinless, boneless chicken thigh, cut into
    ¼-inch-thick bite-sized slices

1 tablespoon finely shredded ginger

1 teaspoon plus 1 tablespoon Shao Hsing rice wine
    or dry sherry

1 teaspoon cornstarch

1 teaspoon plus 1 tablespoon soy sauce

1 teaspoon salt

¼ teaspoon ground white pepper

2 tablespoons peanut or vegetable oil

¼ teaspoon red pepper flakes

3 cups thinly sliced Napa cabbage (about 5 ounces)

4 ounces fresh shiitake mushrooms, stems
    removed and caps thinly sliced (about 2 cups)

½ cup finely shredded scallions

1. In a 3-quart saucepan bring 2 quarts water to a boil over high heat. When the water comes to a rolling boil, add the noodles. Return to a rolling boil and boil according to package directions until al dente. Carefully pour the noodles into a colander and rinse several times with cold water. Drain the noodles, shaking well to remove excess water. Return the noodles to the unwashed pot, add the sesame oil, and toss until well combined. Set aside.

2. Put the chicken in a shallow bowl and add the ginger, 1 teaspoon of the rice wine, cornstarch, 1 teaspoon of the soy sauce, ¼ teaspoon of the salt, and pepper. In a small bowl combine the remaining 1 tablespoon rice wine and 1 tablespoon soy sauce.

3. Heat a 14-inch flat-bottomed wok over high heat until a bead of water vaporizes within 1 to 2 seconds of contact. Swirl in 1 tablespoon of the peanut oil, add the red pepper flakes, then, using a metal spatula, stir-fry 10 seconds or until the pepper flakes are fragrant. Push the pepper flakes to the sides of the wok, carefully add the chicken mixture and spread it evenly in one layer in the wok. Cook undisturbed 1 minute, letting the chicken begin to sear. Stir-fry 30 seconds or until the chicken begins to brown. Add the cabbage and mushrooms and stir-fry 1 minute or until the cabbage is just wilted but the chicken is not cooked through. Transfer the chicken and vegetables to a plate.

4. Swirl the remaining 1 tablespoon peanut oil into the wok. Add the noodles and stir-fry 15 seconds. Restir the soy sauce mixture, swirl it into the wok, add the scallions and chicken mixture, and sprinkle on the remaining ¾ teaspoon salt. Stir-fry 1 to 2 minutes or until chicken is cooked through and noodles are heated through.

Serves 3 as a main dish or 4 as part of a multicourse meal.

Crabmeat Fried Rice

Crabmeat fried rice is both light and rich, a decadent main course or an elegant side dish for any meal. My fishmonger sells three different brands of lump crabmeat and each varies in how much cartilage remains in the meat. I choose the brand that has the least and then I check the crabmeat carefully by hand. Finding a piece of cartilage will ruin the pleasure of this scrumptious rice.

2 tablespoons peanut or vegetable oil

1 tablespoon minced garlic

1 cup ¼-inch diced carrots

4 cups cold cooked Classic Rice (page 283)

1 cup diced ripe tomatoes

1 cup chopped scallions

1 large egg, lightly beaten

¾ teaspoon salt

¼ teaspoon ground white pepper

8 ounces lump crabmeat, picked over to remove
    cartilage (about 1½ cups)

⅓ cup chopped cilantro

Heat a 14-inch flat-bottomed wok over high heat until a bead of water vaporizes within 1 to 2 seconds of contact. Swirl in the oil, add the garlic, then, using a metal spatula, stir-fry 10 seconds or until the garlic is fragrant. Add the carrots and stir-fry 1 minute or until the carrots begin to brown. Add the rice and stir-fry 1 to 2 minutes, breaking up the rice with the spatula until it is heated through. Add the tomatoes, scallions, and egg, sprinkle on the salt and pepper, and stir-fry about 1 minute or until the egg is just set. Add the crabmeat and cilantro and stir-fry 30 seconds or until just heated through.

Serves 3 as a main course or 4 as part of a multicourse meal.

Sandpot Stir-Fried Chicken Rice

This old-fashioned Cantonese recipe exemplifies the fuel efficiency of Chinese cuisine. Chicken and mushrooms are stir-fried with peppery ginger, and before the cooking is complete they are placed on top of hot rice in a sandpot. The heat of the rice finishes cooking the chicken, while the juices from the stir-fry give the rice richness. I have written this recipe for cooking in a saucepan and provided directions for cooking it in the traditional sandpot. When cooking with a sandpot, you must always start on low heat and allow the pan to heat slowly. Any sudden temperature changes can damage the pot. Sandpots are available in specialty cookware shops in Chinatown and in some Chinese markets. A new sandpot should be soaked in cold water for one day before using. When I serve this dish I use a large serving spoon and scoop up the rice with the chicken mixture. You can also stir the rice and chicken together before serving.

6 medium dried shiitake mushrooms

8 ounces skinless, boneless chicken breast or thigh, cut into ¼-inch-thick bite-sized slices

2 tablespoons finely shredded ginger

1 tablespoon egg white, lightly beaten

2 teaspoons Shao Hsing rice wine or dry sherry

1 teaspoon soy sauce

1 teaspoon dark soy sauce

2 teaspoons cornstarch

½ teaspoon salt

¼ teaspoon ground white pepper

1 teaspoon plus 1 tablespoon peanut or vegetable oil

1⅓ cups long-grain rice

2 cups chicken broth

1 scallion, finely shredded

3 slices prosciutto, julienned (about ½ cup)

1. In a medium bowl soak the mushrooms in ¾ cup cold water for 30 minutes or until softened. Drain and squeeze dry, reserving ½ cup of the soaking liquid. Cut off the stems and thinly slice the mushrooms to make about ½ cup.

2. In a medium bowl combine the chicken, ginger, egg white, rice wine, both soy sauces, cornstarch, salt, and pepper. Stir in 1 teaspoon of the oil.

3. Put the rice in a 2-quart saucepan. Wash the rice in several changes of cold water until the water runs clear. Drain. Add the broth, level the rice, and bring the broth to a boil over high heat. Reduce the heat to medium-low and simmer the rice 4 to 5 minutes or until most of the liquid has evaporated and little craters appear on the surface. Reduce the heat to low, cover, and simmer 10 minutes or until all of the broth is absorbed.

4. After the rice has simmered 7 minutes, heat a 14-inch flat-bottomed wok or 12-inch skillet over high heat until a bead of water vaporizes within 1 to 2 seconds of contact. Swirl in the remaining 1 tablespoon oil. Carefully add the chicken, spreading it in one layer in the wok. Cook undisturbed 1 minute, letting the chicken begin to sear. Add the mushrooms, then, using a metal spatula, stir-fry 1 minute or until the chicken is lightly browned on all sides but not cooked through and is well combined with the mushrooms. Swirl the reserved ½ cup mushroom liquid into the wok and stir-fry 10 seconds to combine.

5. Uncover the rice and quickly spread the chicken mixture and scallion on top. Immediately cover the pan and cook 5 to 7 minutes, or until the chicken is just cooked through and the rice is tender. Sprinkle

the prosciutto over the mixture. Bring the pot to the table and serve immediately.

Serves 2 to 3 as a main dish or 4 as part of a multicourse meal.

Sandpot Variation:
Follow steps 1 and 2 of the main recipe.

Put the rice in a 2-quart sandpot. Wash the rice in several changes of cold water until the water runs clear. Drain. Add the broth and level the rice. Place the cover on the sandpot. Set the sandpot over low heat 5 minutes. Increase the heat to medium for 3 to 5 minutes or just until the mixture begins to simmer. Uncover, increase the heat to medium-high, and bring broth to a boil. Reduce the heat to medium-low, and simmer 4 to 5 minutes or until most of the liquid has evaporated and little craters appear on the surface. Reduce the heat to low, cover, and simmer 10 minutes or until all of the broth is absorbed.

Finish the recipe by following steps 4 and 5 of the main recipe.

Stir-Frying Bagels in Beijing

Lejen Chen

The very idea of stir-frying bagels made no sense to me. In fact, a big chewy bagel is the last thing any sane person would even attempt to stir-fry. Surely I had misunderstood. But no, in Beijing I was told a small group of Chinese did, in fact, love to eat stir-fried bagels. My informant was Lejen Chen, a Chinese American. Born in Taiwan and raised in Brooklyn, she has been producing bagels in Beijing's Shunyi district since the mid-1990s. Sold as "Mrs. Shanen's Bagels," they are a favorite among expat Americans craving a taste of home. But for Chen's employees, who had never seen, let alone tasted, a bagel before working for her, this was a foreign food indeed.

As Chen tells it, one day, a Ms. Wong, who happened to be a terrific cook, decided to try a bagel. Rather than split it and smear it with butter or cream cheese, she had the bright idea to use it to prepare the popular Beijing street food *caobing*—typically a stir-fry of pork and cabbage—combined with *laobing*, which is a type of Chinese bread. *Laobing* looks and tastes like a Chinese scallion pancake, only without the scallions; for *caobing*, it is cut into ⅛-inch-wide strips that look like fine linguine. Ms. Wong's inspiration was to substitute plain bagels cut into crouton-sized cubes, for *laobing*, then stir-frying them with cabbage, sliced pork, dried chilies, Sichuan peppercorns, ginger, and a little rice vinegar. Sometimes the ingredients would vary depending on what was available at the market. Chen explains, "Basically, it's like a stir-fried noodle dish, but it tastes like a hot bread salad or a drier version of stuffing." Chen's employees loved the dish and ate it every day for lunch.

Not long after my talk with Chen, I received a rather heavy package from Beijing. It contained two large bags of Mrs. Shanen's bagels and *laobing*, delivered by Chen's friends, Carl and Lesley Walter. The Walters had packed the precious bagels in their luggage on their annual holiday trip back to the States

Lejen Chen

so that I could replicate the stir-fry. The irony of receiving Beijing bagels in New York City did not escape me. As I prepared the ingredients, it felt odd just seeing a bowl of cubed bagels alongside the sliced ginger. Chen's description of the dish was accurate. The stir-fry was indeed tasty, but, to be honest, given that I am not fond of either bread salad or stuffing, it is not a dish I will make often.

On the other hand, I have rarely been so fascinated with a recipe; in this case, as a curious example of how a stir-fry can evolve, however improbably, via a Chinese American whose longing for the quintessential New York nosh inspired an unlikely Beijing bagel business. And the ingenious Ms. Wong, who managed to deconstruct a traditional Jewish food, thereby making it Chinese. Historically, the Chinese have assimilated many foreign ingredients into their cooking. The Spanish and Portuguese explorers gave China corn and sweet potatoes, and it was only one hundred years ago that tomatoes and chili peppers became part of the Chinese diet. Even as global culinary borders become less distinct, who could have ever predicted the possibility of a bagel stir-fry in Beijing, China?

Stir-Fried Bagels with Cabbage and Bacon

Should you like to try Ms. Wong's highly unorthodox stir-fried bagels, here is the recipe courtesy of Lejen Chen, opposite page. She told me the staff likes to use pork belly, but for Americans she thinks bacon would be a great substitute. If the bacon is very lean and does not release much fat, you may need to add a tablespoon or two of oil. To my surprise, instead of Napa cabbage, Lejen uses ordinary green cabbage. I am accustomed to roasting and grinding Sichuan peppercorns before cooking with them, but Lejen says that is unnecessary. A wok is recommended for this dish; I tried stir-frying this in a skillet and the ingredients stuck badly to the pan. If day-old bagels are used, sprinkle a tablespoon of water over the bagel-cabbage mixture before covering the wok.

1 tablespoon soy sauce

1 tablespoon rice vinegar

2 tablespoons peanut or vegetable oil

1 dried red chili pepper, snipped on one end

2 slices ginger, smashed

½ teaspoon Sichuan peppercorns

5 slices bacon, cut crosswise into ½-inch-wide pieces (about 4 ounces)

1 tablespoon coarsely chopped garlic

6 cups cubed green cabbage (about 1 pound)

2 large plain bagels, cut into ½-inch cubes (about 6 cups)

½ teaspoon salt

1. In a small bowl combine the soy sauce and vinegar.

2. Heat a 14-inch flat-bottomed wok over high heat until a bead of water vaporizes within 1 to 2 seconds of contact. Swirl in the oil, add the chili, ginger, and peppercorns, then, using a metal spatula, stir-fry 10 seconds or until the aromatics are fragrant. Add the bacon, reduce the heat to medium, and stir-fry 3 minutes or until the bacon is slightly crispy on the edges. Add the garlic and stir-fry 10 seconds or until the garlic is just fragrant. Add the cabbage, increase the heat to high, and stir-fry 1 minute or until the cabbage leaves just begin to wilt. Swirl the soy sauce mixture into the wok, add the bagels, and stir-fry 1 minute or until well combined. Cover, reduce the heat to medium-low, and cook 1 minute or until the bagels have softened. Uncover, sprinkle on the salt, and stir-fry until well combined.

Serves 4 as part of a multicourse meal.

Peppery Vegetarian Rice

The key to a tasty vegetarian fried rice is to use brown rice, with its mild, nutty flavor and chewy texture. The beauty of this recipe is its total flexibility. I like the meaty texture of mushrooms and will sometimes use cremini or button mushrooms. The pine nuts can also be replaced with chopped roasted cashews, almonds, or pecans. For more protein, sometimes I add defrosted shelled edamame. I cook the rice the day before I want to serve this.

1 cup brown rice

2 teaspoons plus 2 tablespoons peanut
  or vegetable oil

2 large eggs, beaten

2 tablespoons minced ginger

¼ teaspoon red pepper flakes

1 cup ¼-inch diced carrots

4 ounces fresh shiitake mushrooms, cut into
  ¼-inch dice (2⅓ cups)

½ cup vegetable broth

½ cup chopped scallions

¼ cup pine nuts, roasted

2 tablespoons soy sauce

½ teaspoon salt

¼ teaspoon ground white pepper

1. Put the rice in a 1-quart saucepan and wash in several changes of cold water until the water runs clear. Drain and level the rice. Add 2 cups cold water. Bring the water to a boil uncovered over high heat. Reduce the heat to medium, and simmer the rice until most of the water has evaporated and little craters appear on the surface, 4 to 5 minutes. Reduce the heat to low, cover, and simmer 10 minutes or until the liquid is absorbed. Turn off the heat and let stand 5 minutes.

Fluff the rice, cover, and allow to cool completely before refrigerating.

2. When ready to stir-fry the rice, heat a 14-inch flat-bottomed wok over high heat until a bead of water vaporizes within 1 to 2 seconds of contact. Swirl in 2 teaspoons of the oil, making sure the bottom of the wok is completely coated in oil. Add the eggs and cook 30 seconds to 1 minute, tilting the pan so that the egg covers the surface as thinly as possible to make a pancake. When the bottom is just beginning to brown and the pancake is just set, using a metal spatula flip the pancake and allow it to set, about 5 seconds, before transferring it to a cutting board. Cool, then cut the pancake into bite-sized pieces.

3. Swirl 1 tablespoon of the remaining oil into the wok, add the ginger and red pepper flakes, then, using a metal spatula, stir-fry 10 seconds or until the ginger is fragrant. Add the carrots and mushrooms and stir-fry 30 seconds or until all the oil is absorbed. Swirl the broth into the wok and stir-fry 1 minute or until almost all the broth has evaporated. Swirl in the remaining 1 tablespoon oil, add the scallions and rice, and stir-fry 2 to 3 minutes, breaking up the rice with the spatula until it is heated through. Add the pine nuts and soy sauce, sprinkle on the salt, pepper, and the reserved egg pieces, and toss to combine.

Serves 2 to 3 as a main dish or 4 as part of a multicourse meal.

Fried Rice: The Stir-Fry for Rookies

In the old days, when young Chinese chefs learned to stir-fry, one of the first dishes they were taught was fried rice, which was regarded as one of the "safest" dishes to cook. Stir-frying the dish involves minimal spattering because of the relatively low moisture of the rice and because the grains absorb any excess oil. It is a favorite dish for novice chefs to practice the *pao* action, required in restaurant-style stir-frying, which entails jerking the wok in small circular movements to toss ingredients in the air and then catch them. Fried rice also has no complicated sauces to master, but rather is flavored with basic seasonings. To this day, fried rice remains a favorite dish for every home cook, beginner or expert, to make.

I love fried rice not only for its ease of cooking, but also because it is the quintessential one-pot meal. Such classic combinations as Yangchow Fried Rice (page 259) cleverly marry the rich flavors of shrimp, ham, and peas. Recipes such as Chinese Cuban Fried Rice (page 264), Chinese Indian Vegetarian Fried Rice (page 265), and Chinese Jamaican Jerk Chicken Fried Rice (page 262) exemplify fried rice's universal appeal and its ability to adapt to the tastes of any culture.

I find that when I make fried rice it feeds my creative and practical instincts. It is an opportunity to creatively repurpose leftovers. But the beauty of the dish is that it never looks or tastes like a frugal offering. Instead, that lonely half onion, the single carrot left in the vegetable bin, the handful of shiitake mushrooms, the leftover roast chicken leg, and those last lively sprigs from a bunch of cilantro can all be tumbled together in a wok and reinvented as fried rice.

If I want a vegetarian fried rice, I add a beaten egg or heighten the protein with a little edamame or tofu. Haphazardly combining leftovers sometimes creates a masterful concoction that is deeply satisfying but equally disappointing because it can never be replicated. What is striking about fried rice is that it encourages variation, typifying the adaptability of stir-fries.

Day-old rice is a blank canvas for everything from classic recipes to stir-fry experimentation, and the simple secret for great fried rice is leftover cold rice. Freshly cooked rice produces a sticky mess that clumps, because hot or even warm rice is too moist for the grains to remain separate. But day-old rice that has been refrigerated is easy to stir-fry and produces lustrous individual grains. For this reason, I often cook more rice than is necessary for a meal so I have extra rice in the refrigerator, especially welcome when I'm pressed for time and in need of comfort food.

Yangchow Fried Rice

Yangchow fried rice is one of the classic dishes served at a Chinese banquet, customarily toward the end of the meal. The dish originated in eastern China, in Yangchow, but it is popular throughout China. It is lightly seasoned and deliberately does not have any soy sauce so that the rice grains remain white. Yangchow fried rice is prized for its clean and fresh flavors. The Cantonese make this rice with Chinese Barbecued Pork (page 285), in place of the ham.

2 tablespoons peanut or vegetable oil

4 ounces small shrimp, peeled, deveined, and cut into ½-inch pieces

4 cups cold cooked Classic Rice (page 283)

1 cup frozen peas

1 cup ¼-inch diced baked or boiled ham

½ cup chopped scallions

¾ teaspoon salt

¼ teaspoon ground white pepper

Heat a 14-inch flat-bottomed wok over high heat until a bead of water vaporizes within 1 to 2 seconds of contact. Swirl in 1 tablespoon of the oil, add the shrimp, then, using a metal spatula, stir-fry 1 minute or until the shrimp just turn orange but are not cooked through. Swirl in the remaining 1 tablespoon oil, add the rice and peas, and stir-fry 2 to 3 minutes, breaking up the rice with the spatula until it is heated through. Add the ham and scallions, sprinkle on the salt and pepper, and stir-fry 1 minute or until the shrimp are cooked and the mixture is well combined.

Serves 2 to 3 as a main dish or 4 as part of a multicourse meal.

Fried Sweet Rice with Sausages and Mushrooms

I had never had fried rice made with sweet rice until I tasted it in Guangzhou, China. The sweet rice gives an extra richness and bite that is addictively delicious. I cook the rice the day before I want to serve this. The dish must be made with cold cooked rice; otherwise the grains will stick together. If you cook the rice with a homemade chicken broth instead of canned broth, the dish is even more decadent. The Chinese sausage called lop chong *in Cantonese looks like skinny salami and is sold in Chinese butcher shops and some Asian markets.*

2 cups sweet or sushi rice

2 cups chicken broth

8 medium dried shiitake mushrooms

2 tablespoons peanut or vegetable oil

1 tablespoon minced ginger

1 Chinese sausage, cut into ¼-inch dice

½ cup chopped scallions

1 tablespoon soy sauce

½ teaspoon salt

⅛ teaspoon ground white pepper

1. Put the rice in a 1½ quart saucepan and wash in several changes of cold water until the water runs clear. Drain and level the rice. Add the broth and set aside to soak 30 minutes. Bring the broth to a boil uncovered over high heat. Reduce the heat to low, cover, and simmer until the liquid is absorbed, about 10 to 15 minutes. Remove from the heat and let stand 10 minutes. Fluff the rice, cover, and allow to cool completely before refrigerating.

2. When ready to stir-fry the rice, in a small bowl soak the mushrooms in 1 cup cold water 30 minutes or until softened. Drain and squeeze dry. (The soaking liquid can be reserved for stocks.) Cut off and discard the stems and roughly chop the caps.

3. Heat a 14-inch flat-bottomed wok over high heat until a bead of water vaporizes within 1 to 2 seconds of contact. Swirl in the oil, add the ginger, sausage, and mushrooms, then, using a metal spatula, stir-fry 1 to 2 minutes or until the mixture is lightly coated in oil and the sausage begins to brown. Add the rice and stir-fry, breaking up the rice with the spatula, 1 to 2 minutes or until the rice is heated through. Add the scallions and soy sauce, sprinkle on the salt and pepper, and stir-fry about 1 minute or until well combined and the sausage is cooked through.

Serves 2 to 3 as a main dish or 4 as part of a multicourse meal.

Chinese Jamaican Jerk Chicken Fried Rice

I never dreamed I would write a recipe for jerk chicken in a Chinese cookbook. I first tasted jerk chicken fried rice in a Chinese Jamaican restaurant in New York City and was blown away by what an unexpected combination it was—without a doubt this was a truly great fried rice. All the Chinese Jamaicans I have interviewed have never heard of this dish. Jerk chicken fried rice catered to the tastes of Jamaican customers, just as chop suey appealed to Americans. I am told it is also served in Chinese Jamaican restaurants in Toronto, Canada, and in a Chinese Guyanese restaurant in England.

I like my version even better than what I tasted in the restaurant; I'm sure that's because a homemade jerk sauce is superior to the bottled sauce the restaurant was probably using. The other key is to stir the pan drippings into the rice. I roast the chicken in a roasting pan lined with aluminum foil so it's easier to add the drippings to the rice. If you're concerned with fat, skim it off; it does add to the great flavor, though.

The jerk marinade makes twice what you'll need for one recipe of fried rice, but you'll want the extra so you can make this again soon. You can refrigerate the extra marinade for up to 1 week or freeze it for up to 2 months.

1 cup plus ½ cup chopped scallions
1 tablespoon roughly chopped garlic
2 tablespoons ketchup
2 tablespoons fresh lime juice
1 tablespoon distilled white vinegar
2 tablespoons soy sauce
1 tablespoon fresh thyme leaves
2 teaspoons ground allspice
2 teaspoons brown sugar

1 teaspoon plus 1 tablespoon dark soy sauce
1 teaspoon plus 2 tablespoons peanut or vegetable oil
1¼ teaspoons salt
½ teaspoon ground cinnamon
½ teaspoon freshly ground pepper
½ to 1 teaspoon red pepper flakes
½ teaspoon cayenne
2 whole chicken legs, well trimmed (about 1¾ pounds)
⅓ cup chopped onions
⅓ cup diced carrots
4 cups cold cooked Classic Rice (page 283)

1. In a mini food processor combine 1 cup of the scallions and garlic and pulse until just combined. Add the ketchup, lime juice, and vinegar and process 1 minute, pausing once to scrape down the sides of the bowl, or until the mixture is almost smooth. Add 1 tablespoon of the soy sauce, thyme, allspice, sugar, 1 teaspoon of the dark soy sauce, 1 teaspoon of the oil, 1 teaspoon of the salt, cinnamon, pepper, red pepper flakes, and cayenne. Pulse until well combined to make about ½ cup. Put ¼ cup in a covered container and refrigerate; use within 1 week, or freeze for up to 2 months.

2. Make several 1-inch slits on both sides of the chicken legs. Put the chicken legs in a large shallow bowl and pour on the reserved ¼ cup jerk marinade, making sure the marinade reaches under the skin and completely coats the chicken. Cover and refrigerate for 2 hours or overnight. Thirty minutes before roasting remove the marinated chicken from the refrigerator.

3. Preheat the oven to 425°F. Put the chicken skin

side up in a roasting pan lined with aluminum foil and roast 30 minutes or until the chicken is golden brown and a meat thermometer registers 170°F when inserted at the meatiest point of the thigh but not touching the bone. Transfer the chicken to a cutting board, reserving the pan drippings. If desired, skim any surface fat from the pan drippings. Allow the roasted chicken to rest 10 minutes before cutting it into bite-sized pieces to make about 2½ cups. Discard the bones. In a small bowl combine the remaining 1 tablespoon soy sauce and 1 tablespoon dark soy sauce.

4. Heat a 14-inch flat-bottomed wok over high heat until a bead of water vaporizes within 1 to 2 seconds of contact. Swirl in the remaining 2 tablespoons oil, add the onions and carrots, then, using a metal spatula, stir-fry 30 seconds or until the onions begin to wilt. Add the rice and stir-fry 2 minutes, breaking up the rice with the spatula until it is heated through. Swirl in the soy sauce mixture and stir-fry 1 minute or until all the rice grains are evenly colored with the soy sauce. Stir in the remaining ½ cup scallions, ¼ teaspoon salt, pan drippings, and chicken and stir-fry 10 seconds or until just combined.

Serves 3 as a main dish or 4 as part of a multicourse meal.

Chinese Cuban Fried Rice

In New York City there used to be a number of Chinese Cuban restaurants. Typically, the menu would be divided equally between Chinese and Cuban food; however, there are a few dishes that reflect the fusion of both cuisines. This fried rice is inspired by the one served at La Caridad 78, a restaurant on the Upper West Side that has been in business for over thirty years. The last time I went with my friend Barbara Chan she observed that eating in the restaurant felt like a step back in time. La Caridad 78 uses old-fashioned diner-style chinaware, and the all-male waitstaff, fluent in Chinese, Spanish, and English, reminded her of the old Chinese bachelorhood society. Every meal, whether Chinese or Cuban, is served with bread and butter.

La Caridad 78's fried rice is "plain," reminiscent of the Peruvian and Mexican fried rice I have tasted. At first I was surprised that there was no garlic, ginger, or chilies, but Chinese Hispanic–style fried rice is very simple, made with dark soy sauce as the main seasoning. This is very different from fried rice in China, which is rarely seasoned with dark soy sauce. The other unusual distinction is the rice is served with fried plantains and garnished with iceberg lettuce and a tomato slice. If bay shrimp are not available, use 1 cup diced cooked shrimp.

2 tablespoons peanut or vegetable oil

½ cup chopped onions

1 cup bean sprouts, rinsed and patted dry

1 cup cooked bay shrimp (about 4 ounces)

4 cups cold cooked Classic Rice (page 283)

2 tablespoons dark soy sauce

½ cup chopped scallions

½ teaspoon salt

1. Heat a 14-inch flat-bottomed wok over high heat until a bead of water vaporizes within 1 to 2 seconds of contact. Swirl in 1 tablespoon of the oil, add the onions, then, using a metal spatula, stir-fry 30 seconds or until the onions begin to wilt. Add the bean sprouts and shrimp and stir-fry 30 seconds or until the bean sprouts are lightly coated in oil. Transfer the shrimp mixture to a plate.

2. Swirl in the remaining 1 tablespoon oil, add the rice, and stir-fry 2 minutes, breaking up the rice with the spatula, until it is heated through. Add the soy sauce and stir-fry 1 minute or until all the rice grains are evenly colored with the soy sauce. Stir in the shrimp mixture and scallions, sprinkle on the salt, and stir-fry 10 seconds or until just combined.

Serves 2 to 3 as a main dish or 4 as part of a multicourse meal.

Chinese Indian Vegetarian Fried Rice

This recipe was inspired by a very spicy Sichuan vegetarian fried rice I tasted at Chinese Mirch, a Chinese Indian restaurant in New York City. As I watched the Chinese chef stir-fry the rice I was shocked to see him use freshly cooked hot rice. When I mentioned that Chinese fried rice is always made with cold cooked rice, the chef explained that they use basmati rice to suit Indian tastes. Basmati rice is naturally fluffier and drier than the more traditional long-grain rice, so it can be stir-fried right out of the pot. Traditionally, basmati rice is first cooked with a little ghee or oil before being cooked in water. To simplify this recipe, I eliminated that step because the cooked rice is eventually stir-fried in oil.

The chefs at Chinese Mirch make their own chili garlic sauce. I use the commercial chili garlic sauce made by Huy Fong Foods, Inc., which is available in most Asian markets, and it replicates the taste surprisingly well. The restaurant's fried rice is very spicy. I have given a range for the amount of chili garlic sauce for those who want their rice a little milder. The restaurant makes its vegetarian fried rice with carrots, green beans, and scallions; you should feel free to use whatever vegetables you like.

1½ cups basmati rice

2 tablespoons soy sauce

2 tablespoons ketchup

2 to 3 teaspoons chili garlic sauce

¼ teaspoon ground white pepper

2 tablespoons peanut or vegetable oil

½ cup ¼-inch diced carrots

½ cup ¼-inch diced green beans

½ cup chopped scallions

1. Put the rice in a 1½-quart heavy saucepan. Wash the rice in several changes of cold water until the water runs clear. Drain. Level the rice in the pan and add 1¾ cups cold water. Bring the water to a boil over high heat, reduce the heat to low, cover, and simmer 15 minutes or until all of the water is absorbed. Turn off the heat and let stand 5 minutes. Meanwhile, in a small bowl combine the soy sauce, ketchup, chili garlic sauce, and pepper.

2. Heat a 14-inch flat-bottomed wok over high heat until a bead of water vaporizes within 1 to 2 seconds of contact. Swirl in the oil, add the carrots and green beans, then, using a metal spatula, stir-fry 1 minute or until the vegetables are barely beginning to brown. Add the hot rice and stir-fry 30 seconds, breaking up the rice with the spatula or until the rice is well combined with the vegetables. Swirl the ketchup mixture into the wok and stir-fry about 30 seconds or until just combined. Stir in the scallions and remove the pan from the heat.

Serves 2 to 3 as a main dish or 4 as part of a multicourse meal.

Stir-Fried Cilantro Chili Noodles with Egg

Just the fragrance of fresh cilantro at the farmers' market in the summer makes me hungry to make this stir-fry. Rice noodles are so fine and delicate and especially delicious when infused with cilantro, along with spicy fresh chilies and ginger. For a vegetarian dish, use vegetable broth in place of the chicken broth. If I'm in the mood for a little more protein, I add a cup of lump crabmeat or julienned smoked ham.

8 ounces (½ package) thin rice stick noodles (vermicelli)

½ cup chicken broth or vegetable stock

2 tablespoons soy sauce

2 teaspoons rice vinegar

2 teaspoons plus 2 tablespoons peanut or vegetable oil

2 large eggs, beaten

1 to 2 tablespoons minced Anaheim chilies, with seeds

1 tablespoon minced ginger

1 cup chopped cilantro sprigs and stems

½ teaspoon sugar

¼ teaspoon salt

⅛ teaspoon freshly ground pepper

2 teaspoons sesame oil

Cilantro sprigs

1. Soak the noodles in a large pan or bowl with enough warm water to cover for 20 minutes or until they are soft and pliable. Drain the noodles in a colander, shaking well to remove excess water. Using kitchen shears, roughly cut the noodles into 6- to 8-inch-long pieces. In a small bowl combine the broth, soy sauce, and rice vinegar.

2. Heat a 14-inch flat-bottomed wok over high heat until a bead of water vaporizes within 1 to 2 seconds of contact. Swirl in 2 teaspoons of the peanut oil, making sure the bottom of the wok is completely coated in oil. Add the eggs and cook 30 seconds to 1 minute, tilting the pan so that the egg covers the surface as thinly as possible to make a pancake. When the bottom is just beginning to brown and the pancake is set, using a metal spatula flip the pancake and allow it to set, about 5 seconds, before transferring it to a cutting board. Allow to cool, then cut the pancake into ¼-inch-wide shreds.

3. Swirl the remaining 2 tablespoons peanut oil into the wok. Add the chilies and ginger, then, using the spatula, stir-fry 10 seconds or until the aromatics are fragrant. Swirl the broth mixture into the wok, add the drained noodles, reduce the heat to medium, and stir-fry 2 minutes or until the noodles are just tender and almost all the liquid has been absorbed by the noodles. Add the cilantro and egg shreds, sprinkle on the sugar, salt, and pepper, and stir-fry 1 minute or until well combined. Stir in the sesame oil. Garnish with the cilantro.

Serves 2 as a main dish or 4 as part of a multicourse meal.

Beef Chow Fun

This beloved noodle dish is a favorite in Cantonese restaurants. It is a classic example of the technique of dry stir-frying (see Dry Stir-Frying and Moist Stir-Frying, page 121) and is revered for its caramelized, toasty flavors and the deliberate absence of sauce. In contrast, an example of moist stir-frying is Chicken Chow Fun (page 276), made with a sauce that lightly coats the noodles and chicken.

Broad rice noodles are made fresh daily and sold in specialty noodle shops in Chinatown, but they can also be found in some Asian markets. Made with rice flour, the noodle batter is poured onto lightly oiled jelly-roll pans, and then steamed. After steaming, the noodle sheets are folded like kitchen towels and sold unrefrigerated. These are best used the day of purchase. Once they are refrigerated, they become hard and must be resteamed before stir-frying.

8 ounces lean flank steak

2 teaspoons soy sauce

1½ teaspoons cornstarch

1 teaspoon sesame oil

1 pound fresh broad rice noodles (1 sheet)

2 tablespoons oyster sauce

1 tablespoon Shao Hsing rice wine or dry sherry

2 tablespoons peanut or vegetable oil

2 teaspoons minced ginger

2 teaspoons minced garlic

1 tablespoon fermented black beans, rinsed and
   mashed

3 cups bean sprouts, rinsed and patted dry (about
   6 ounces)

½ cup finely shredded scallions

¼ teaspoon ground white pepper

1. Cut the beef with the grain into 2-inch-wide strips. Cut each strip across the grain into ¼-inch-thick slices. Put the beef in a shallow bowl and add the soy sauce, cornstarch, and sesame oil. Stir to combine. Leaving the noodles as a slab, cut it crosswise into ½-inch-wide strips. Using your hands, separate and loosen the strips to make about 4 cups. In a small bowl combine the oyster sauce and rice wine.

2. Heat a 14-inch flat-bottomed wok over high heat until a bead of water vaporizes within 1 to 2 seconds of contact. Swirl in 1 tablespoon of the peanut oil, add the ginger and garlic, then, using a metal spatula, stir-fry 10 seconds or until the aromatics are fragrant. Push the aromatics to the sides of the wok, carefully add the beef and spread it evenly in one layer in the wok. Cook undisturbed 1 minute, letting the beef begin to sear. Add the fermented beans and stir-fry 30 seconds or until the beef is lightly browned but not cooked through. Transfer the beef to a plate.

3. Swirl the remaining 1 tablespoon peanut oil into the wok, add the noodles, and spread evenly in one layer in the wok. Cook undisturbed for 1 minute or until the noodles are slightly crusty. Add the bean sprouts and stir-fry 1 minute or until the sprouts are just limp. Return the beef with any juices that have accumulated to the wok, add the scallions, sprinkle on the pepper and oyster sauce mixture, and stir-fry 1 minute or until the beef is just cooked.

Serves 2 as a main course or 4 as part of a multicourse meal.

Noodle Soup with Stir-Fried Scallops and Enoki Mushrooms

This is an example of how a stir-fry is also excellent over soup noodles. The enoki mushrooms, which add a delicate flavor, are wonderful for stir-fries because they hardly need to be handled and cook quickly. When purchasing enoki, look for mushrooms with firm, creamy white caps and stems. If bay scallops are not available, substitute sea scallops cut into quarters.

12 ounces fresh bay scallops
2 tablespoons Shao Hsing rice wine or dry sherry
1 teaspoon chili bean sauce
6 teaspoons soy sauce
4 teaspoons sesame oil
Ground white pepper
4 ounces enoki mushrooms (about 2 cups)
1 quart chicken broth
3 ginger slices, smashed, plus 1 tablespoon
　　minced ginger
2 tablespoons peanut or vegetable oil
1 cup julienned carrots
8 ounces bok choy, trimmed and cut crosswise into
　　¼-inch-wide pieces
¾ teaspoon salt
1 pound fresh Chinese thick, round egg noodles

1. Rinse the scallops in cold water, removing any visible bits of shell or grit. Drain well in a colander and pat dry with paper towels. In a small bowl combine the rice wine and chili bean sauce. Pour 1½ teaspoons of the soy sauce and 1 teaspoon of the sesame oil with a pinch of white pepper into each of 4 large soup bowls.

2. Trim off the roots of the enoki mushrooms up to the point where the individual stems can be separated, about 1¼ inch. Separate the mushrooms into smaller clusters or individual stems.

3. In a 2-quart saucepan bring the broth and the 3 slices of ginger to a boil over high heat. Cover, reduce the heat to low, and simmer until ready to use. In a 3-quart saucepan bring 1½ quarts water to a boil over high heat. Cover, reduce the heat to low, and simmer until ready to use.

4. Heat a 14-inch flat-bottomed wok or 12-inch skillet over high heat until a bead of water vaporizes within 1 to 2 seconds of contact. Swirl in the peanut oil, add the remaining 1 tablespoon minced ginger, then, using a metal spatula, stir-fry 10 seconds or until the ginger is fragrant. Push the ginger to the sides of the wok, and carefully add the scallops, spreading them evenly in one layer. Cook undisturbed for 1 minute, letting the scallops begin to sear. Add the mushrooms, carrots, and bok choy and stir-fry 1 minute or until the bok choy starts to wilt. Sprinkle on the salt, swirl the rice wine mixture into the wok, and stir-fry 1 minute or until the scallops are just cooked through and the vegetables are crisp-tender. Remove the wok from the heat and set aside.

5. Return the water in the saucepan to a boil over high heat. Add the noodles and cook according to the package directions or until al dente. Drain the noodles in a colander and divide the noodles among the soup bowls. Toss the noodles in each bowl with the soy sauce mixture. Divide the scallop mixture. Divide the broth among the soup bowls. Serve immediately.

Serves 4 as a main dish.

Barbecued Pork Lo Mein

Chinese barbecued pork, also known as cha siu *in Cantonese, is available in Chinese restaurants that display prepared poultry such as roast duck in the window for takeout. When I have the time, I prefer to make barbecued pork; it's easy and homemade* cha siu *is so delicious. Unlike the restaurant variety, my recipe does not have red food coloring.*

When stir-frying noodles, I like to use a spatula and a pair of chopsticks to loosen the noodles so that they can be tossed like a salad to mix in all the other ingredients. Only do this if your wok is stabilized on a wok ring or someone is holding the handle of your wok to prevent the pan from sliding off the burner.

In New York City I live near a wonderful Italian pasta shop called Raffetto's, and I sometimes buy the fresh Italian tagliarini *in place of the egg noodles. This recipe is an example of a "cooked stir-fry" because it requires a precooked ingredient.*

12 ounces fresh Chinese thick, round egg noodles

3 tablespoons peanut or vegetable oil

2 tablespoons soy sauce

1 tablespoon oyster sauce

½ teaspoon salt

3 slices ginger, smashed

1 tablespoon minced garlic

8 ounces Chinese Barbecued Pork (page 285), julienned (about 2 cups)

4 cups bean sprouts, rinsed and patted dry (about 8 ounces)

1 tablespoon Shao Hsing rice wine or dry sherry

2 scallions, finely shredded

1. In a 3-quart saucepan bring 2 quarts water to a boil over high heat. When the water comes to a rolling boil add the noodles. Return to a rolling boil and cook according to the package directions until al dente. Carefully pour the noodles into a colander and rinse with several changes of cold water. Drain the noodles in the colander, shaking well to remove excess water. Return the noodles to the unwashed pot, add 1 tablespoon of the oil, and toss until well combined. In a small bowl combine the soy sauce, oyster sauce, and the salt.

2. Heat a 14-inch flat-bottomed wok over high heat until a bead of water vaporizes within 1 to 2 seconds of contact. Swirl in the remaining 2 tablespoons oil, add the ginger, garlic, and pork, then, using a metal spatula, stir-fry about 1 minute or until the pork is lightly coated in oil. Add the bean sprouts and rice wine and stir-fry 30 seconds or until the bean sprouts just begin to wilt.

3. Restir the oyster sauce mixture, swirl it into the wok, add the noodles and scallions, and stir-fry 2 minutes or until the pork and noodles are heated through.

Serves 2 to 3 as a main course or 4 as part of a multicourse meal.

Singapore Noodles

This is the "traditional" version of Singapore noodles, made with curry powder, shrimp, and Chinese barbecued pork. In Singapore this is one of the great street foods to enjoy. For the best flavor be sure to use a high-quality Madras curry powder. There are many versions of this classic noodle dish, including Nyonya-Style Singapore Noodles (page 278). This is also an example of a moist stir-fry (see Dry Stir-Frying and Moist Stir-Frying, page 121) that does not have a sauce. The rice noodles are stir-fried in about ⅔ cup of liquid until they are just tender and all the liquid has been absorbed.

8 ounces (½ package) thin rice stick noodles
    (vermicelli)

½ cup chicken broth

1 tablespoon soy sauce

1 tablespoon Shao Hsing rice wine or dry sherry

3 tablespoons peanut or vegetable oil

1 tablespoon minced garlic

1 tablespoon minced ginger

¼ teaspoon red pepper flakes

4 ounces small shrimp, peeled and deveined

1 cup thinly sliced green bell peppers

1 tablespoon curry powder

¾ teaspoon salt

½ teaspoon sugar

⅛ teaspoon freshly ground pepper

4 ounces Chinese Barbecued Pork (page 285),
    julienned (about 1 cup)

1 cup finely shredded scallions

1. Soak the noodles in a large pan or bowl with enough warm water to cover for 20 minutes or until they are soft and pliable. Drain the noodles in a colander, shaking well to remove excess water. Using kitchen shears, roughly cut the noodles into 6- to 8-inch-long pieces. In a small bowl combine the broth, soy sauce, and rice wine.

2. Heat a 14-inch flat-bottomed wok over high heat until a bead of water vaporizes within 1 to 2 seconds of contact. Swirl in 1 tablespoon of the oil, add the garlic, ginger, and red pepper flakes, then, using a metal spatula, stir-fry 10 seconds or until the aromatics are fragrant. Add the shrimp and stir-fry 1 minute or until the shrimp have just turned orange but are not cooked through. Transfer the shrimp to a plate.

3. Swirl the remaining 2 tablespoons oil into the wok, add the bell peppers, and stir-fry 30 seconds or until the peppers are bright green. Add the curry powder and stir-fry 5 seconds or until the curry is fragrant. Swirl the broth mixture into the wok, add the drained noodles, and stir-fry until they are completely coated in the curry mixture. Sprinkle on the salt, sugar, and pepper and stir-fry 2 minutes, or until the noodles are just tender. Add the shrimp and pork and stir-fry 1 to 2 minutes or until the shrimp are just cooked through and all the liquid has been absorbed by the noodles. Stir in the scallions.

Serves 2 to 3 as a main dish or 4 as part of a multicourse meal.

Chicken Chow Fun

I had never made chow fun with a sauce until Raymond Leong, who has taught cooking for over thirty years, demonstrated this dish for me. Chow fun can be prepared "dry" or "moist" with a sauce (see Dry Stir-Frying and Moist Stir-Frying, page 121). You'll notice that after swirling the oil into the wok Leong adds the salt. According to Leong, this disperses the salt more evenly. Southeast Asian cooking authority Joyce Jue told me her mother also taught her this technique, explaining that less salt is necessary in a stir-fry when it is added this way. For more information on broad rice noodles, see Beef Chow Fun (page 269). Leong serves the stir-fried chicken and vegetables poured over the noodles. You can also return the noodles to the wok and combine all the ingredients.

8 ounces skinless, boneless chicken breast, cut into
 ½-inch cubes

1 teaspoon minced plus 1 teaspoon sliced garlic

1 teaspoon minced plus 1 teaspoon finely
 shredded ginger

3 teaspoons Shao Hsing rice wine or dry sherry

½ teaspoon plus 1 tablespoon oyster sauce

½ teaspoon plus 1 tablespoon soy sauce

1¾ teaspoons cornstarch

⅛ teaspoon ground white pepper

1 pound fresh broad rice noodles (1 sheet)

½ cup chicken broth

1 teaspoon sesame oil

4 teaspoons plus 1 tablespoon peanut
 or vegetable oil

¼ teaspoon salt

8 ounces bok choy, cut into 2-inch pieces (about
 4 cups)

12 medium fresh shiitake mushrooms, stems
 removed and caps halved (about 6 ounces)

1. In a medium bowl combine the chicken, the 1 teaspoon minced garlic, the 1 teaspoon minced ginger, 1 teaspoon of the rice wine, ½ teaspoon of the oyster sauce, ½ teaspoon of the soy sauce, ¾ teaspoon of the cornstarch, and pepper. Stir to combine. Leaving the noodles as a slab, cut it crosswise into ½-inch-wide strips. Using your hands, separate and loosen the strips to make about 4 cups noodles. In a small bowl combine the broth, sesame oil, the remaining 1 tablespoon oyster sauce, 1 tablespoon soy sauce, and 1 teaspoon cornstarch. In a small cup measure the remaining 2 teaspoons rice wine.

2. Heat a 14-inch flat-bottomed wok over high heat until a bead of water vaporizes within 1 to 2 seconds of contact. Swirl in 2 teaspoons of the peanut oil, sprinkle on the salt, and add the noodles, spreading them evenly in one layer in the wok. Cook undisturbed for 1 minute, or until the noodles are slightly crusty. Then, using a metal spatula, stir-fry 1 minute or until the noodles are loosened, slightly crusty, but not browned. Transfer the noodles to a platter.

3. Swirl 2 teaspoons of the peanut oil into the wok, add the remaining 1 teaspoon sliced garlic and 1 teaspoon shredded ginger, and stir-fry 10 seconds or until the aromatics are fragrant. Push the aromatics to the sides of the wok, carefully add the chicken, and spread it evenly in one layer in the wok. Cook undisturbed 1 minute, letting the chicken begin to sear. Swirl in the remaining 2 teaspoons rice wine and stir-fry 1 minute or until light brown. Transfer the chicken to a plate.

4. Swirl the remaining 1 tablespoon peanut oil into the wok. Add the bok choy and mushrooms and stir-fry 1 minute or until the bok choy is bright green and the

mushrooms begin to wilt. Return the chicken with any juices that have accumulated to the wok. Restir the broth mixture and swirl it into the wok and stir-fry 1 to 2 minutes or until the chicken is just cooked and the sauce is slightly thickened. Pour the mixture over the noodles.

Serves 2 to 3 as a main course or 4 as part of a multicourse meal.

Raymond Leong stir-fries outdoors using a portable wok stove fueled with propane gas.

Nyonya-Style Singapore Noodles

Mei Ibach, a Chinese Malaysian born in Malaysia and raised in Singapore, shared this recipe with me, which shows how dramatically different Singapore Noodles (page 274) are in Southeast Asia. In the nineteenth century, many Chinese immigrated to Malaysia and Singapore, creating their own cuisine, called Nyonya—a term that refers to the female descendants of these Chinese settlers who married local Malay women. Nyonya cuisine is highly seasoned. In this case, in addition to curry powder the noodles are flavored with soy sauce, kecap manis (a thick, sweet soy sauce), chili bean sauce, and ketchup. This is another example of moist stir-frying, but it's done in a slightly different manner from the one in the Singapore noodle recipe.

Ibach calls for fried tofu, which is sold in the refrigerator section of many Asian markets. If you are unable to find it, you can pat dry 1 square (about 4 ounces) of extra-firm tofu with paper towels to remove excess moisture. Pan-fry it in 1 teaspoon of oil over medium heat for 2 minutes, flipping it midway through cooking, then dice the tofu into ½-inch pieces. Ibach teaches Asian cooking in the Culinary Arts Program at Santa Rosa Junior College in California.

8 ounces (½ package) thin rice stick noodles (vermicelli)

½ cup chicken or vegetable broth

2 tablespoons soy sauce

2 tablespoons kecap manis or dark soy sauce

2 tablespoons ketchup

1 tablespoon curry powder

2 to 3 teaspoons chili bean sauce or sambal

1 teaspoon sugar

2 teaspoons plus 3 tablespoons peanut or vegetable oil

2 large eggs, beaten

1 cup chopped scallions

2 tablespoons minced shallots

1 tablespoon minced garlic

1 cup diced fried tofu

½ cup cooked bay shrimp (about 2 ounces)

2 cups bean sprouts, rinsed and patted dry

Cilantro sprigs

Salt

Pepper

1. Soak the noodles in a large pan or bowl with enough warm water to cover for 20 minutes or until they are soft and pliable. Drain the noodles in a colander, shaking well to remove excess water. Using kitchen shears, roughly cut the noodles into 6- to 8-inch-long pieces. In a medium bowl combine the broth, soy sauce, kecap manis, ketchup, curry powder, chili bean sauce, and sugar.

2. Heat a 14-inch flat-bottomed wok over high heat until a bead of water vaporizes within 1 to 2 seconds of contact. Swirl in 2 teaspoons of the oil, making sure the bottom of the wok is completely coated in oil. Add the eggs and cook 30 seconds to 1 minute, tilting the pan so that the egg covers the surface as thinly as possible to make a pancake. When the bottom is just beginning to brown and the pancake is just set, using a metal spatula flip the pancake and allow it to set, about 5 seconds, before transferring it to a cutting board. Allow to cool, then cut the pancake into ¼-inch-wide shreds.

3. Swirl the remaining 3 tablespoons oil into the wok, add ½ cup of the scallions, shallots, and garlic, and then, using a metal spatula, stir-fry 1 minute or until the scallions are wilted. Swirl the broth mixture into

the wok, add the drained noodles, reduce the heat to medium, and stir-fry 2 minutes. Add the tofu and stir-fry 2 minutes or until the noodles are just tender and all the liquid has been absorbed. Add the cooked bay shrimp, bean sprouts, and the remaining ½ cup scallions and stir-fry 1 minute or until just combined. Garnish with the egg pancake shreds and cilantro. Season with salt and pepper to taste.

Serves 3 as a main dish or 4 as part of a multicourse meal.

Stir-Fried Cellophane Noodles with Enoki Mushrooms

Cellophane noodles are made of mung bean flour. Like rice sticks, they need to be softened in warm water before cooking. The texture is almost silky and is very different from that of noodles made from wheat or rice. I always keep several packages on hand because they are excellent for making a light meal. This is a moist stir-fry so quite a bit of broth is added; it gets totally absorbed by the noodles. Naturally, if you can use a homemade broth, the noodles will have a much richer flavor. I suggest roughly cutting the noodles into 6- to 8-inch lengths; otherwise the noodles will form a solid mass that will be difficult to mix with the rest of the ingredients. If you don't have enoki mushrooms, use an equal amount of thinly sliced fresh shiitake mushrooms or button mushrooms.

One 3.5-ounce package cellophane noodles

¾ cup chicken broth or vegetable stock

2 tablespoons soy sauce

4 ounces enoki mushrooms (about 2 cups)

3 tablespoons peanut or vegetable oil

2 teaspoons minced garlic

¼ teaspoon red pepper flakes

1 cup julienned carrots

1 cup julienned snow peas

½ teaspoon salt

1 teaspoon sesame oil

1. Soak the noodles in a bowl with enough warm water to cover for 20 minutes or until they are soft and pliable. Drain the noodles in a colander, shaking well to remove excess water. Using kitchen shears, roughly cut the noodles into 6- to 8-inch-long pieces. In a small bowl combine the broth and soy sauce.

2. Trim off the roots of the enoki mushrooms up to the point where the individual stems can be separated, about 1¼ inch. Separate the mushrooms into smaller clusters or individual stems.

3. Heat a 14-inch flat-bottomed wok over high heat until a bead of water vaporizes within 1 to 2 seconds of contact. Swirl in the peanut oil, add the garlic and red pepper flakes, then, using a metal spatula, stir-fry 10 seconds or until the aromatics are fragrant. Add the carrots and mushrooms and stir-fry 1 minute or until the carrots just begin to wilt. Add the cellophane noodles and stir-fry 30 seconds or until the noodles just begin to soften. Swirl in the broth mixture, add the snow peas, cover the wok, and cook 1 minute or until the mixture just begins to simmer. Uncover, sprinkle on the salt, and stir-fry 1 minute or until the noodles are just tender and almost all the liquid has been absorbed. Remove the pan from the heat, add the sesame oil, and toss to combine. Serve hot, warm, or at room temperature.

Serves 2 as a main dish or 4 as part of a multicourse meal.

Stir-Frying in Brooklyn's Great Outdoors

George Chew

George Chew is no ordinary home cook. On our first get-together in his New York City loft, he was casually preparing a ten-course home-style Chinese dinner for a dozen friends, something he does regularly. Chew is legendary for his parties: on Thanksgiving, New Year's Eve, and July Fourth, he and his wife, Marilynn, invite fifty or sixty guests and he spends days preparing. His spacious kitchen is equipped with a powerful Wolf range and a serious exhaust system that leaves no trace of cooking odors.

Every year Chew also prepares his extended family's Chinese New Year's dinner at his brother's home in Brooklyn. The ordinary stove there used to drive him mad. Then six years ago he discovered a portable wok stove, called the Big Kahuna, on a visit to Chicago's Chinatown. "I went nuts. I'd never seen anything like it and I knew I had to have it," recalls Chew. He lugged it back to New York City in his checked luggage and installed it in his brother's backyard.

The stove has over 60,000 BTUs, a power Chew came to realize was unnecessary. "The first time I stir-fried with it, I used full power and incinerated everything," he confesses. In fact, it took Chew several attempts at cooking on the stove outdoors before he

George Chew (Photo by Marilynn K. Yee)

stopped burning all of the ingredients. "The Kahuna requires a constant adjustment of heat, especially when cooking with multiple ingredients," he adds. "I modify the heat depending on how much I have in the wok." Over time Chew learned how to accommodate the difference between cooking on his powerful Wolf home range and cooking with the Kahuna's even more intense level of heat. For example, instead of mincing his garlic, he began to dice it to prevent instant burning with the Kahuna. "I prepare a *mise en place* in which every ingredient is cut and measured, as you would for a professional kitchen, so that I can fully concentrate on the cooking and prevent scorching. There's no time to be doing anything last minute once the stir-frying begins," says Chew.

Cooking outdoors is ideal because it provides a natural exhaust system. Throughout Asia, street cooks use woks set on braziers, charcoal burners, or units similar to Chew's portable stove. In the Chinese countryside many people cook in outdoor kitchens, using a wok set over a traditional hearth stove.

Chew uses the Kahuna only for stir-frying: the enormous 22-inch carbon-steel wok can easily handle two pounds of Asian greens. On his brother's indoor stove that same amount would require stir-frying in several smaller batches. Two of his favorite dishes for stir-frying for the Chinese New Year's feast are Chinese American Shrimp with Lobster Sauce (page 179) and Stir-Fried *Yau Choi* with Oyster Sauce (page 196).

Chew warns that the Kahuna should never be used

by novice cooks. "Unless you know your way around a professional stove, it is really intimidating. Once it heats, it roars," says Chew. The stove generates far more power than a home cook needs. In fact, the speed and intensity of heat it produces is dangerous if the cook is not thoroughly experienced (see Stir-Frying with Proper Heat and Control, page 52). Its instructions suggest having a fire extinguisher handy. There are several other portable wok stove options that produce more heat than an average American range but at a more manageable power.

Recently, Chew's brother renovated his kitchen and he now has a stove with decent power, so this past year's Chinese New Year's dinner was successfully cooked indoors. As much as Chew enjoyed stir-frying with the Kahuna, there are several things he does not miss. It was always a pain to wash the gigantic wok as it did not fit into the kitchen sink. And, of course, because the Chinese New Year falls between January 21 and February 19, Chew sometimes had the unusual experience of stir-frying outdoors in 15-degree weather, but there was no need to wear full winter gear—the reflective heat from the Kahuna was intense enough to keep him warm.

The traditional clay brazier is found throughout China and Asia. This inexpensive portable wok stove can be fueled with wood or charcoal briquettes.

Supplemental Recipes

Classic Rice

Stir-fries are incomplete without rice. This is an old-fashioned recipe for cooking rice in a saucepan; I do not own a rice cooker. The method is simple and makes perfect rice every time. If you are planning on using the rice for fried rice, be sure to fluff it soon after it is cooked. Without fluffing, the rice will harden into a solid block after it is refrigerated and it will be difficult to separate into individual grains when you stir-fry it.

1⅓ cups long-grain rice

Put the rice in a 1½-quart heavy saucepan. Wash the rice in several changes of cold water until the water runs clear. Drain. Level the rice in the pan and add enough cold water to cover by 1 inch, or add 1⅔ cups water. Bring the water to a boil uncovered over high heat. When the water comes to a boil, reduce the heat to medium-low and simmer uncovered until most of the water has evaporated and little craters appear on the surface, about 4 to 5 minutes. Reduce the heat to low, cover, and simmer 10 minutes or until all of the water is absorbed. Turn off the heat and let sit 5 minutes before serving.

Makes about 4 cups. Serves 4 as part of a multicourse meal.

Homemade Chicken Broth

Every few weeks I make a batch of homemade chicken broth. There is no comparison between the flavor of homemade broth and canned. Homemade broth is less expensive than canned, but, more important, it has a richness that will greatly enhance the flavor of dishes. My butcher sells chicken backs. If you cannot find them substitute with a 3-pound whole chicken. Salt is not added in this recipe on the assumption that it will be added to the dish in which the broth is used. I freeze the broth in 1-pint plastic containers.

3 pounds chicken backs
2 slices ginger, smashed

Remove any fat pockets from the chicken. Remove as much skin as possible and rinse the chicken under cold water. Place the chicken backs in a 6-quart stockpot. Add enough cold water to cover (about 2½ quarts), then set the pot over high heat. As the water heats, skim the scum that rises to the surface, adjusting the heat so the broth never boils; skim until most of the scum has been removed. Add the ginger and bring to a boil over high heat. Cover, reduce the heat to low, and simmer 3 to 4 hours. Allow the broth to cool and then strain it, discarding the chicken backs and ginger; cover the broth and refrigerate. The next day, remove and discard the hardened fat on top.

Makes about 2½ quarts.

Chinese Barbecued Pork

Chinese barbecued pork is called for in two recipes in this book: Singapore Noodles (page 274) and Barbecued Pork Lo Mein (page 273). This recipe makes more than you'll need for either dish, but homemade barbecued pork is excellent served warm. If you don't want to make it yourself and you live near a Chinatown, you'll see it hanging in the windows of some Cantonese restaurants. The homemade is, of course, far superior to store-bought, which often has red food coloring.

1 pound pork shoulder or butt, well trimmed

2 tablespoons sugar

1 tablespoon soy sauce

1 tablespoon hoisin sauce

1 tablespoon dark soy sauce

1 tablespoon Shao Hsing rice wine or dry sherry

1 tablespoon bean sauce

1 teaspoon sesame oil

1/8 teaspoon ground white pepper

1 tablespoon honey

1. Quarter the pork lengthwise. In a large bowl rub 1 tablespoon of the sugar over the pork and set aside for 15 minutes. Pour off any excess liquid. In a small bowl combine the soy sauce, hoisin sauce, dark soy sauce, rice wine, bean sauce, sesame oil, pepper, and the remaining 1 tablespoon sugar. Pour the mixture over the pork, making sure the pork is well coated. Loosely cover with plastic wrap and refrigerate overnight, turning the pork from time to time.

2. When ready to roast, let the pork come to room temperature for 30 minutes. Preheat the broiler. Place a rack that stands at least ½ inch high in a roasting pan and add enough water to reach a depth of ¼ inch in the pan. Remove the pork from the marinade, reserving the marinade. Place the pork on the rack, leaving about 1 inch of space between the pieces. Using a spoon, drizzle the honey as evenly as possible over the pork.

3. Carefully place the pan under the broiler. The pork should be about 4 inches from the broiler element. Broil until the meat is just beginning to char slightly, 7 to 10 minutes. Monitor the water level in the roasting pan to make sure it never falls below ¼ inch. Turn the pork over, brush with the reserved marinade, and broil until the meat just begins to char, 7 to 10 minutes, or until the pork registers 155°F when tested with a meat thermometer. If the pork is getting too charred, lightly cover with a small piece of aluminum foil. Carefully remove the barbecued pork from the broiler and set on a cutting board to cool for 10 minutes. Cut the pork into ¼-inch-thick slices and serve warm or at room temperature.

Serves 4 as part of a multicourse meal.

Sources

The Wok Shop
718 Grant Avenue
San Francisco, CA 94108
415-989-3797
888-780-7171
www.wokshop.com
Owner Tane Ong Chan will take the time to figure out what wok is best for you. If you have the pleasure of visiting this charming shop, you'll be impressed to see that Chan stocks carbon-steel, Chinese-made cast-iron, and hand-hammered woks; cleavers; and every kind of wok accessory, including the clay brazier for a wok, plus the Kinipira Peeler and the Negi Cutter, as well as Asian vegetable seeds.

Flamtech Appliance, Inc.
114 Bowery
New York, NY 10013
212-274-8820
www.flamtech.com
This Asian kitchen showroom specializes in professional and residential wok stoves and exhaust hoods. Consultants give in-depth advice on setting up a wok kitchen.

Uwajimaya
600 Fifth Avenue South
Seattle, WA 98104
206-624-6248
www.uwajimaya.com
This unique Asian supermarket has an impeccable selection of fresh produce and an equally impressive choice of Asian dry goods available.

Kalustyan's
123 Lexington Avenue
New York, NY 10016
212-685-3451
800-352-3451
www.kalustyans.com
One of the best shops for fine spices, a wide variety of Asian ingredients, and West Indian pepper sauces such as Pickapeppa Sauce and Matouk's Calypso Sauce.

Melissa's World Variety Produce, Inc.
P.O. Box 21127
Los Angeles, CA 90021
800-588-0151
www.melissas.com
An excellent source for fresh chilies, exotic fruits, and Asian vegetables.

Bonnie Slotnick Cookbooks
163 West Tenth Street
New York, NY 10014
212-989-8962
www.bonnieslotnickcookbooks.com
bonnieslotnickbooks@earthlink.net
Owner Bonnie Slotnick carries an incredible collection of hard to find out-of-print cookbooks, including Chinese cookbooks.

Bibliography

Au, M. Sing. *Chinese Cookery: Genuine Chinese Dishes You Can Prepare in Your Kitchen.* Honolulu: Creart, 1932.

Bak-Geller, Sarah. "Chinese Cooks and Mexican Tastes: The Encounter of Two Culinary Practices in Mexico's Chinese Restaurants." *Journal of Chinese Overseas* 1, no. 1 (May 2005): 121–29.

Barbas, Samantha. "'I'll Take Chop Suey': Restaurants as Agents of Culinary and Cultural Change." *Journal of Popular Culture* 36, no. 4 (Spring 2003): 669–87.

Bosse, Sara, and Onoto Watanna. *Chinese-Japanese Cook Book.* 1914. Reprint, Bedford, Mass.: Applewood Books, 2006.

Chang, K. C., ed. *Food in Chinese Culture: Anthropological and Historical Perspectives.* New Haven: Yale University Press, 1977.

Chao, Buwei Yang. *How to Cook and Eat in Chinese.* Third, Revised, and Enlarged eds. New York: Random House, 1963.

Chu, Grace Zía. *The Pleasures of Chinese Cooking.* New York: Simon & Schuster, 1962.

Claiborne, Craig. "New Cookbook Covers Chopsticks to Chop Suey." *New York Times*, September 27, 1962.

———, and Virginia Lee. *The Chinese Cookbook.* Philadelphia: J.B. Lippincott Company, 1972.

Collins, Julie K., Guoyao Wu, Penelope Perkins-Veazie, Karen Spears, Larry Claypool, Robert A. Baker, and Beverly A. Clevidence. "Watermelon Consumption Increases Plasma Arginine Concentrations in Adults." *Nutrition* 23, no. 3 (March 2007): 261–66.

Corriher, Shirley O. *Cookwise: The Hows and Whys of Successful Cooking.* New York: William Morrow, 1997.

———. "Sticky Situation." *Saveur* no. 108 (January-February 2008).

Creasy, Rosalind. *The Edible Asian Garden.* Boston: Periplus, 2000.

Dahlen, Martha. *A Cook's Guide to Chinese Vegetables.* Hong Kong: The Guidebook Company, 1995.

Davidson, Alan. *The Penguin Companion to Food.* New York: Penguin Books, 1999.

Dunlop, Fuchsia. *Land of Plenty.* New York: W.W. Norton & Company, Inc., 2003.

Eng-Wong, John, and Imogene L. Lim. "Chow Mein Sandwiches: Chinese American Entrepreneurship in Rhode Island." In *Origins and Destinations: 41 Essays on Chinese America*, 417–36. Los Angeles: Chinese Historical Society of Southern California and UCLA Asian American Studies Center, 1994.

Epstein, Jason. "Chinese Characters." *New York Times Magazine*, June 13, 2004.

Feng, Doreen Yen Hung. *The Joy of Chinese Cooking.* New York: Grosset & Dunlap, 1950.

Geerligs, P. D. Prinsen, B. J. Brabin, and A. A. A. Omari. "Food Prepared in Iron Cooking Pots as an Intervention for Reducing Iron Deficiency Anaemia in Developing Countries: A Systematic Review." *Journal of Human Nutrition and Dietetics* 16, no. 4 (August 2003): 275–81.

Girnau, Fredric H. *Girnau's Chinese Chop Suey, Chow Mein Cook Book.* Los Angeles: Fredric H. Girnau, 1931.

Hahn, Emily, and Editors of Time-Life Books. *The Cooking of China.* Foods of the World. New York: Time-Life Books, 1968.

Hom, Ken. *Chinese Technique: An Illustrated Guide to the Fundamental Techniques of Chinese Cooking.* New York: Simon & Schuster, 1981.

———. *Easy Family Recipes from a Chinese-American Childhood.* New York: Alfred A. Knopf, 1997.

———. *The Taste of China.* London: Pavilion Books, 1996.

Huang, H. T. *Fermentations and Food Science, Pt. 5 of Vol. 6, Biology and Biological Technology*, in *Science and Civilisa-*

tion in China, by Joseph Needham. Cambridge: Cambridge University Press, 2000.

Jen, Gish. "A Short History of the Chinese Restaurant: From Stir-fried Buffalo to Matzoh Foo Young." *Slate*, April 27, 2005. http://www.slate.com/id/2117567 (accessed May 26, 2009).

Johnson, Kim. *Descendants of the Dragon: The Chinese in Trinidad 1806–2006*. Kingston, Jamaica: Ian Randle, 2006.

Jung, John. *Chopsticks in the Land of Cotton*. San Francisco: Yin Yang Press, 2008.

Kan, Johnny, and Charles L. Leong. *Eight Immortal Flavors*. Berkeley, California: Howell-North Books, 1963.

Kuo, Irene. *The Key to Chinese Cooking*. New York: Alfred A. Knopf, 1989.

Kwan, Cheuk, director and producer. *Chinese Restaurants*. DVD. Toronto: Tissa Films, 2005.

Lamb, Corrinne. *The Chinese Festive Board*. Peking: Henri Vetch, 1938.

Lee, Jennifer 8. *The Fortune Cookie Chronicles: Adventures in the World of Chinese Food*. New York: Twelve, 2008.

Lee, M. P. *Chinese Cookery: A Hundred Practical Recipes*. New York: Transatlantic Arts, 1945.

Lee Lum, Winnie. *Caribbean Chinese Cooking*. Kingston, Jamaica: Periwinkle, 1999.

Levin, Gail. *Edward Hopper: An Intimate Biography*. New York: Alfred A. Knopf, 1995.

Li, Li. "Cultural and Intercultural Functions of Chinese Restaurants in the Mountain West: An Insider's Perspective." *Western Folklore* 61, nos. 3 & 4 (2002): 329–46.

Lin, Florence. *Florence Lin's Chinese Regional Cookbook*. New York: Hawthorne Books, 1975.

Lin, Yutang. *The Importance of Living*. New York: William Morrow and Company, 1965.

Liu, De-Yu, Zuan-Guang Chen, Huan-Qiang Lei, Mei-Qiong Lu, Li Rui, and Lan-Xin Li. "Investigation of the Amount of Dissolved Iron in Food Cooked in Chinese Iron Pots and Estimation of Daily Iron Intake." *Biomedical and Environmental Sciences* 3, no. 3 (September 1990): 276–80.

Liu, Dolly. *Chow! Secrets of Chinese Cooking*. Hong Kong: Kelly & Walsh, 1939.

Lo, Kenneth. *Chinese Food: An Introduction to One of the World's Great Cuisines*. London: Faber and Faber Ltd., 1996.

———. *Food the Chinese Way*. Secaucus, N.J.: Chartwell Books, 1976.

Loewen, James W. *The Mississippi Chinese: Between Black and White*. 2nd ed. Prospect Heights, Ill.: Waveland Press, 1988.

Low, Henry. *Cook at Home in Chinese*. Hong Kong: Pacific Printing & Mfg., n.d.

Look Lai, Walton. *The Chinese in the West Indies, 1806–1995: A Documentary History*. Kingston, Jamaica: The Press, University of the West Indies, 1998.

———, ed. *Essays on the Chinese Diaspora in the Caribbean*. St. Augustine, Trinidad and Tobago: History Department, University of the West Indies, 2006.

Lu, Henry C. *Chinese Foods for Longevity: The Art of Long Life*. New York: Sterling Publishing, 1990.

McGee, Harold. *On Food and Cooking: The Science and Lore of the Kitchen*. Completely rev. and updated ed. New York: Scribner, 2004.

Miller, Gloria Bley. *The Thousand Recipe Chinese Cookbook*. New York: Atheneum, 1966.

Moskin, Julia. "Craving Hyphenated Chinese." *New York Times*, September 21, 2005.

Nathan, Joan. "Home Cooking; East Meets South at a Delta Table." *New York Times*, June 4, 2003.

Newman, Jacqueline M. *Food Culture in China*. Food Culture Around the World. Westport, Conn.: Greenwood Press, 2004.

New York Times, "Chop Suey Resorts: Chinese Dish Now Served in Many Parts of the City," November 15, 1903.

Pang, Ching Lin. "Beyond 'Authenticity': Reinterpreting Chinese Immigrant Food in Belgium." In *Eating Culture: The Poetics and Politics of Food*, edited by Tobias Döring, Markus Heide, and Susanne Mühleisen, 53–70. American Studies Monograph Series 106. Heidelberg: Universitätsverlag Winter, 2003.

Quan, Robert Seto, and Julian B. Roebuck. *Lotus Among the Magnolias: The Mississippi Chinese*. Jackson: University Press of Mississippi, 1982.

Schlarbaum, Scott E. "Step Into the Past at Omaha's King Fong Restaurant." *Vox Populi Nebraska* 3, no. 6 (June

2002). http://www.voxpopuline.com/2002_06/page51.html (accessed May 26, 2009).

Shepherd, Ted. *The Chinese of Greenville, Mississippi.* Greenville, Miss.: Burford Brothers Printing, 1999.

Solimano, Georgio R., and Sally A. Lederman, eds. *Controversial Nutrition Policy Issues.* Springfield, Ill.: Charles C Thomas, 1983.

Sutton, David E. *Remembrance of Repasts: An Anthropology of Food and Memory.* Materializing Culture. Oxford and New York: Berg, 2001.

Thornell, John. "Struggle for Identity in the Most Southern Place on Earth: The Chinese in the Mississippi Delta." *Chinese America: History & Perspectives* 17 (2003): 63–70.

Wilkinson, Endymion. "Chinese Culinary History," *China Review International* 8, no. 2 (Fall 2001): 285–304.

———. *Chinese History: A Manual.* Cambridge, Mass.: Harvard University Asia Center, 2000.

Wolke, Robert L. *What Einstein Told His Cook 2: The Sequel: Further Adventures in Kitchen Science.* New York: W.W. Norton & Company, Inc., 2005.

Wu, David Y. H., and Sidney C. H. Cheung, eds. *The Globalization of Chinese Food.* Honolulu: University of Hawai'i Press, 2002.

Young, Grace. *The Wisdom of the Chinese Kitchen: Classic Family Recipes for Celebration and Healing.* New York: Simon & Schuster, 1999.

Young, Grace, and Alan Richardson. *The Breath of a Wok: Unlocking the Spirit of Chinese Wok Cooking Through Recipes and Lore.* New York: Simon & Schuster, 2004.

Yu, Renqiu. "Chop Suey: From Chinese Food to Chinese American Food." *Chinese America: History and Perspectives* 1 (1987): 87–99.

Zhou, Yang-Dong, and Helen C. Brittin. "Increased Iron Content of Some Chinese Foods Due to Cooking in Steel Woks." *Journal of the American Dietetic Association* 94, no. 10 (October 1994): 1153–56.

EQUIVALENCY TABLES

Common Measurements

VOLUME TO VOLUME

3 tsp = 1 tbsp

4 tbsp = ¼ cup

5⅓ tbsp = ⅓ cup

4 ounces = ½ cup

8 ounces = 1 cup

1 cup = ½ pint

VOLUME TO WEIGHT

¼ cup liquid or fat = 2 ounces

½ cup liquid or fat = 4 ounces

1 cup liquid or fat = 8 ounces

2 cups liquid or fat = 1 pound

1 cup sugar = 7 ounces

1 cup flour = 5 ounces

Metric Equivalencies

(Liquid and Dry Measure Equivalencies)

CUSTOMARY	METRIC
¼ teaspoon	1.25 milliliters
½ teaspoon	2.5 milliliters
1 teaspoon	5 milliliters
1 tablespoon	15 milliliters
1 fluid ounce	30 milliliters
¼ cup	60 milliliters
⅓ cup	80 milliliters
½ cup	120 milliliters
1 cup	240 milliliters
1 pint (2 cups)	480 milliliters
1 quart (4 cups)	960 milliliters (.96 liter)
1 gallon (4 quarts)	3.84 liters
1 ounce (by weight)	28 grams
¼ pound (4 ounces)	114 grams
1 pound (16 ounces)	454 grams
2.2 pounds	1 kilogram (1,000 grams)

Oven Temperature Equivalencies

DESCRIPTION	°FAHRENHEIT	°CELSIUS
Cool	200	90
Very slow	250	120
Slow	300–325	150–160
Moderately slow	325–350	160–180
Moderate	350–375	180–190
Moderately hot	375–400	190–200
Hot	400–450	200–230
Very hot	450–500	230–260

Index

Note: Page numbers in italics refer to illustrations.

pine nuts:

    Peppery Vegetarian Rice, 5, 256

popcorn, 25

pork, 66

    Chinese American Shrimp with Lobster Sauce, 179

    Barbecued Pork Lo Mein, *272*, 273

    Cantonese-Style Stir-Fried Pork with Chinese Broccoli, *76*, 77

    for Chinese New Year, 194

    Dry-Fried Sichuan Beans, 121, 233

    Minced Pork in Lettuce Cups, 82–83, *83*

    Sichuan Pork with Peppers and Peanuts, 95

    Spicy Long Beans with Sausage and Mushrooms, 55, 212, *213*

    Stir-Fried Bagels with Cabbage and Pork, 254, 255

    Stir-Fried Cucumber and Pork with Golden Garlic, *72*, 73, 109

    Stir-Fried Fuzzy Melon and Ginger Pork, 230, 232

    Stir-Fried Garlic Eggplant with Pork, 62, 228

    Stir-Fried Hoisin Pork with Peppers, 94

    Yin Yang Beans, 206, *207*

portable wok stove, 5, *277*, 282, *282*

Portuguese cooking traditions, 117

potatoes:

    Chinese Peruvian Stir-Fried Filet Mignon (*Lomo Saltado*), 60, 92–93

    Stir-Fried Aromatic Potatoes, 210

potato flour, 79

poultry:

    adding liquid ingredients, 69

    avoid overfilling the wok, 69

    cutting, 66

    essentials for stir-frying, 66–69

    fresh, 66

    marinating, 69, 79, 94

    preparing, 7

    room temperature, 68

    searing, 69

    sizzle, 69

    see also chicken; duck

preheating wok, 6, 15, 20, 52, 53, 54

prosciutto:

Stir-Fried Napa Cabbage with Prosciutto, *198*, 199

    Sandpot Stir-Fried Chicken Rice, 252–53, *253*

proteins, searing, 54–55, *54*

Pu, Sen, 58

Q

Quon, Frieda, 58

R

raw stir-fries, 49

    Stir-Fried Mussels with Ginger and Scallions, *158*, 159

recipes:

    general instructions for, 6–7

    notes on, 5

redcook.net, 26

Red Egg, New York City, 92

rice:

    basmati, 265

    Chinese Cuban Fried Rice, 263

    Chinese Indian Vegetarian Fried Rice, 265

    Chinese Jamaican Jerk Chicken Fried Rice, 264

    Classic Rice, 283

    cold cooked, 246, 257

    Crab Meat Fried Rice, 251

    day-old, 257

    dry seasonings added to, 247

    egg pancake with, *248*

    essentials for stir-frying, 246–47

    fluffing, 246, 283

    fried, *see* fried rice

    Fried Sweet Rice with Sausages and Mushrooms, 260

    in Hakka cooking, 144–45

    Peppery Vegetarian Rice, 256

    rinsing, 246

    Sandpot Stir-Fried Chicken Rice, 252–53, *253*

    sizzle in, 247

    stir-frying tips, 246–47

    sweet, 260

    wok used in cooking, 247

    Yangchow Fried Rice, 259